Bridging the Gap

Popular Music and Music Education

Bridging the Gap

Popular Music and Music Education

Edited by Carlos Xavier Rodriguez

Based on a Northwestern University
Music Education Leadership Seminar

 The National Association for Music Education

Production Editor: Teresa K. Preston

© 2004
MENC: The National Association for Music Education
1806 Robert Fulton Drive
Reston, VA 20191

ISBN 1-56545-158-9

Contents

Preface
The Northwestern University
Music Education Leadership Seminars

The music education profession, like all others, must engage itself in continual efforts to improve its effectiveness and viability. Such efforts need to be made at a variety of levels, reflecting the complexity of this field. One of these levels, often neglected, requires the profession to nurture the expertise of its most influential members.

The Northwestern University Music Education Leadership Seminars (NUMELS) were conceived as a means to elevate all aspects of the music education profession by providing an intensive learning experience for its top-level leaders, thinkers, and activists. A relatively small number of music educators exercise a high degree of influence on the profession's fortunes. These are the professionals who are the most visible, productive, active, well-regarded people in their particular area of music education expertise. A great deal of the success of music education, in refining its understandings and reforming its practices, depends on their wisdom.

The continuing education of these national and international leaders occurs largely by their own self-directed efforts to keep abreast of issues most relevant to their work. Seldom, if ever, is there an opportunity for them to expand their expertise by coming together with people as advanced as they, specifically to serve their needs for continued growth by learning from each other and from experts in related fields. The luxury, intensity, and excitement of being a student rather than a teacher is rare indeed for people at that high level of attainment, but it is no less needed if their intellectual horizons and professional efficacy are to continue to expand.

In alternate summers starting in 1996, a dozen people who are among the leading music educators in the particular aspect of music education on which that seminar focused were invited to participate. They spent five days at Northwestern University in Evanston, Illinois, in informal discussions (led, in turn, by each participant), in interactions with guest instructors from outside music education who were identified as being able to add useful dimensions to their expertise, in strategy sessions on needed professional initiatives in which they saw themselves playing key roles, and in various other activities they mutually devised.

The 1996 NUMELS focused on the topic "Performance in the Context of the National Standards for Music Education." The 1998 seminar was on "Issues of Multiculturalism in Music Education." The 2000 Seminar dealt with "Composing in the Schools: A New Horizon for Music Education." The topic in 2002, leading to the publication of this book, was "Popular Music and Music Education: Forging a Credible Policy."

The seminars are not product oriented in the sense of creating a final report or policy recommendation or consensus document. Their purpose is to deepen and expand the leadership capacities of the attendees in whatever way they choose to apply the learnings they have gained. However, the participants in each seminar expressed their desire to capture the insights of the group—those they brought to the meeting and those they gained from it in a book from which the profession as a whole could benefit. MENC has published all the books produced by the Seminars: *Performing With Understanding: The Challenge of the National Standards for Music Education* (2000), *World Musics and Music Education: Facing the Issues* (2002), and *Why and How to Teach Music Composition: A New Horizon for Music Education* (2003).

The topic of the 2002 seminar and of this book is of particular importance to the relevance of the music education profession in the United States and around the world. One reason for an uncomfortably high degree of artificiality in school music programs across the globe has been a pervasive attitude by music educators that only the classical (and to some extent folk) musics of their culture are worthy of study in school settings. This posture ignores, even denigrates, the music most enjoyed and treasured by the great majority of people in practically every culture, particularly by people of school age. For a variety of reasons discussed by authors in this book, popular musics are held in low esteem by many, if not most, music educators. Therefore, they tend to be represented inauthentically in their programs. That is, they are often altered to conform to styles of music deemed "acceptable," or they are used to demonstrate their inferiority to the approved styles or as tokens to demonstrate that the teacher is "with it," or they are simply ignored under the pretense that students already know as much about "their" music as there is to know.

Such practices, examined in a variety of ways in the chapters of this book, have the effect of distancing "school music" from "real music" in the minds and hearts of young people. No one has argued that popular musics should be the only ones studied in schools. But, conversely, many are realizing that misrepresenting or ignoring them prevents music education from enhancing the learnings of students in ways directly pertinent to the actualities of their musical lives. Including popular musics as one dimension of a comprehensive general music education, and as an opportunity for specialized electives along with a variety of other opportunities, will bring school music programs into the real world of music as it actually exists. If approached honestly and respectfully, popular music engagements can deepen the musical understandings and pleasures of all students—the reason, after all, for music to exist as an essential school subject. This book will go a long way toward helping the profession achieve a more realistic, more balanced curriculum.

As director of the NUMELS, I have benefited from the generosity of the dean of the

Northwestern University School of Music, Bernard Dobroski, who supplied the financial wherewithal required and offered an extraordinary level of hospitality, making each seminar personally as well as professionally memorable. His far-seeing vision has embraced a variety of initiatives from which music education has reaped many rewards. I will be forever grateful for his support of my diverse professional projects.

I have also been affected greatly by my association with all the attendees of this and the previous three NUMELS. Their expertise has amazed me, their generosity has impressed me, their dedication to music education has inspired me, and their friendship has warmed my life.

—Bennett Reimer
Professor Emeritus
Northwestern University

Introduction

Bringing It All Back Home: The Case for Popular Music in the Schools

Carlos Xavier Rodriguez

In his introduction to the book *World Musics in Music Education: Facing the Issues,* Bennett Reimer stated emphatically, "The study of popular music in focused, relevant ways remains largely unaddressed in music education to this day."[1] This statement foreshadowed the leadership seminar dedicated to this topic for which the authors of this book gathered in June 2002. The question of how to teach popular music in the school music curriculum was eagerly anticipated by the group, which was well equipped with a diversity of expertise and experience, yet mindful of the complexity and urgency of the issue for music education. Popular music has always been problematic for music educators because, while it meets the public need for musical understanding, it does not inhere in the principles and processes of formal music instruction. As music educators and participants in or advocates of popular music, our seminar participants were concerned with upholding the sensibilities of the two distinct traditions to which we belong. Our task then, as it evolved, was to explore whether formal music teaching and learning might incorporate the essential aspects of popular music in mutually supportive and balanced ways.

There were, and are, of course, impediments to our approach. Traditional music instruction has typically not made use of popular music except on a perfunctory level, such as when popular tunes have made their way into performance repertories or practice manuals. Conversely, the creation of popular music has never significantly depended upon standardized, systematic instructional methods. The two traditions could not be more different nor more independent. We did, however, direct much of our discussion toward these key questions:

- How do we define popular music, and what accounts for its extraordinary commercial success?
- How and why do popular styles change?
- How do popular musicians learn?
- What learning processes are implicit in popular music making?
- Is it possible or desirable to teach popular music in music education?
- What are the key issues in bridging the

gap between popular music and traditional school music?

• What are the implications for teacher education?

This collection of writings begins with my essay comparing the classical music and popular music traditions, and it opens a section of the book that deals with the more pervasive issues surrounding the use of popular music in music education, issues that have challenged teaching professionals throughout our history. As a participant in both traditions, I have benefitted and suffered in pursuit of my own musicianship, as I imagine others have as well. This essay, then, is my attempt to make greater sense of the dialectic relationship between the traditions and encourage new conceptions of musicality that I hope readers will find promising for music education.

Wayne Bowman is a trombonist and jazz educator, although he is best known for his extensive writings in music philosophy. As a teacher of improvisation and jazz pedagogy, he has confronted, and shares with us here, the hard questions of what music we should teach, how we might teach it, and why. His chapter sets forth the proposal that we must examine whether and how the inclusion of popular music in the music curriculum can bring about changes that are socially relevant and beneficial to all students. A useful feature of his approach is careful scrutiny of the term "popular," in all its manifestations and ambiguities, in which he isolates some of the more enduring values that have kept popular music and "school music" separate spheres of activity. He then ruminates on this analysis as it pertains to education, "schooling," and the responsibilities of teaching professionals.

Theodore Gracyk teaches and writes in the area of philosophy and aesthetics but is best known for his books on rock music. I venture to call him a rock musicologist, the result of a lifetime spent honing writing skills and listening to rock and roll. The "What I Am Listening To" feature on his Web site (www.mnstate.edu/gracyk) demonstrates his ability to craft insightful, succinct, and humorous commentaries on a broad variety of popular music recordings. His writing reveals the marvelous array of understandings that listeners bring to popular music and how principles of relational structures of music are developed and transformed through the listening experience. Gracyk also confronts the formidable question of expressive qualities in popular music, citing an impressive array of considerations that affect listeners' perceptions, leaving little doubt that the integrity of this process is on par with the highest levels of classical music listening.

Martha Bayles, a teacher, writer, and critic of popular culture, concludes this opening section with a critique of the social forces that have brought change in popular music. She theorizes that the role of Afro-American influences on popular music, which were so significant in the formation of blues, jazz, rhythm and blues, gospel, soul and which helped define popular music in the early to mid-twentieth century, has markedly decreased as these styles have found increasing acceptance as educational material. She contends that popular music is now driven by forces and values that emphasize visual elements and participatory lifestyles suggested by performers in various musical subgroups. These changes in popular music and culture have distanced consumers from the emotionally and aesthetically gratifying aspects of musical experience, as Bayles so convincingly argues in her book *Hole in Our Soul: The Loss of Beauty and Meaning in Music* (University of Chicago Press, 1996) and with which many music educators would agree. However, Bayles offers a practical suggestion for approaching popular music in the music classroom, one that may empower future consumers to make informed choices about musical quality.

The second section of this book traces the historical antecedents of popular music in music education. Jere Humphreys, an internationally recognized scholar in the history of music education, observes America's hesitation to embrace popular music as didactic material in light of its acceptance in the music curricula of other countries. He further points out that most of the reasons why popular music, and in particular rock music, is resisted by the music teaching profession are historically rooted, among them: (1) that music teachers collectively aspire to cultivate higher-level tastes than the public cultivates for itself, (2) that rock music is associated with the youth culture that wielded it to express antiestablishment, antiwar, proyouth, and profreedom sentiments, (3) that lack of federal control over the public school system permits the predominantly middle-class American society to perpetuate its traditional values regarding what is and isn't appropriate music for study. After his delineation of the pragmatic and philosophical

issues that separate school music and popular music, Humphreys suggests that the coalition of these two musical cultures is not only inevitable, but also democratic.

William Lee is a historian and a composer, and he makes few qualitative distinctions between types of music appropriate for music education, claiming that they need only be grounded in a context to ensure meaning and continued learning. He reaches far into the possibilities for contextual connections and explains how the historical, cultural, social, aesthetic, and age-specific aspects of musical experience inform that experience and comprise its wholeness. Writing in a straightforward voice and using examples from multiple styles, Lee asserts the importance of embracing and utilizing historical context for a variety of instructional applications, including what is certainly a major concern for music educators—how to develop good judgment in selecting popular music for the classroom. Finally, he outlines a set of themes that he has found useful for creating a historical perspective for any type of popular music, including change, multiple causes, evidence, choices, origins, material context, and social patterns.

George Odam's essay begins the section on international perspectives of popular music in music education. An Englishman, he has taught music at all age levels, authored textbooks, and composed extended works, including an opera and a cantata. These activities have given him many opportunities to examine the role of popular music in music education, and he has also formulated some insightful impressions of American music education. One is what he calls our "fear of transience," an unwillingness to adopt new teaching materials that have not proven their longevity. Another is "nostalgia," the mistaken belief that an educator's own favorite popular music is necessarily the most significant or of the highest quality. Odam further observes that there is a tendency for American music educators to perpetuate the nineteenth-century ideal of separate composer and performer roles, apparently due to their own training in Western European common practice, leaving them ill prepared to appreciate or understand the aesthetics and practices of popular music. Odam's metaphor of the "Age of Aquarius" to represent the phenomenal ascent of popular music and culture in the late twentieth century suggests that our profession has much to lose by continuing to ignore its importance in the lives of teachers and students alike.

Kathryn Wemyss, an Australian who has written on such topics as popular music in the school curriculum, Aboriginal music, instrumental pedagogy, and songwriting, takes a step back to examine the interaction between the cultures of popular music and formal education and the process of change that results from their interaction. Tracing the history of Australian secondary schools in adopting the tools and practices of popular music, she analyzes the negotiation of these cultures in the school setting, attributing its success not to policies or administrative leadership, but to individual teachers committed to transforming music instruction to meet student interests. A successful singer/songwriter and popular musician, Wemyss has experienced firsthand the

remarkable power of music to institute social changes and unite individuals with a common view of the world, and she believes students can experience this power by systematically developing their skills in popular music production. She describes how several critical aspects of the curriculum, including technology, composition, performance, and notation, can all contribute to a new form of musicianship and culture making that thrives as a consequence of, rather than in spite of, formal music education.

What do these challenges imply for music teacher education? Scott Emmons has taught a university-level course in popular music as well as numerous music education methods courses, and he is well poised to address this question. He outlines the behaviors and attitudes needed for understanding and teaching popular music styles and explains how these might be delivered as part of preservice education. An experienced guitarist, Emmons explains what is involved in teaching instruments, collaborative composition, and digital recording techniques. He shares the results of an independent study suggested by one of his graduate students, in which the two of them conducted a four-month project with a group of middle school students who wanted to form a rock band. The students' compositional activities supported a model developed by Emmons's earlier research, in which he found the creative process to be nonlinear, nonsequential, and consisting of three distinct stages: formation, preservation, and revision. The results further provided a microcosm of the knowledge, skills, and reactions implicit in such work, with direct implications for larger-scale efforts to prepare teachers to use popular music in their classrooms. With this end in mind, Emmons provides information to new teachers, or those inexperienced in teaching popular music, on how to negotiate the scheduling and administration of popular music performance programs.

Craig Woodson is an ethnomusicologist, music educator, inventor, professional percussionist, and administrator for the Rock and Roll Hall of Fame in Cleveland, Ohio. In his capacity with the Rock Hall he has assisted in the development of a curriculum that is offered to in-service music educators as a professional enrichment program. Woodson's extensive experience in playing and teaching, both in the U.S. and abroad, has contributed to a particularly rich collection of global themes, principles, and practices in popular music. His narrative description of this curriculum, which includes American, Hispanic, African, Asian, and European influences on rock music, provides a stunning array of possibilities for the music classroom. Quite helpful is the manner in which the artists have been selected for inclusion—they are Rock and Roll Hall of Fame inductees, whom national experts have deemed the most representative of and successful in their given styles. Woodson also contributes extensive information on teaching the "roots" of rock and roll, which truly belong to the United States and which have received far too little focus as the logical starting point for popular music study.

Numerous issues that surround the creation and performance of popular music comprise the final section. George Boespflug is a classical pianist who now heads the music program at Biola University, a small liberal arts college. While developing a popular music component there, he has extensively conceptualized the inner workings of the popular music ensemble. These include its history as an educational entity, the skills required to participate, the ways in which it does and does not support more traditional ideas about formal musicianship, the specific resources it demands to operate efficiently, and how these factors compare to traditional school performance ensembles. He then proposes how the popular music ensemble might operate in the junior high, high school, and college settings in terms of their outcomes, use of technology, classroom management, and other curricular issues. Boespflug makes extensive use of the latest music technology to assist his ensemble, leading him to confront the changing roles of musicians in the digital recording process, in which he finds single musicians functioning as performer, composer, engineer, and producer of a recording. In an effort to reconcile this creative freedom in the context of group work, he proposes the "virtual studio," a completely digital musical environment in which participants communicate through headphones in a carefully controlled physical space. This proposal brings to mind the oft-spoken conviction among arts educators that the optimal use of computers is to help students exercise greater personal creativity.

Randall Allsup approaches similar issues from a different perspective, asking how the principles and processes of popular music can be applied to existing performance ensembles. Examining the trajectory of activities throughout the music-learning continuum, Allsup finds that most truly creative music opportunities end abruptly as students enter performance ensembles in middle and secondary school, precisely the time at which they become more reliant on music as a source of culture making and identity. In contrast, Allsup contends, the characteristics of music learning as it occurs informally (e.g., in garage bands) models more closely the conditions for "democratic learning," since its ideals arise from the behavior of its participants, rather than vice versa, as occurs in traditional school music ensembles. Allsup tallies the overwhelming benefits of allowing students to create their own music, including the articulation of identity, the management of public and private emotions, the preservation of significant events in one's personal history, and the discernment of ownership as a functional aspect of artistic development. Allsup's efforts to compare "classical" and "popular" forms of group music making reveal basic differences and indicate how and why certain steps might be taken in traditional performance ensembles to render them more democratic and rewarding for students.

Lucy Green has studied the behavior of popular musicians in England for some years now and has published well-known books on the topic that emphasize the implications of these behaviors for formal music education. Her rationale for this approach is especially strong—that formal music instruction has very limited practical benefits for the majority of those who participate in it and that most of the world's population prefers music created without the formalized skills and knowledge taught in the music classroom. Using the essential musical behaviors of performing, listening, and creating as a comprehensive platform, Green analyzes the particular behaviors that arise from attempts to make popular music. These include copying recordings, "jamming," using and not using notation, developing playing techniques, sharpening aural skills, developing a "feel" for pop music performance, building friendships, increasing self-esteem, and cultivating an open mind toward other styles and genres of music. Green's central thesis is that while popular music has gradually made its way into formal music instruction around the world, it is the incorporation of popular-music-making processes that represents the more significant challenge and change. The increased role of enculturation, so richly present in popular music learning, and typically absent from classical music training, is given special treatment in her recommendations for formal music education.

The "final word" is given to Rob Cutietta, an eminent music researcher, composer, and electric bass player, who poses the probing question, "When we question popular music in education, what is the question?" The ostensible question is whether popular music belongs in formal music instruction, to which Cutietta answers no, not with the performance ensembles typically found in secondary music settings. Cutietta proceeds to define quality in music, identifying the significant overlaps between the classical and popular traditions. He further explains progress in music, again noting significant similarities in the ways that musical forms, performance practices, and idiomatic advantages and constraints of instruments impact changes in styles and periods. On the matter of authenticity, it is here that Cutietta insists that popular music has no place in the school curriculum unless we are prepared to reinvent it through performance ensembles, a statement that has strong implications for what instruments we teach, when we teach them, and how.

This collection of essays is not meant to be the final word on popular music in music education, but an orientation to the complex philosophical and practical issues that accompany this important topic for music education. Easy questions abound, such as whether it may be desirable for a music teacher to allow a classroom full of students to listen to their favorite music while engaging in meaningful discourse that invokes the music vocabulary being introduced and practiced in that classroom. The more difficult question is how we are going to prepare music teachers in their undergraduate programs to elevate that learning to a more meaningful level when, in fact, there are exceptionally few opportunities to for them learn how to do this in schools of music and colleges of education. The participants in this seminar possessed the common denominator of some form and amount of popular music learning, this despite their formal music training. Yet this learning does not form a unified body of information, nor does it collectively comprise a sufficient base for practice or advocacy. In short, this is an emergent topic to which we intend to devote further thinking and action. I invite you to share with us the exciting possibilities of popular music as an instructional medium, for, ultimately, you will decide whether they are worthy of our best efforts.[2]

Notes

1. Bennett Reimer, ed., *World Musics and Music Education: Facing the Issues* (Reston, VA: MENC, 2002), 3.

2. I am grateful to graduate assistants Michael Knight and Sarah Bobenhouse and intern Lauren Flittner for their help with this book.

The Broader Perspective

Popular Music in Music Education: Toward a New Conception of Musicality

Carlos Xavier Rodriguez

In this chapter, I reflect on some of the issues confronting music educators as they consider whether and how to integrate popular music into the music curriculum. My purpose is to suggest a broader conception of musicality that incorporates the study of music in multiple contexts, specifically music in popular media, based on my belief that didactic models of musical experience are limited forms of "real-world" musical experiences. Such changes in our thinking might help us meet our students' need and right to learn more about the music that surrounds them. I discuss various definitions of popular music and compare how the parallel cultures of "popular" and "classical"[1] music affect the learning, notating, creating, and performing of music. These comparisons are vital for assessing the promises and problems of including popular music in existing music curricula.

I qualify my remarks here by first explaining my own experiences and education in music. I was raised in a family of musicians who learned and play mostly by ear, and I am the first in my family to study music formally in a college or university.

My relatives reminded me that I had to choose between being "good" or "smart" in music, and while I chose what they would consider "smart," I had always hoped to achieve both. I have maintained close ties with my colleagues since choosing the university life, owing to sustained immersion in the "classical repertory," dating from when from my mother relentlessly played Toscanini recordings of Beethoven symphonies in my preschool years.

However, I remain, first and foremost, a pop musician. I learned guitar at age eleven, performed and recorded with various bands, and eluded formal training until entering college as a music major. I struggled to develop a conceptual knowledge of what I intuitively knew about music, believing that fully realized musicianship requires both types of knowledge. Along the way, I frustrated my professors as well as my band mates, because these people belong to autonomous music cultures. I now witness the same disparity between music teachers who are unconvinced that popular music belongs in formal educational settings and students who remain wary of learning their "own" music at school.

Much of the debate over whether popular music is appropriate for systematic music instruction is rooted in conflicting views over what constitutes musicality, or how we define the "musical person." Certainly we should include music performing, listening, and creating in our definition, but we nurture these behaviors for grander outcomes, such as helping students meaningfully express and interpret musical ideas, which rightfully belong to the definition as well. The grander outcomes, rather than the discrete behaviors, help us conceptualize musicality. The term "musicality" has traditionally carried specific meaning in music education, but it must be broadened to include the skills and thinking implicit in popular music, since our students evidently find it profoundly relevant and worth their finest efforts. I will first attempt to explain what I mean by "popular music," since the term has pedagogical implications as well as stylistic meanings.

Defining Popular Music

What is popular music? It is so formidable a presence in our lives, and of such rich and sustained history, that the term inevitably has different meanings to people. There are certainly generational differences—when I speak of popular music, I mean a *different* kind of music than did my father when he spoke of popular music, or than my children do now—but there are also gender, economic, and ethnic differences. What distinguishes the various forms of popular music are the cultures that consider them popular. (The term "culture" is used here to mean a group of individuals who share the same beliefs and understandings about themselves, each other, and the world around them.) The variability of the term "popular music" has ensured ongoing changes in what people regard as "popular" over time and across cultures.

Three characteristic approaches are used to determine if a certain type of music is popular.[2] The first is the measurable consumption of the music, for instance, its position on the *Billboard* charts or other ranking system. These lists are widely disseminated in local and national newspapers for a reason—people are generally influenced by, or a least curious about, what *other* people think is good music. Listening to the local Top 40 radio station is another way of experiencing the same music. CD stores prominently display their most popular sellers, making them the most convenient to find and buy. Top-ten lists are targeted at specific age-groups—mostly the young—and getting younger all the time. While most music educators can remember quite well what music was on their own top-ten lists, what is currently on the *Billboard* charts may be completely unfamiliar and/or unappealing.

The second approach for determining the popularity of music is its delivery mode. Certain media can validate the popularity of music, such as when songs appear as sheet music, on movie soundtracks, on jukebox selection lists, and so forth. The introduction of new media is also a very important popularity indicator—when the recording industry embraced CD technology over long-playing vinyl records, the first CDs to appear were of the big hits of the time.

The third approach for determining the popularity of music is its alignment with a particular group of people. This is a critical approach, because the target audience usually exerts some control over which features of the music are retained and revised as the style develops over time, making it all the more attractive to group members. It is an empowering aspect of popular music because listeners perceive the style as an emulation of their dress, language, preferred activities, or temperament.

This very issue of what constitutes popular music troubles many teachers who fear there is no consensus between themselves and their students. Equally disconcerting for teachers is their inability to relate to, or find quality in, the music that is popular with students. Regarding the former concern, I suggest that the issue is pedantic. In the early days of multicultural music education, one of the most urgent concerns was that of authenticity. Presenting the music of a culture without its true setting, instruments, language, and performance practices was worse than not presenting the music at all. We are now satisfied with knowing that each culture's settings, instruments, language, and performance practices differ, and we do our best to inform students of them as we perform the music as authentically as we can. We should do the same with popular music. Rather than hesitate because we cannot relate to or do not know enough about the music of our students, we might remember that our students too frequently possess similar attitudes about the music we choose instead.

Considering the diverse perspectives of the three approaches to defining what it popular, it is clear how ballroom, ethnic, folk, jazz, rap, Christian, reggae, rhythm and blues, rockabilly, funk, disco, punk, and country can be popular, at different times, for different audiences, and for different reasons. Some people acknowledge the more broad colloquial use of the term "pop" while recognizing a style of music called "pop"—a style with its own distinctive sound that reflects American and British music from the later decades of the twentieth century. However, most people simply believe that popular music is intended for a broad audience that may not have substantive background in music history, theory, and literature; thus, they do not expect the music to reference any of those cognate areas.[3] Fueling this belief are commonly used pop "formulas" such as simple, memorable melodies, catchy "sing-along" choruses, and instrumental "hooks" that provide immediate, albeit short-term, appeal.[4] Often, "pop music" serves as an umbrella term for many types of music that people of all ages enjoy. Music educators may find it useful to think carefully about the music they consider "popular," either now or in the past, and decide how and why the music is popular. It is the first step in developing a didactic approach to the study of popular music, and it is a step that our students should take as well.

what is "pop"? what we consider pop, our students.

public schools. Teaching music is highly challenging, and educators rely on their own disciplined musical pasts to set standards and protocols for the instructional present. Popular music learning, on the other hand, circumvents the well-known routine of European classical training, eliciting indignant attitudes from classically trained music educators. ("Anybody can make music like that!" is a common reaction to Top 40 music.) This attitude arises from numerous preexisting beliefs about popular musicians, including the following: (1) they don't really know what they are doing—success is fortuitous rather than skillful or planned, (2) they don't grow musically at the same rate as classically trained musicians, and (3) they have trouble communicating with other musicians and preserving their work efficiently. The two traditions present very different "effort-to-success" ratios, leading many music educators to believe that there is not much worth *teaching* about pop musicianship. Supporting this belief is the tendency of successful pop performers to relinquish greater creative roles to producers and arrangers, so they can spend more time promoting their images.

Ironically, these same qualities strengthen the status of popular musicians with students who interpret them differently. They see pop musicians having "fun" because their music so easily combines with other activities (surfing, dating, dancing, etc.). They are motivated by the prospect of becoming famous without exceptional musical talent or substantial investment of time and practice. While we hope they find musicianship the most enviable quality, students are distracted by pop stars' physical attractiveness and dancing skills. Popular music definitely influences students, but even while many impressions

that the music conveys are superfluous or detrimental to artistic thinking and doing, the medium does appeal to students' natural interests, aspirations, and belief that, simply by being themselves, they will have endless opportunities for personal success.

Despite the foregoing stereotypes of pop performers, relatively few achieve the kind of extraordinary success that permits a reliance on attributes besides musicianship. Most have worked as hard to achieve professionalism as their counterparts in classical music, and in many cases they have endured additional obstacles related to the oral nature of the learning context. One example is Robbie Robertson, the guitarist of the long-defunct group the Band, which gained fame as Bob Dylan's touring band in the 1960s. As a Canadian youth, Robertson was committed to learning the guitar. He encountered country sounds on a Nashville radio station and was mesmerized by the electrifying style of blues great Muddy Waters. These sources projected the same sliding sound in the guitar part, and Robertson practiced laboriously to master it. Eventually, he perfected an unusual vibrato style that closely resembled it. Only later did he realize that the country and blues musicians produced the sound by pushing a glass or metal slide across the strings. However, in his naive attempt to achieve this sound, he began developing the intensive work habits that would serve him throughout his career, earning him a reputation as a highly original guitarist with impeccable technique.[5]

Imitation is a basic learning process in formal music training and in popular music training. However, in popular music training, the imitation is neither sequential nor deliberate (which is why it seems awkward to use the term "popular music training"). In informal learning environments, beginning musicians usually acquire what they can when they can, learning bits and pieces that eventually form entire songs. This protocol is confounding to music educators, since it would seem to require individualized instruction and separate developmental tracks for each student. However, there are procedural similarities between the two types of learning. For instance, every learning stage contains various elements and skills the student has mastered, is currently learning, and will encounter later; this planned, forward movement can bring greater comprehension and effectiveness to the learning process.

Another difference between the two types of learning is in *what gets imitated*. Pop images and lifestyles motivate young people. They want to be like the performers whose styles they emulate. (In contrast, it is not likely that a young pianist would be motivated to practice through the desire to be like Beethoven or Liszt.) Guitarist and singer Sully Erna of the group Godsmack relates:

> When I was fourteen I bought Aerosmith's *Live Bootleg*, and inside the record there's a collage of pictures. One of them changed my life. It's Joe Perry. He's standing on a stadium stage or something—it's kind of a small picture— but he's holding up this guitar, and his hair's in his face, and he just looked so [expletive] cool. I remember going, "That's what I wanna do!"[6]

Several years ago, I offered a guitar soloing class to a small group of beginning guitarists as part of their summer camp program. Dressed in clothes that signified an allegiance to heavy metal, these young men were solely interested in learning blues, well aware that their idols thought the blues represented the "basics" of rock. Popular music performers can and do influence what their fans believe is worth their attention,[7] and this influence stimulates connection-making within and between styles, as students analyze how playing techniques, song forms, timbres, and lyrics evolve in popular music. We do, in fact, strive to help students "transfer and link" musical concepts and skills, of which style sensitivity is an advanced example. When they do, it reaffirms the validity of what and how we teach.

There is the temptation to believe that popular music, moving forward as it does without consistent adherence to previous trends, lacks a significant or teachable legacy. It does, in fact, have a rich history that is tied to our social, political, cultural, and economic history. What it lacks, in comparison to, say, Western European music, is the passage of sufficient time to determine which practices, structures, persons, and places have most influenced the genre. Listeners have always loved Elvis and considered him the King, but as time advances they are much more likely to clearly understand his contributions to the American sound. When I was in high school, I listened raptly to Johnny Winter as he obtained from his amplifier what guitarists fondly call "tone, tone, and more tone." I listened mostly because he unleashed his feral instincts on every track, creating a tremendous slashing sound with his guitar and voice. It was only as a college student that I realized how much Winter owed to his mentor Muddy Waters, whose playing evidenced many of the same techniques but in the more pristine and original form that pushed the blues to urbanization. Only recently did I realize how much Muddy Waters owed to Son House and Robert Johnson, the two legendary Delta bluesmen from whom Muddy took the idea of sliding the same notes on the guitar that were being sung, letting the slide imitate the nuances of voice, and vice versa.

There is a historic foundation for popular music in the United States, and it rightfully belongs to American roots music. Its origins lie in the music of European Americans in the rural south, but it soon encompassed the songs of African Americans, Mexican Americans, Cajuns, Native Americans, and others. While these individual music traditions expressed the activities and thinking of "ordinary" people, they also reflected their cultural beliefs and values. When radio broadcasts began in the 1920s, Americans everywhere could experience the music of other folk and ethnic cultures. Popular styles, such as jazz, blues, rhythm and blues, and rock and roll, developed from these sources throughout the century. During the 1950s and 1960s, the folk music revival brought national attention to these early and influential music traditions, and they have since collectively become known as examples of American roots music.

Students should learn about the relevant history of the sounds and styles they know best. American roots music is a collection of interrelated vernacular traditions that

has shaped the forms, rhythms, textures, tonalities, and lyrical themes of popular music in the United States, and it can and should be studied systematically in music classrooms. With guidance from music educators, students should also become more cognizant of how pop musicians present themselves, how they develop their skills, what pop music traditions are upheld in its performance and recording, and what antecedents are evident in the style.

Notating Music

One expectation of formal musical training is the attainment of some measure of musical literacy. Musical literacy has varied definitions, but it primarily refers to the ability to hear notes and encode them into symbols and to see symbols and decode them into sounds.[8] We remain grounded in this definition of literacy primarily through its relatedness to reading instruction, in which it means the ability to encode and decode discursive symbols. However, for the same reason that we may call someone "illiterate" for not knowing a historical fact, our use of the term in music means something much more than using notation. Listeners who can hear a piece of music and identify it as a "madrigal" are "literate" in that they demonstrate style sensitivity, that is, they recognize secular text, imitative writing, and so forth, as belonging to the madrigal. While some may argue that this skill is best taught and learned through music performance, that is, by active interaction with musical symbols, certainly it can also be learned without symbols, as demonstrated by the many astute people who write about madrigals but are not necessarily performers.

Popular music learning is so varied that it is not easy to determine a specific role of music reading and writing. For those who learn in garage bands, or "on the fly" in improvisational ensembles, the role of notation is nonexistent or minimal. However, for those who create stage musicals, notational skills are necessary to create scores and parts. In each of these cases, however, performers may be regarded as more or less literate contingent upon their fluency in stylistically appropriate "licks," in the former case, or in the scripting of conducting cues, in the latter case.

Nowhere are the differences between classically trained and aurally trained musicians more clear than in their reactions to their own backgrounds when it comes to music reading and writing. Accomplished musicians who have learned by ear often regret not being able to read music, which might help them to communicate more efficiently with other performers and to preserve their work. Conversely, classically trained musicians often lament being "tied to the page" and unable to improvise or otherwise play from intuition. Both types of performers regard music reading and writing as a detriment to the fullest expression of their musicianship. Still, we might determine both types of musicians to be "literate" if they perform expressively—whether they use notation is not important to our determination.

Successful musicians, whether classically or orally/aurally trained, share many of the same attributes, such as a developed musical memory, sensitivity and competence in ensemble playing, self-critical analysis and evaluation, effective practicing strategies,

creative energy, and a sufficiently strong ego to perform regularly and well for audiences. I propose here that the *differences* between these types of musicians are, in contrast, largely irrelevant.

While popular music is often conceived "by ear," it is an overgeneralization to state that notation has no role in popular music or its history. Professional string and horn arrangers, by virtue of their formal music training, have helped songwriters accentuate the sonorous possibilities of their core ideas. The most conspicuous example of this practice was George Martin's marshaling of the Beatles' raw talent and energy. A classically trained musician, he is well-known to have influenced the structure, harmonic progression, and orchestration of virtually every song he produced. His contributions were a major reason why the Beatles had such widespread appeal and prevailed over all their contemporaries. Some of the most beloved popular songs of the twentieth century have been conceived notationally, such as those written by George Gershwin and Leonard Bernstein.

While these examples illustrate the advantages of notational skills in popular music, notation can also impede the oral music-making process. For example, many songs made popular by the folk revival movement have formed the initial repertory for those learning to accompany their voices with the guitar. Songbook collections are widely available, but the arrangements, in order to remain "easy to read," reduce the melodies, strumming patterns, and chord changes to their simplest form. They do not adequately represent "how the song goes" because the songs are conceived aurally and possess features that are not efficiently captured with notation. Players may at first use songbooks to locate points where certain chords and melodic tones coincide, but they eventually use them only as sources of lyrics for songs, since many in this genre have extended verses.[9]

Perusing a recent issue of *Guitar Player* magazine, I found "pro tips" consisting of guitar solos notated as single-line melodies above the same melody notated in tabulature (a notation system showing graphically where to place fingers on which strings for the correct notes). It also featured technical explanations of picking and style technique above the staves. Conversely, in the product reviews, I found a newly developed guitar trainer that helps players who learn by ear to master recorded guitar solos that are performed too fast to decode. The user inserts a CD, and the machine plays a solo at half speed without altering the pitch and provides a guitar preamp so the learner can play along until mastering the solo.[10] These features demonstrate that popular musicians do rely on notation to learn new music, and those who can read music have more learning options than those who can't. However, an important aspect of popular music culture is the ability to see, listen, absorb, and play along by ear, mastering details that are not conceived and are thus difficult to capture using notation.

The life of the ragtime performer Scott Joplin provides another view of the role of notation in popular music and carries implications for classroom instruction. Born in the 1860s in rural Texas, his mother was a housekeeper for a wealthy lawyer who permitted her son to play his piano while she

was working. Later, determined to provide their child with a better life (his father was born a slave) and encouraged by his incipient musical skills, Joplin's parents sought formal training under the German pianist Julius Weiss, who taught Scott to read and write music—an unusual opportunity for a poor African-American in the late 1800s. By the time Joplin was twenty, he was proficient at playing "by ear," having traveled and worked extensively as a dance musician and saloon entertainer, and he was steadily developing the ragtime style that would make him famous. In 1899, Joplin composed "Maple Leaf Rag," the first piece of sheet music to sell over one million copies, earning him the title "King of Ragtime." He also composed a large-scale ragtime opera, *Treemonisha,* for which he was posthumously awarded the Pulitzer Prize in 1976. Joplin's notational skills elevated his musical and commercial reputation above all other ragtime performers. However, ragtime as a musical style was not necessarily conceived notationally. Joplin most likely wrote the music in his unencumbered "by ear" style and subsequently reproduced it notationally, attesting to the cumbersome look of ragtime when it is notated and the tendency for learners to figure out "how it goes" so they no longer need the score to perform it.[11] This example demonstrates the effectiveness of notation for disseminating musical ideas, and at the same time, testifies to the importance of developing facility on one's instrument, unmediated by symbol systems.

Creating Music

When students are given the opportunity to compose "in their own style," their music almost invariably resembles popular music. The most immediate explanation for this is the ever-present sound of popular music in their lives—they are saturated with it. Today, pop music is aimed at increasingly younger audiences, causing this saturation to overlay a more developmentally critical time span.[12] Popular music has become the vernacular music of the young, suggesting they are more fluent in it (in terms of basic skills like describing, performing, creating, and responding) than in other types of music.

Having asserted that student compositions resemble popular music, I further propose that student compositions *are* popular music. While a tendency in some professional circles is to credit music with reflecting social organization and values, a view popularized by Blacking[13] and others, a related but distinct view is that creating music *generates* social history and culture. Simon Frith explains:

> Music not only represents social relations, it also and simultaneously enacts them ... and too often attempts to relate musical forms to social processes ignore the ways in which music is itself a social process. In other words, in examining the aesthetics of popular music, we need to reverse the usual academic argument: the question is not how a piece of music, a text, "reflects" popular values, but how in performance it produces them.[14]

Students imitate much of what they understand from the sound of popular music when they create music, and this actual *doing* of what they experience as consumers of popular music is a vital and affirming part of the creative process. It helps students discern more tangibly that popular music reflects what they know about themselves, each other, and their world. In this sense, students satisfy two important artistic needs—the impetus to invent, or build, something and the search for coherency between what they know and the medium itself. Peter Abbs states:

> As teachers, we have to keep in touch with the biological roots of art-making, ... that obscure, interior movement that animates, connects, and spontaneously creates inner figurative and narrative patterns. ... At the same time we have to draw on and draw in the inherited culture, all the artefacts [sic] that relate to the particular art discipline, all the techniques that have been laboriously evolved, and as much of the relevant discourse as can be understood.[15]

A significant part of the "inherited culture" of popular music is in the unconscious accumulation of perceptions and appraisals about quality compositions and performances. Students become more judicious in this skill with age; as their compositional skills develop, so does their ability to be productively self-critical and to differentiate between structural aspects of the music and its performance. I have witnessed this emerging ability in some of my own students, who have learned to trust their compositional instincts even while they remain insecure about their performance skills.[16] This disposition is echoed by Ray Charles in his claim, "When you write a good song, it will be good even if it's sung by somebody with a bad voice."[17]

Composing music helps students participate in culture by contributing artifacts, influencing others, and determining new artistic directions for the future. While the immediate effects on culture may initially be evident only in the classroom, they can spread across classrooms, age-groups, schools, and communities. Contemporary education, with its emphasis on social responsibility and respect for individuality, is all about teaching students to *expect* to contribute to culture in positive ways, and the musical arts, by virtue of their importance to our lives, are particularly effective for this purpose. Students can express ideas in and with their music, and herein lie the cultural contributions.

Performing Music

The classical music repertory provides structural and stylistic models for musical performance, and these models reinforce excellence standards within the tradition. It is not unusual to organize performance curricula around exemplary pieces that serve as focal points for addressing all the objectives in the curriculum. The pop music repertory, however, does not have its own exemplary pieces. There are no pop "models" that enable students who have learned them to be functional in popular music performance. Instead, popular music is a flexible medium that adapts itself to, and is defined by, the new performance techniques that even (and, sometimes, especially) inexperienced performers contribute to the genre. For instance, feedbacking, bass "slapping," turntabling, sampling, deejaying, and a host of other performing techniques were not the products of high-level performance practice but arose from a search by novices and professionals alike for new, compelling sounds from available

resources. This is an important draw of popular music—it belongs to young people, accommodating their experimentation and need for musical self-expression.

The evaluation criteria for classical and popular music performance differ widely because they are relatively fixed in the classical music tradition and more protean in popular music. Consider, for example, the desirable characteristics of the singing voice. In the classical tradition, there is consensus on how a trained singing voice sounds. However, in popular music, there may be any number of standards for judging singing skill and quality, since there are so many accepted vocal styles, some bearing little resemblance to others. What is more important is whether the singer is able to express clearly an emotion or feeling through the music. Popular music vocalists are well-known for presenting specific attitudes and emotions in their singing, such as defiance (Bob Dylan, Grace Slick), sadness (Johnny Cash, Robert Wyatt), irony (Loudon Wainwright III), joyfulness (Al Jarreau), tenderness (James Taylor), street smarts (Bonnie Raitt), and youthful defiance (Avril Lavigne). Some singers appear to be trying to eliminate any identifiable emotion in their voices, which suggests indifference (Juliana Hatfield, Liz Phair, Beck). I list these singers to make two distinct points: (1) there is remarkable creative latitude for musicians in the creation and performance of popular music, and (2) our students are drawn to the emotional richness they perceive in popular music.

Another example that highlights the differences in evaluative criteria for popular and classical music is the likelihood of, and even preference for, environmental noise when experiencing music. While the classical music tradition has distinct rules for optimal listening, such as quiet rooms and concentrated attention, the popular music listening tradition suggests the exact opposite. Most likely, listeners will encounter the music with varied, intensive, and even desired interference. So widespread and conscious is this expectation that pop performers have begun accounting for it when mixing and producing new music. Wil S. Hylton, in an imaginary conversation with the pop artist Beck, whose *Sea Changes* had just been released, explained the phenomenon this way:

> The construction workers on the job were jamming to a small, shabby radio, with sh—ty speakers, and you noticed that they did not mind, or even notice the crackle and fuzz. Something crystallized for you in that. You realized that sound quality is a luxury that rarely surfaces in real life. You realize that in real life music usually arrives through a filter of ambient noise. Maybe a faucet is running. Maybe you're in the car, or on a busy street. Maybe the music is droning through the walls of your neighbor's apartment. It doesn't matter what kind of interference you get—just that there *will be* interference most of the time, something between your ears and the speakers to annul the precision of the recording. It was then that you came up with the Other Room Test. Before you can release a new album, you have to give it the ORT: play it on a boom box and listen from another room, letting the sound enter your ears sideways and distorted.[18]

Another profound difference between the popular and classical traditions is their relative view of the purposes of creative and performance activity. In the classical tradition, the artist gradually acquires a conception of the music through practice, undertaking extensive refinements, commensurable with experience, until the final performance represents a summative artifact of its preparation. The listeners' scrutiny of this artifact helps them understand the effort and skill involved in the process. In popular music, summative artifacts are not as important because pop music audiences expect a certain degree of spontaneous charm, a certain level of sincerity that precludes technical perfection. This is why pop concertgoers feel "ripped off" when an artist or group performs exactly as on the recording. This also accounts for the remarkable popularity of cover versions of popular songs, in which the performances are offered as interpretations of the originals: they are successful tributes insofar as they *do not* sound like the originals.[19] Additionally, pop music audiences are fascinated by "demos," earlier, rougher versions of songs that artists assemble to secure recording contracts, to preserve their emerging ideas for songs,[20] or to help producers choose material for an album. Recent reissues of landmark albums have begun featuring additional tracks of demos or outtakes, reflecting and fueling interest in the *process* of artistic creation rather than polished final products.[21]

These and other characteristics of popular music consumers' values have strong implications for the music classroom. Students expect music to allow them and others to extend their personalities through the medium. Students relate to their

favorite performers because those performers reveal something of themselves that tran-
scends the sounds in the music. When students craft their own music, they try to do
likewise—this is partly what makes their
own style "pop." Developing an individual
"voice" in music is thus achieved, and students are motivated to experiment with
other sound sources and production strategies that more efficiently articulate their
personal style. This type of progress is the
best there is in music teaching and learning.

Reconceptualizing Musicality

As a way of summarizing some of the
points raised in this chapter, we should
revisit the task of defining "musicality," since
it is linked to whether we believe popular
music deserves a rightful place in school
music instruction. The following is an explanation of musicality by Roger Reggeri:

> On its most general levels, to be musical is
> to sound right, to be notably satisfying to
> both experienced and inexperienced lis-
> teners. It means playing adequately in
> time, in tune, with an appealing sound,
> and with appropriate dynamic contours.
> After years of performing and hearing
> countless auditions at all levels of achieve-
> ment, I remain impressed by how easy
> that sounds, but how enduringly difficult
> it is to actually rise to its challenges.[22]

The use of the words "satisfying," "adequately," "appealing," and "appropriate"
presupposes agreement on what these
words represent in terms of sound. Also
evident is the opinion that achievement of
musicality is arduous. Compare Reggeri's
statement here of what musicians need to
do to make good music with the following

explanation by the rock performer Al
Kooper, in an excerpt from a record review
he wrote in the 1960s:

> This album was made along the lines of
> the motto "honesty is the best policy."
> The best part of pop music today is
> honesty. The "She's Leaving Home," the
> "Without Her's," the "Dear Landlord's"
> etc. When you hear a dishonest record
> you feel you've been insulted or turned
> off in comparison. It's like the difference
> between "Dock of the Bay" and "This
> Guy's in Love with You." Both are excel-
> lent compositions and both were num-
> ber one. But you believe Otis while you
> sort of question Herb Alpert. You can
> believe every line in this album and if
> you choose to it can only elevate your
> listening pleasure immeasurably.[23]

Kooper's statements focus on the single
criterion of honesty, but they do not tell us
how "honest" music sounds. They are, like
Reggeri's criteria, decidedly subjective, but
they have more to do with *intention* than
with *performance within specified boundaries.*
These statements highlight differences in
standards and values regarding the nature
and purpose of music.

The traditional organization in contemporary Western culture of a few who produce music and a majority who only consume it[24] is vanishing with the advent of
digital recording technology. Since virtually
anyone can produce a polished CD recording economically, virtually everyone is. This
trend strengthens the possibility of students
as active contributors to popular culture,
since the roles of former mediators such as
talent agents, producers, and record companies have severely diminished. Now, all our
students are in the driver's seat. Many con-

temporary issues about intolerable volume levels, relentless rhythms, inappropriate lyrics, and derogatory stereotypes of female pop stars are challenges that we can negotiate with students because they will be *creating* the issues. But the students continue to need our guidance, and we should mediate what they want to know and learn with what we know and have learned, just as music teachers have been doing for years.

To revise what we believe musicality means, we must take into account what our training and intuition tell us is important, but we must also factor in what the training and intuition of our students tell them is important. Teachers, students, and the cultural world at large must negotiate together the meaning of "musicality"—what it represents and how it mediates classroom activities—lest we lose the battle of conflicting values, which has too long been the case in music education. I have seen the smiles on the faces of in-service music teachers as I play popular music for them, music that I am sure triggers all kinds of reactions. Imagine how sweet it would be if our students think of us when they, as adults, hear the favorite songs of their own past.

Notes

1. Here and elsewhere, I will use the term "popular" to describe musicians who have acquired their skills and knowledge primarily through the aural/oral tradition and "classically trained" to describe musicians who have acquired their skills and knowledge primarily through formal training in music.

2. Richard Middleton, "Popular Music in the West," in *The New Grove Dictionary of Music Online,* ed. Laura Macy (Oxford: Oxford University Press, n.d.[cited 28 July 2003]); available at www.grovemusic.com. Middleton offers these three approaches with a word of caution—that the term "popular" is much more fluid than the approaches reflect and that it is susceptible to a broad array of criticisms and social/technological forces that constantly redefine it.

3. In John Blacking, *How Musical Is Man?* (Seattle: University of Washington Press, 1973), the author argues that Western European societies elevate the very best musically trained individuals as a way of distinguishing them from the rest of society, which is partly accomplished by preserving the status of the majority as untrained.

4. This synopsis of pop music is similar to many found in music reference books, notably in Nicolas Slonimsky, ed., *Baker's Dictionary of Music* (New York: Schirmer Books, 1997).

5. Robbie Robertson, "Rick Danko—Robbie Robertson," interview by Steve Caraway, The Band Web site (Halden, Norway: Jan Søiberg, n.d.[cited 14 September 2003]); available at http://theband.hiof.no/articles/gpm_rr_rd_dec _76.html. Previously published in *Guitar Player,* December 1976, this interview contains a concise version of this well-known story about Robbie Robertson. It is also worth noting that Robertson used a widely imitated "banjo-roll" method of outlining chords that requires realignment of the picking fingers on adjacent strings with the voicing of various chord inversions, one right after the other, in the chording hand, which is indicative of intensive, sustained practice.

6. Sully Erna, interview by Austin Skaggs, *Rolling Stone,* 29 May 2003, 24.

7. A clear example of this influence is the manner in which early proponents of grunge resurrected the career of their personal idol, Neil Young, who proceeded to become a hero of the movement. He was brought onstage for encores with various groups and cheered wildly by young fans, even though most of them were unaware of his past recordings and their connection to grunge.

8. A more comprehensive explanation of music literacy can be found in Patricia Shehan Campbell and Carol Scott-Kassner, *Music in Childhood: From Preschool through the Elementary Grades* (New York: Schirmer Books, 1995).

9. On a recent visit to a local bookstore, I found six different Bob Dylan songbooks in the music section. I bought one for my daughter, who I have observed using it precisely as described here. One of his classic songs, "Sad-Eyed Lady of the Lowlands," has five verses of eight lines, an average of nine words per line, and a nonlinear story line featuring unusual conceptual relationships and imagery.

10. *Guitar Player,* September 2003.

11. One explanation why notation may be cumbersome in ragtime performance is that two different playing techniques are required, one for each hand. The right hand outlines the (usually) syncopated melody, rich with the cross-rhythms of vernacular music from the Deep South, while the left hand plays more metrically, usually in octaves, offering stability reminiscent of Sousa marches. It is much like rubbing your head and patting your tummy, and since performing a rag requires concentrated independence of hands, having to read notation adds needless complexity to the process.

12. When I visit my son's kindergarten class to lead music time, none of the students, including my son, know the Mother Goose nursery rhymes, but all of them request selections from the *Lion King.*

13. John Blacking, *How Musical Is Man?* Blacking made these assertions based on his extensive observations of the Venda people of Africa.

14. Simon Frith, *Performing Rites: On the Value of Popular Music* (Cambridge: Harvard University Press, 1996), 269.

15. Peter Abbs, *A is for Aesthetic: Essays on Creative and Aesthetic Education* (New York: Falmer Press, 1989), 23. In the first chapter, "Creativity, the Arts and the Renewal of Culture," Abbs proposes that these two forces of creative thinking are best viewed as opposing axes, with the conscious/unconscious represented by the vertical axis, and the traditional/ innovative represented by the horizontal axis.

16. Carlos Xavier Rodriguez, "Designing the Music Composition Matrix: Tasks, Tools, Working Styles, and Contingencies" (paper presented at the European Society for the Cognitive Sciences of Music, University of Liège, Belgium,

April 2002). The subjects in this study were undergraduate music education majors whose critical responses to their compositions were examined for experience-related changes.

17. Ray Charles, "What I've Learned: Ray Charles," interview by Mike Sager, *Esquire,* August 2003, 98.

18. Wil S. Hylton, "The Master of Everything (and Nothing at All)" [imaginary conversation with the pop artist Beck], *Esquire,* November 2002, 159.

19. One notable divergence from this practice was the work of Todd Rundgren, the pop music wizard who compiled an album of covers titled *Faithful,* in which his versions were dead-on remakes of the originals, ostensibly to exercise his consummate skills in performing, recording, mixing, and producing.

20. XTC, *Homegrown* [liner notes]. TVT Records, TVT3330-2. Band members of the English band XTC were reportedly frustrated with principal songwriter Andy Partridge when, in preparation for the recording of their album *Wasp Star,* Partridge overdeveloped his personal demo version of the song "We're All Light," leaving the band no opportunities for additional creative changes.

21. I recently purchased a reissue of my all-time favorite pop music record, *Harmony Row* by Jack Bruce, featuring "bonus tracks" of some early takes. A discarded rhythm track from the song "Escape to the Royal Wood (on Ice)" triggered an intense aesthetic reaction.

22. Roger Ruggeri, "What Does It Mean to Be Musical?" *American String Teacher* 50, no. 1 (2000): 132.

23. Al Kooper, review of *Music from the Big Pink* by the Band, The Band Web site (Halden, Norway: Jan Søiberg, n.d. [cited 14 September 2003]); available at http://theband.hiof.no/ albums/rs_15_music_from_big_pink.html. This review was originally published in *Rolling Stone* in August 1968.

24. Ian Cross, "Music, Mind and Evolution," *Psychology of Music* 29, no. 1 (2001): 95–102.

Carlos Xavier Rodriguez is associate professor of curriculum and instruction and associate director of undergraduate studies in the School of Music at the University of Iowa in Iowa City. An active writer, clinician, and musician, his research and teaching interests include musical development, interpretation, and expression.

2
"Pop" Goes …?
Taking Popular Music Seriously

Wayne D. Bowman

Stiff in opinions, always in the wrong.
—*John Dryden*

You know something is happening here,
but you don't know what it is—do you,
Mister Jones?

—*Bob Dylan*

The gap between conventional music curricula in North American schools and the musical practices in which most people engage in everyday life is enormous, and it is growing wider at a breathtaking rate. This point is illustrated concisely and provocatively by Daniel Cavicchi:

> I would think it safe to say that the stead-fast school music rituals of singing folk songs in unison, learning music notation, and playing an instrument in a marching band are quite removed from most students' musical lives, not only in terms of genre and style but also in terms of defining what "music" is supposed to be about. If outside of school a student's musical life mainly consists of trading MP3 files of obscure emo and grunge songs on his computer or dancing with friends at an all-ages club, then a music class where he studies how to play the clarinet is going to seem incredibly bizarre.[1]

This "disconnect" between the experiences that typify students' school-based musical activities and their out-of-school musical lives is no minor curiosity, no idle or passing concern. It is, if critics like Cavicchi are to be believed, part of a broader trend with far-reaching and profoundly troubling consequences. Formal, institutionalized music studies and actual musical practices have, Cavicchi asserts, "parted ways."

The music education community's increasing obsession with advocacy is, I believe, a clear reflection of this trend, as more and more resources (both financial and imaginative) become necessary to justify instructional practices whose meaning and relevance are apparent neither to those for whom they are intended nor to those who provide financial support. At the same time, ironically, people's belief in the value of music is as evident as ever. Music occupies vast amounts of people's time and expendable income and plays a constitutive role in vast ranges of daily activity. Clearly, something is amiss in the way we conceive of and engage in music education; for where people find meaning and value in what they do, there is seldom a need to convince them of the importance of becoming more proficient or knowledgeable about it.

One strategic response to this legitimation crisis is to endeavor to make school music more relevant to students' lives by replacing old or anachronistic musical content with music believed to have greater currency. However, this strategy is not nearly as straightforward as it may seem. On the one hand, it must be weighed against the important educational aim of enhancing access to the less common, less accessible, and therefore less "relevant." On the other hand, it is necessary to ask whether the factors that make for relevance are compatible with or capable of survival in the context of formal schooling.

The case of jazz is illustrative. The incorporation of jazz into the school music curriculum was motivated at least in part by concerns about relevance and currency. But it is important to note that jazz became "safe," "respectable," and "legitimate" musical content for school study only as its commercial viability and popularity in the broader social realm waned. It is also noteworthy that the kind of jazz practices that eventually gained sufficient legitimacy to warrant bona fide musical and educational status became, in that process, school jazz. Its recognition of the legitimacy of jazz notwithstanding, institutionalized music education was able to accommodate relatively few of the divergent sociomusical priorities presented by jazz—priorities like individuality, independence, innovation, nonconformity, and creativity. Because adding jazz to the curriculum did little to

transform the way music educators conceptualized music, or curriculum, or the nature of education, jazz practices paid a steep price for admission to the academy.

The significance of these observations for our interest in popular music is twofold. First, the inertia of school music and the institutions it serves is a force that must not be underestimated. Second, and as a consequence, popular music cannot improve or revitalize the curriculum without radically reforming the way it is conceived. Put differently, the introduction of popular music into the curriculum will change little unless we examine explicitly its implications for how and why we do what we do—unless we take advantage of the opportunity to retheorize our instructional and educational practices. An educational program that attempts to incorporate popular music without addressing its powerful cultural resonances and contradictions—without situating it amidst issues of struggle, resistance, defiance, identity, power, and control—is an educational program that seeks to use popular music to achieve safe, preordained ends, ignoring the very things that account for its popularity in the first place. If our intent in adding popular music studies to the curriculum is to maintain "what is," or to enable us simply to keep doing what we already do—to simply "add 'the popular' and stir"—we would probably do well to forego the effort. Our interest in popularity and things popular should not revolve around the maintenance of the existing system. Rather, we should use it to reopen possibilities for critical and creative thought and action, both in our students and in ourselves. The issues attending the incorpo ration of popular music studies into the school curriculum are both extensive and complex, and they involve concerns at the very heart of music education and curriculum theory. They offer an exceptional opportunity to open up dialogue on the ways music education might need to change if popular music were to become paramount among the things we deem worthy of teaching and learning. We need, in other words, to examine that into which we would incorporate these popular phenomena—to help make unfamiliar our overfamiliar world of music education. To that end, taking popular music seriously is a stance rich in transformative potential for North American music education.

Let me identify at the outset several of the assumptions and convictions that frame this essay. First, I believe that the problems created by excluding popular music far outweigh the perceived perils of including it. Second, I believe that North American music education must and eventually will (whether of choice or necessity) find ways to incorporate popular music studies meaningfully into its public school and university curricula. Third, I do not believe that this can be achieved without major, perhaps even radical, reconceptualizations of what music is, and what music education means (how it is best done, by whom, for whom, and to what ends). Fourth, these reconceptualizations do not (and must not) mean that "serious" or "classical" music studies will be eliminated. This suggests that, fifth, it is imperative that we develop instructional frameworks and teacher competencies that accommodate both musics at once.[2] These concerns point collectively to a need

for close interrogation and philosophical analysis of the taken-for-granted beliefs and values that undergird current educational practice in music.

Whence "Popularity"?

Let us begin at the beginning, because we ought to agree on what we are talking about. What might be meant by the phrase popular music, and what is it about popularity that interests (or ought to interest) us? The difficulties begin here. The adjective "popular" has many, many meanings— some of them contradictory, some of them incompatible with the aims and nature of education, and many of them more implicit than explicit. Popular music's meaning is a question, as one scholar puts it, "riddled with complexities."[3]

The most facile answer is, as usual, not very helpful: popular music is that which is not unpopular.[4] Not only is this annoyingly circular, it points us in the direction of statistical rather than musical or educational issues.[5] How extensive or pervasive or enjoyable must a musical practice be in order to warrant educational inclusion on the basis of its popularity? The limited statistical perspective replaces questions of musical value with concerns about the extent to which music is programmed, purchased, or consumed—an approach made familiar by the Top 40 hit parade.[6] It replaces qualitative concerns with quantitative ones. One might argue that the most popular (i.e., the most statistically pervasive) should be represented proportionally in the curriculum, and the least popular should receive minimal attention. But that flies in the face of the idea of education as an endeavor intended to introduce people to the less pervasive, the uncommon, the rare, and the precious. It also fails to acknowledge that many broadly popular things do not appeal to a homogenous mass of people for reasons they all share, but rather achieve their popularity by connecting with diverse and divergent subgroups for different, even contradictory, reasons.

A more revealing way to proceed is by asking to what the term "popular" stands as *other* in general usage—what the term is presumed to exclude—and, consequently, what we mean implicitly when we designate music as popular. The list in Table 1 helps demonstrate the magnitude and complexity of this definition problem.

Each of the contrasts listed in Table 1 is deeply flawed. Collectively, they not only distort our understanding of popular and classical music, they also pervert our understanding of the entire musical field. Yet at the same time there is in each contrast, from some strongly held perspective, a degree of validity. Each represents a way people (music educators among them) tend to talk about and conceive of popularity. In light of the liberal mix of laudatory and condemnatory ideas, it should be evident that popularity means many things to many people—not a very sanguine situation for a profession potentially interested in embracing music that is popular or in endorsing music for its popularity.

What contrasts like these share more fundamentally and disturbingly is their dualism—their reduction of potentially useful distinctions to dichotomous differences. Most criticism and praise of popular music is, I believe, implicated in one or more of these dichotomous systems of thought—systems rooted in comfortable, unexamined assumptions that what popularity means is perfectly clear and that its nature is quite different from "the rest" of music (whatever "the rest" means). The real challenge for music education, then, lies in learning to deconstruct these binaries in ways that breathe life into the supposedly moribund classics, while at the same time recognizing the educational integrity of the popular—and in the process, showing the continuity and unity of all human musical endeavor.

The most recalcitrant and misleading myths about popular art and music stem from certain biases of philosophical idealism, biases Richard Shusterman aptly calls "ascetic."[7] These ascetic biases become manifest in three near-phobic aversions I like to designate "plethorophobia" (aversion to multiplicity), "temporophobia" (anxiety about temporal transience and change), and "somatophobia" (fear of the body). Not coincidentally, music that is popular often manifests multiplicity, transience, and corporeality in abundance.

Thus, popular music affords pleasures that are often considered cheap, quick, or easy (unlike the "deferred gratification"[8] supposedly associated with genuinely artistic music). Its gratifications are spurious, or fraudulent—the musical equivalent of junk food or self-gratification. It titillates the body rather than nourishing the mind. Its effects are superficial and fleeting, not durable; subjective rather than objective. Popular music is created for passive consumption and is bereft of intellectual effort and reward. It is boringly simple, banal,

Table 1

Defining the Popular

"The Popular" *is Other* to ...	And therefore *Is* ...
The elite, rare	Down to earth
The special, exceptional	Everyday, mundane, common
The pretentious and haughty	Real, authentic, honest
The pretentious and haughty	Prosaic
The classical, "classy"	Un-classy, uncouth
The aristocratic, for "the few"	Democratic, of "the people"
The select	Accessible
The complex	Simple
The restrained, refined	Indulgent, crass
The mindful	Visceral
The cerebral and somber	Vital, fun
The respectful, polite	Defiant, irreverent, rude, unruly
The serious, profound	Capricious, trivial, lightweight, trite
The stuffy, dull, dying, or dead	Vital, living, energetic
The intrinsically valuable	Commercial, of primarily extrinsic value
The objective or absolute	Subjective, functional, social, political
The formally autonomous	Socially determined
The intellectual	Human, real
The challenging, demanding	Banal, predigested
The genuine, authentic	Fraudulent, fake
The time-tested and validated	Transient, fleeting
The museum	The street
The transcendent	Worldly
The contemplative	Entertaining, diversionary
The appreciated	Participatory
The expressive and vital	Formulaic, trite dulling
The acoustically produced	Electronically mediated
The formal, calculated	Informal, casual
The sophisticated, elevated	Vernacular, everyday
The premeditated, planned	Spontaneous, unrestrained
Broad and richly various	Narrow[a]
The learned	Socialized, absorbed
The controlled, orderly	Out of control
The high	Low
The musical	Premusical, submusical, extramusical
That with sufficient cohesion, integrity, and interest to have a name of its own	Residue, someone else's music

Note: [a] Note that this contrast is the view of the outsider, to whom other people's music "all sounds the same." For many who are unfamiliar with so-called classical musical traditions, the classical music field appears narrow and predictable–precisely the same claim devotees of the classics frequently make about other musics.

and predigested, so as to relieve the listener of any real effort or responsibility. It caters more to sensation than to cognition. Its products are not creative or original, but trendy and derivative. They enter into and fall out of fashion rather than standing the test of time. Popular music is music of the herd—music that numbs individual and critical awareness. It all sounds the same: formulaic, predicable, rhythmic, and obvious. It is designed to pander to the lowest common denominator of human taste.

The most cogent and convincing advocate of such views is Theodore Adorno, who was probably right in many aspects of his argument. He was wrong, however, in one of his most fundamental assumptions: that popular music is all of one cloth, hopelessly enmeshed with a "culture industry" whose influence renders it incapable of critical resistance, cognitive substance, or challenge. Still, any attempt to mount a balanced understanding of popular music must proceed through Adorno's arguments; they cannot be bypassed.[9]

Again, the chief failing of these arguments is their failure to acknowledge that not all popular music is identical. Popular music is not an "it" but a "them"—a vast, multifarious, and fluid range of musical practices with remarkably different and divergent intentions, values, potentials, and affordances. Much of it speaks to the body, or more properly, the incorporated (embodied) mind; but there is nothing inherently cheap, substandard, or second-class in that. Much of it is accessible and enjoyable without major intellectual effort, but there is no reason significance must be difficult, nor is the intellect the primary

determinant of musical worth. Much of it is trite, banal, and insipid, but it is not inherently or invariably so. It caters to large audiences, but these are by no means uniform. Its commodity character—its commercial side—is an important part of what it is, but that by no means exhausts its appeal or its semiotic (thought- and behavior-shaping) potential. What we get from the one-sided views of music represented in Table 1 are grossly distorted views of music.

So, What *Is* Popular Music?

We have discounted the utility of the statistical approach to defining popularity. We have also observed that our common discursive uses of the term "popular" point to a deeply ideological field with contested and contradictory parameters. We have suggested as well that many dismissals of the popular follow from the prudishness of philosophical idealism and its worries over the trustworthiness of things bodily, multitudinous, or transient. This leads us to the further question of whether popular music may be best understood along lines of social class, a view with its substantial share of adherents among both sociologists and musicians.

The list of implicit meanings advanced in the previous section of this chapter makes evident two opposing class-based views of popular music, one from "above" and one from "below."[10] Both views are rooted in essentialism—the naive and seriously mistaken belief that popularity is the kind of thing that has an "essence" and that this essence can be traced more or less along social class lines. The view from above is that popular music is a mass, standardized, commercial phenomenon, shaped and defined by the manipulative interests of a capitalist culture industry. Seen from below, popular music is the music of "real people"—authentic, grounded, vital, and connected to day-to-day human existence. From the first perspective, popularity threatens to replace superior music that is, for variously valid reasons, inherently unpopular; from the latter, the elitism of art music poses a threat to the music of common folk. Both perspectives err in their assumption that popularity has a stable essence—whether, as Middleton puts it, "the people" is regarded as "an active, progressive historical subject or a manipulated dupe."[11] The trouble with essentialist views of popularity is that they attempt to disentangle what is by its very nature entangled, to make concrete what is fluid and immaterial, to unify what is diverse and contradictory.

In opposition to essentialist views, Middleton takes the stance that popular music "can only be viewed within the context of the *whole musical field,* in which it has an active tendency; and this field, together with its internal relationships, is never still— it is always *in movement.*"[12] What this phrase "popular music" does, then, is attempt to "put a finger on that space, that terrain, of contradiction—between 'imposed' and 'authentic,' 'elite' and 'common,' predominant and subordinate, then and now, theirs and ours, and so on—and to organize it in particular ways."[13] Clearly, this is a project replete with ideological ramifications.

The musical field to which Middleton refers is the field Keil and Feld characterize as "culture"—fermenting, "morphing," bubbling—as opposed to the domain of "civilization," in which most such activity

has subsided, or spent itself.[14] The field of popular music is, in other words, continuous with the whole field of musical agency and action; it is always contested, never stable, and ever and unavoidably political.[15] There are no pure or stable cultures, let alone cultures that can be segregated hierarchically so that the terms "high" and "low" describe accurately people's involvements and engagements. Individuals and groups have multiple and fluid subjectivities, identities, and affinities that may be simultaneously or alternatively "high" and "low," above or below—as circumstances and propensities warrant.

So where does this leave us in our quest for a definition? *Without one,* if we expect something handy-dandy, neat, and definitive. The only definition that seems defensible is one that is open, provisional, and subject to revision—one that foregoes the idealist's yearning for the eternal, exhaustive, and final. This does not negate the possibility of definition, but it does render untenable the idea that popular music and all its associated values and pleasures can be accounted for in some simple, timeless, monolithic way. Popular music is, as Middleton shows, a field whose area is extensive and whose inner structure is highly complex.

All this said, it might be argued, we know what popularity means, even if that meaning is fluid, various, and contested. We know more or less what sort of practices we speak of when we talk about popular music, even if we are sometimes unable to agree whether a particular practice warrants the label. Let us ask, then, how popular music tends to be characterized.

It tends, at least in this age of late capitalism and technology, to be *mass-mediated*.[16] Its *commodity character* is an important part of what it is, a prominent source of what makes its popularity possible. It tends as well to be designed or intended for a *broad audience*, however constituted, an audience often *without formal training* or the kind of technical understanding musicians call musicianship. Its audience is comprised extensively of *amateurs*—those whose interest stems not from professional involvement but more simply and directly from love ("amateur" derives from the Latin, *amare*) of the music at hand. Likewise, its practitioners—tend to be less formally schooled and more inclined to learn and transmit their craft *aurally*,[17] if enhanced by recorded media. Popular music is, to this extent, music created by, and especially for, the enjoyment and enrichment of *everyday people* in their *everyday lives*.

By these criteria, "classical" music and jazz once were, but no longer are, popular. Their practice has become highly specialized, reliant upon formal training, and aimed extensively at fellow practitioners—although obviously, this does not preclude enjoyment and use by others, especially those with the benefit of some kind of formal tuition or other means of induction into the norms of the practice.

Thus another common tendency of music we tend to regard as popular: its relative *informality* and its seeming indifference to concerns like stylistic purity or authenticity.[18] Popular music tends to be music that is not intended to transcend time, place, and circumstance; it is more a music of and for the *here and now*—though in today's mediated world "here" can range

from the local to the global. This is not to say that certain of its products may not eventually achieve the kind of ongoing cultural resonance that transforms them into cultural icons of sorts, but their origins (precisely like much music that has subsequently attained "artistic" status) are more *pragmatic,* more concerned with use than transcendental status. Popular music is *used music.* (That nonpopular or artistically elevated musics are also "used"—albeit for purposes less immediately obvious—is both further evidence of the need for contingent definitions and of the depth of the ideological roots of these issues.) Because popular music has a pragmatic orientation, stylistic modulation, mutation, and hybridity are regular features: popular musics tend to approach the musical field as a place for *play and experimentation* more often than as the ground for the creation of works.

An important corollary of these tendencies is popular music's linkage to *embodied or corporeal experience*.[19] Popular music is not generally or primarily intended for cerebral or contemplative perception. It often emphasizes rhythm, timbre, volume, and other attributes that align themselves with process, gesture, and "feel." Rather than revolving around syntactical and hierarchical structural concerns or the cognitively mediated anticipations/expectations with which these are associated,[20] popular music tends to speak to the body or to appeal to a bodily mode of engagement that demands familiarity but not formal tuition.[21]

The "definition" I have been reluctantly developing in this section[22] thus includes the following tendencies: (a) breadth of intended appeal, (b) mass mediation and commodity character, (c) amateur engagement, (d) continuity with everyday concerns, (e) informality, (f) here-and-now pragmatic use and utility, (g) appeal to embodied experience, and (h) emphasis upon process.

One final matter demands our consideration before we move on: the fact that popular music in today's world seems by and large to mean youth music. The question of whether this is a function of "the music" or of the way it is marketed and the disposable income of young people is a revealing one, because the difficulty in answering it points to the inextricable links between popularity and capitalist systems of production and distribution. The popularity of music is a function of the creation of consumer demand, a factor that has no inherent connection to the value of the music itself. People like what they know and are given, rather than knowing what they like. In light of this, we would probably do well to draw a distinction between "pop" music and music that is popular in the more broadly democratic sense. "Pop" is more purely commodity music, designed foremost with market in mind. Whether the more democratic sense of popularity even remains a possibility in the age of commodity capitalism is very much an open question. The punk movement, for example, has raised in particularly acute form the question "whether, in a capitalist society, a really popular music is in fact possible."[23]

On closer reflection, then, these last matters—these afterthoughts about youth, consumerism, commodity exchange, and the industrial creation of taste—are not incidental "asides" at all. They are among the most important attributes of popular music as constituted in our postmodern, late capitalistic world. And they bring to the fore once more the economic and ideological underpinnings of popular culture—reminding us that popularity is never straight ahead, never as obvious as it seems, never "popular" in the one-dimensional sense advocates and detractors would have us believe.

Despite my best efforts at definition, then, the only defensible answer to the question used to frame this section (What is popular music?) is, "That depends!" "Popular music" is like "art"; it does not and cannot mean any one thing, or even any single combination of things. Terms like these are tools; what they mean depends on who is using them and to what ends. Their meaning cannot be settled once and for all and will always be contested. (I hope, therefore, that readers have found significant counterexamples to each of the components in my compound "definition.") Popular music is not commodity or mass music for those who most care about and are most intimately involved with it,[24] nor is it always "youth" music, nor is it invariably connected to everyday concerns, and so on. Popular music's status is ever unsettled and contested, and indeed, these may be its most salient characteristics. These characteristics are, at the same time, among the greatest challenges to those who would make it an integral part of music education.

Education and the Popular

Adding education to the popular music equation expands exponentially the complexity and contradictions the music education profession must consider. Thus far, we have been concerned with identifying what popular music "is" (or "isn't"), because such determinations constitute an important preliminary step in the selection of curricular content. Definition provides us with a basis for indicating what to incorporate and exclude. Yet in this case, it is arguable that what we have identified significantly challenges and subverts music education itself—at least as it conventionally understood and practiced. This leads inexorably to political questions about the desirability or necessity of professional change, questions the remainder of this chapter will endeavor to explore.

A serious and thoughtful commitment to popular music in music education would change a great many things, curricular content by no means the least of them. If popular music's meaning and identity are fundamentally unsettled, a music education profession that takes such music seriously can scarcely evade unsettledness itself. Is music education more concerned with cultural preservation or with cultural transformation? To what extent are cultural values and ideological struggles appropriately addressed within musical education? Should music education concern itself with what *is,* or is it more properly concerned with what *could be?* Can educational institutions study without distortion musical practices that are often rebellious, coarse, vulgar, and deliberately offensive? Can musical practices in which individuality, creativity, and change figure so prominently be accommodated in schools that are on many levels devoted to precisely the opposite ends? Even if we agree to some stipula-

tive definition of popularity and presume thereby to have resolved the curricular question of what kind of music is appropriate and desirable for instructional purposes, it remains for us to decide such matters as whose music, for whom, and to what ends—and to judge whether schools lend themselves satisfactorily to such things.

The fact that something *is* popular provides us with no clear reason for teaching it,[25] especially if the nature of popularity alters radically what instruction might entail—unless, of course, current instructional practices are clearly inadequate and in need of alteration. I stated at the outset that popular music might have little effect on music education unless we embrace it as an opportunity to think carefully and critically about how and why we do what we do. If the arguments I have advanced have merit, such thought appears an unavoidable outcome of endorsing popular music.

Let us reflect briefly on the aims of schooling, qualifying what we say with the recognition that such ends are, like the meaning of popular music, various and contested. (In this interesting way, popular music and education might be ideally compatible!) What are the educational ends of schooling by which we might be able to assess the desirability of incorporating popular music into the curriculum?

First, education is concerned with the development of skills, understandings, and dispositions that do not follow easily or naturally from the socialization process alone. For most young people, however, popular music plays a major role in that socialization process, which suggests a kind of overfamiliarity with the subject among those to whom we would teach it (and perhaps an inevitable underfamiliarity among those responsible for instruction). The question, then, is what teaching, learning about, and engaging in popular music can achieve that is educational, not already accomplished informally, and yet desired by society at large. So long as we confine our attention to musical practices that are not widespread and that do not flourish unassisted in society, the case for music education seems fairly clear. (This is not to say it is persuasive, only that a genuinely educational need appears to have been advanced.) But when we turn our attention to something that is thriving without educational interventions, our understandings and justifications for what we are doing must change.

Second, education is concerned with developing and transmitting skills, understandings, and dispositions that are deemed important by society. Though obvious, this cannot go without saying, since informal socialization fails to transmit many things that nonetheless do not warrant the allocation of scarce educational resources. Resources are allocated for the protection or preservation of major human accomplishments and the transmission of indispensable social values.

Although situating popular music among achievements deemed worthy of educational transmission may be controversial, popular music's relevance to social values is less so—again, depending upon what values one has in mind. Among the social values deemed indispensable in Western democracies are those that prepare an informed citizenry for democratic participation by broadening horizons, developing more pluralistic values, and the like. A third educational aim, then, involves preparing students for life by giving them skills that will serve them well. Significant among these in capitalistic democracies are such attributes as empowerment, independence, self-reliance, critical skills, and the inclination to use them. Popular music's cultural significance and its ideologically contested nature may be well suited to ends like these, provided that instruction actually addresses them rather than avoiding them or sweeping them under the rug. From this perspective, it might well be argued that popularity raises complex questions exactly where they need to be raised—particularly in light of music education's historical propensity for technical training rather than education in the broad sense, and in light of the frequent assumption that music education's designated curricular foci are self-evident and directed by values presumed to be intrinsic.

On this view, then, popular music studies might be justified on grounds that they develop the kind of critical awareness that makes people less vulnerable to totalizing (universalizing, or totalitarian) thought, to capitalism's voracious need for willing consumers, or to the potent semiotic forces at work in the musics that now pervade almost every aspect of everyday life.[26] We might argue without contradiction, then, that one reason we should study popular music is precisely because much of it is of dubious quality. That much popular music serves as propaganda or as a substitute for critical awareness may be granted without discounting the importance of addressing it educationally. There are at least two reasons popular music's dangers or deficiencies should not keep it out of schools: first, it is not uniformly defective or deficient; and second, one of the concerns of education is to enhance people's access to what is better, to make them more discriminating in their perceptions and choices. Music education might actually presume to improve the quality of popular music by making students more fully aware and competent.[27]

Adorno's scathing critiques of popular music as mind-numbing indoctrination (training the unconscious for conditioned reflexes), though not universally valid as he believed, are persuasive accounts of what may indeed happen where people are not extended the potential benefits of musical education. From this perspective, education and schooling exist in part to give people more control over their lives and to enable them to make true, informed choices. The educated person makes decisions and acts in light of the desirability of foreseen consequences. The musically educated person is able to use music to enhance and shape time, not simply to "kill" it.[28]

At least one further reason to study popular music remains—one that differs substantially from, but is by no means incompatible with, what has been advanced above. Popular music might be approached as a vital field of action, such that instruction seeks to help students participate in and contribute creatively to the field itself. This orientation would focus on bringing students into a realm of meaningful and potentially rewarding action and is closely aligned with the performance emphasis of conventional music education in North America. Although it is also more closely aligned with

training than with the broader sense of education, its continuity with existing practice would doubtless enhance its appeal and familiarity to music educators. Whether the diverse performance practices of the popular music field are feasible in standardizing institutions like schools or whether the small size of popular music groups render them unviable vehicles for the education of broad student populations remains to be seen. In light of the allegations of selectivity that have plagued large performing ensembles historically, this latter question needs to be considered carefully.

Popular Music and Schooling[29]

I have referred repeatedly to things like diversity, change, complexity, contestedness, and contradiction when characterizing the field of popular music; each of these being inherent features of living human practices, of "culture" in contrast to "civilization." The educational issues raised by such characteristics need to be addressed explicitly, however. Most of these revolve around tensions between living, breathing culture and the standardized and standardizing systems typical of institutionalized instruction. In brief, what often makes popular music popular are things like coarseness, corporeality, casualness, and contradiction—to say nothing of its polysemic nature, its capacity to engage diverse groups of people in simultaneously different ways on simultaneously different levels, not all of them reflective. Musical validity issues aside, many of these characteristics are simply inappropriate to public institutionalized instruction.

But what of the further question: can popular music deemed otherwise appropriate remain viable in such settings? Although none of the potential impediments are insuperable, some do demand careful consideration. In the first place, the comfort of formal institutions can be inimical to the cutting-edge cultural realities that are so often the focus of popular artistry. Secondly, the technical standards of schooled artistry may be at odds with the kinds of raw creative energies at the heart of living, breathing musical practices. Thirdly, the history of any truly creative tradition, as Gracyk reminds us, revolves around individual inventions or achievements that simply cannot be predicted from their predecessors.[30] Therefore, instruction that seeks truly to situate students amid "the action" in popular realms needs not only to allow for but also to incorporate things like divergence, unpredictability, freedom, and radical experimentation—a potential worry, one might think, in institutions that are otherwise devoted so extensively to standardization and conformity. Conservative institutional inertia, as the example of jazz shows, tends to enshrine and refine practices rather than nurture their further evolution. A personal friend and devoted jazz musician, Les Paine, once made a passing comment to me about the standardizing effect of formalized pedagogical systems on jazz performance—a profound comment whose seeming simplicity makes it all the more potent. "If you put ketchup on everything," he observed, "everything is going to taste like ketchup."

By committing seriously to process, one changes almost everything about music education. To the alarmist response that we stand to lose more than we gain by "chang-ing everything," I can only offer that I am not necessarily suggesting we discard current instructional practices and curricular emphases in their entirety—as if that were even possible. One can alter fundamental assumptions, goals, and processes without starting over from scratch. Several fundamental characteristics of the status quo would almost certainly have to be rejected, however—fondness for standardization and uniformity foremost among these.

It is extraordinarily difficult to avoid (mis)representing any culture as frozen when we teach it. Furthermore, there frequently comes with institutionalized study a degree of technical polish and refinement uncharacteristic of praxis in the field outside. Schools are by their very nature artificial, controlled environments. Whether or not this amounts to a seriously stultifying factor, it does entail the creation of musical cultures that differ in fundamental ways from those in the "real world." School cultures are no less "real" than cultures outside school—but they are different. More to the point here, the polish and refinement characteristic of institutional cultures tend to generate cliques or "clubs" where technical virtuosity, for instance, becomes valued above novelty, or where practitioners play and communicate predominantly with each other.[31] "Clubs" like these eventually become "musical museums" and must turn to funding foundations to compensate for dwindling support from "outside" sources. In fact, schools and universities themselves often serve precisely this kind of curatorial function—providing institutional support for musical activity that is no longer financially viable elsewhere. Such commercial supports, as we have seen, are among the distinctive characteristics of popular music in the first place.

Several considerations warrant our attention. First, the values of education and of the commercial sphere are often incompatible.[32] Since commercial value is an important part of what makes the popular "popular," this should give us pause. Change the commercial dimension, one might say, and one has changed what the music is. If this is persuasive, we would do well to stay open to the possibility that the deemed admissibility of a musical practice into the school curriculum may indicate the preliminary onset of "aesthetic fatigue."[33]

The fact that popular musics change so frequently, moving into and out of fashion at sometimes breathtaking speed, poses problems of its own. Among these is the fact that a practitioner who is fluent, successful, or pedagogically astute in the popular music of one era is not necessarily so in another. The transformation from hip to archaic can happen overnight, and this has far-reaching implications for the preparation and professional development of music educators—at least where fluency is considered essential to pedagogical competence, an assumption with a lengthy pedigree in the profession.

Much of what has just been said here makes the assumption, I believe justified in light of past and current practice, that music education would turn to popular music primarily as a mode of performance. However, I have also suggested that we might well embrace popular music with the intent of making students more discriminating listeners and consumers, an end that

might cater to a broader educational "audience" than those specifically interested in developing performance skills. This is not to suggest that performance skills are in any way incompatible with the development of discrimination. The more likely issue is one of efficiency, or breadth of educational contact. If our interest in popular music stems from a concern for the way those we euphemistically call "general" students think about and respond to music in everyday life—a highly laudable educational concern, I submit—other issues demand our scrutiny. Chief among these is a concern raised by Gracyk: the desirability of bringing self-consciousness to an area in which vast numbers of people currently engage un-self-consciously, without benefit of instruction, and "without anxiety or feelings of inferiority." One of popular music's attractions, Gracyk reminds us, is precisely that "it is not regarded as 'art,' something one must work to appreciate."[34] The transformation of popular music into a "serious" enterprise of the kind we have enshrined for the study of the classics and jazz is a concern about which educators need to exercise caution.

I stated earlier that a commitment to process "changes everything."[35] Whether such a claim is greeted with enthusiasm or trepidation depends upon whether one believes things need to change. I believe they do. And thus, I conclude this brief overview of popular music and schooling with the observation that emphasis upon process, action, agency, and cultural engagement—an emphasis that I believe follows from a commitment to including popular music in music education—is fundamentally at odds with the product/reception focus that has typified traditional music studies. That constitutes a serious impediment to the kind of change that popular music seems to require. But in it also lies considerable potential for professional reconceptualization, revitalization, and transformation. With that in mind, let us conclude with a brief inventory of the potential benefits of taking popular music seriously.

Popular Music and the Music Education Profession

Taking popular music seriously, it should be clear, is by no means a utopian solution to all music education's problems. But neither is it anathema to the ideals of music education or an abdication of educational responsibility.[36] Numerous advantages might well accrue to the profession—depending, of course, upon what popular music is taken to mean and how we accommodate it. I suggest that these very contingencies are at once the greatest challenge and the greatest potential benefit to music education. If we are willing to accept the degree of disciplinary change it involves, bringing popular music into the schools can indeed make a significant difference. Recognizing popular music practices as potential purveyors of musical and educational value makes it difficult for us to continue as though answers to the questions, What music? and Whose music? are somehow preordained and self-evident. It takes away from us the comfort and convenience of appeals to "intrinsic" or "inherent" musical value. It can no longer be quite so clear who the beneficiaries or recipients of musical instruction should be. Nor can we proceed

as if the primary ends of instruction are foregone conclusions. It replaces habitual practices with questions—a highly desirable turn of events, in my view.

Taking popular music seriously will force us to recognize the mutual reciprocity of music and culture, the social and political power of music, and in turn its profound importance in human affairs. It will force us to accept taste-group affiliations as crucial components of musical value and move us away from aesthetics-influenced preoccupation with "works" or "pieces" and the supposedly inherent values of their formal or expressive features. It will help both us and our students understand music, in Cavicchi's words, as an "open 'process,' and not a closed 'object.'"[37]

Taking popular music seriously will mean accepting the contradictory, the paradoxical, and the ambiguous as pedagogical assets.[38] It will force us to see and study music and its meanings as sociopolitical constructs—bubbling, fermenting, and part of "the action" at the heart of culture—rather than as artifacts or by-products of such actions.

Taking popular music seriously will change the role of the music educator, who can hardly presume any longer to be an authoritative purveyor of factual insights in a field notable for its effervescence, fluidity, polysemy, hybridity, and mutation. What students bring to the educational experience will of necessity become much more central, a fact that will arguably alter in positive ways what they take away as well.

Taking popular music seriously will draw into the educational realm many students who are traditionally and currently excluded. Thus, whom we seek to educate will become a more salient issue—one to be resolved in a variety of ways in response to diverse local circumstances.

Taking popular music seriously will make the classics—the greatest musical achievements of the past—all the more momentous. They become far more vital concerns to the extent that they are appropriately seen as part of a continuous, dynamic musical field rather than as constituting the whole of it. Rather than museum pieces that demand reverent appreciation, they become part of a broader, living culture—culturally vital, vibrant, and rich in their power to enrich here-and-now experience in the real world.

Taking popular music seriously offers to replace our notions of music as a thing to be appreciated, understood, and respected for its inherent qualities with the recognition that all musics are actions that are *useful* in myriad ways. That musical value is inseparable from questions of use or function is an insight rich with educational and musical implications. One of the unavoidable consequences of accepting popular music as legitimate is the recognition that value is always "value for." Inherent and autonomous value are inspiring, but ideologically loaded, constructs that are designed to privilege music whose "value for" is institutionally hidden. Recognizing all musical value as practical value requires us to renounce the myths perpetrated by an acontextual, ahistorical Kantian aesthetic heritage, rejecting the aloofness from everyday concerns that heritage has attributed to "aesthetic" experience. It has become extraordinarily easy in the wake of aesthetic orthodoxy to take up

music making (and teaching) without paying attention to social or political contradictions. To take popular music seriously is to change that, decisively and irreversibly. Gracyk observes that "all music is historically grounded in the practices of musical communities. Its assessment must be grounded in a community of musicians and listeners, not in a transcendental 'essence.'"[39]

Taking popular music seriously will pose direct and significant challenges to our educational obsession with things clear and distinct, and to our predilection to train rather than to educate.[40] Training and its reliance upon narrow, technocratic models tend to lead people to reject what is at first loose, messy, disturbing, or contradictory. One aim of education should be to help people learn to cling to such images or notions, not rejecting them out of hand but working them through; for it is precisely in such form that original ideas almost always first appear. Instruction preoccupied with the so-called practical ("how-to," as contrasted to ethical concerns like whether to, under what circumstances, to what extent, and so on) is associated with a long history of anti-intellectualism—one that is hardly becoming of a vocation claiming profession status. Giroux reminds us that within the technocratic tradition

> management issues become more important than understanding and furthering schools as democratic public spheres. Hence, the regulation, certification, and standardization of teacher behavior is emphasized over creating the conditions for teachers to undertake the sensitive political and ethical roles they might assume as public intellectuals who

selectively produce and legitimate particular forms of knowledge and authority.[41]

Taking popular music seriously would require music educators to situate such issues at the center of their educational praxis.

Taking popular music seriously would place questions where music education traditionally finds answers. Popular for whom? In what sense? From what direction? There is no inherently popular music, no music that is of its own "high" or "low." It is we who make it so. All music is intentionally constructed and constituted, and any music has a potentially viable claim to artistic or popular status. We can draw contingent distinctions, but there is no inherent or durably objective difference.

Taking popular music seriously entails that we commit to making students less vulnerable to the manipulative consumerist strategies of what Adorno contemptuously calls "the culture industry"—helping students to become more aware and more discriminating toward music that seeks their complicity in its popularity, helping increase the popularity of lesser-known musics that arguably warrant broader recognition, and helping make informed choice and musical agency conspicuous outcomes of musical instruction. In short, taking popular music seriously should require (to close with a decidedly normative claim) that we as music educators accept as part of our educational obligation a deliberate role in what Middleton memorably calls the "struggle to redeem the democratic core of 'the popular.'"[42]

Conclusion

Many words have been devoted here to exploring what popular music is, or is not, and to the attempt to come to grips with what it might mean for music education to "take popular music seriously"—as I have been putting it. But in a way, the real question we need to ask is, How can we *not* take popular music seriously?[43] What do we teach our students when we turn our backs on the vast majority of the musical experience they find meaningful? What do we do to the field of music when we carve it up into neatly dichotomous and mutually exclusive packages? And perhaps most importantly, what do we do to our own understanding of music and its role in human endeavor—we who purport to have special insights and assume responsibility for the education of the public?

If we are to do justice to popular music—to its vitality, its complexity, and its legitimacy as a field of human musical endeavor—we must allow it to change us. We must allow it to complicate our professional lives, to enrich our understandings of music's nature and power, to extend our assumptions about which students we presume to educate, to broaden our vision of the ways music education can occur, and to reconstruct our views of who music educators are, what they do, and how they do it.

Many students we currently fail to reach, and many of those we do reach, know a great deal more about music than we recognize. They think and talk about popular music intelligently, use it in all kinds of ways, and are extraordinarily discriminating in their choices. Indeed, they know a great deal of the field of music better than we do—powerful evidence of our neglect. Popular music is a powerful and influential part of the musical world to which we are largely and complacently oblivious. Such a blind spot seriously compromises our understanding of the whole. In turning our backs on popular musics and all that they entail, we deprive students of our insights while depriving ourselves of theirs.

There will be many who feel the music education profession is incapable of the kinds of change to which I have alluded here, or at least ill-advised to attempt it. We must not underestimate the extent of the challenge, the amount of institutional inertia to be overcome. One might expect the impetus for change to arise from young music educators currently entering the field, but they face enormous pressures to conform to current practices, and the professional intensification created by our recent infatuation with standards and standardization exerts an extraordinarily chilling effect on large-scale change or innovation. The time will come, however—and perhaps sooner than we imagine—when the effort required to keep things as they are will surpass the effort change entails. I would prefer to see us lead rather than respond.

Notes

1. Daniel Cavicchi, "From the Ground Up," *Action, Criticism, and Theory for Music Education* 1, no. 2 (2002). Available at http://mas.siue.edu/ACT/index.html.

2. If it is indeed a "both" with which we are concerned here. In due course, the inadequacy of this dualistic way of thinking should become apparent.

3. Richard Middleton, *Studying Popular Music* (Philadelphia: Open University Press, 1990), 3.

4. My use of the word "unpopular" is deliberate and appropriate in this particular context. Elsewhere in this essay, however, one might well ask whether "nonpopular" would be the more

appropriate choice. It seems these designations have two subtle differences: the former attributes *general dislike* to a music, and the latter suggests that the music in question, whatever its popularity in some quarters, does not warrant inclusion in the broad category "popular." That is, "unpopular" is a more negative designation than "nonpopular."

5. Richard Middleton calls this the "positivist" approach to defining popularity. As Middleton observes, the positivist approach only tells us about *sales*, not the meaning of popularity. "What it can tell us about is limited, first, to the data themselves, as categorized, and second to its own assumptions"—assumptions that attempt to sidestep popularity's ideological repleteness. Richard Middleton, *Studying Popular Music*, 6. The contentiousness and contestedness of popularity are crucial to its proper understanding, I submit, and therefore to its potential educational value.

6. It is worth noting that even this top-forty approach to defining popularity is far from straight ahead. It is not so much a direct reflection of listeners' preferences as of the air time distributors manage to achieve for their wares.

7. Richard Shusterman, "Don't Believe the Hype," in *Performing Live: Aesthetic Alternatives for the Ends of Art* (Ithaca, NY: Cornell University Press, 2000), 35–59. Here I must forego the temptation to argue that much of what the North American music education profession has pursued under the banner of "aesthetic education" might better be described as "ascetic education." I believe the claim can be substantiated, however. Shusterman also indicates, correctly and alliteratively, that such ascetic idealism is "a powerful philosophical prejudice with a Platonic pedigree" (p. 45). See also Richard Shusterman, *Pragmatist Aesthetics: Living Beauty, Rethinking Art* (Oxford: Blackwell, 1992).

8. Leonard B. Meyer, *Emotion and Meaning in Music* (Chicago: University of Chicago Press, 1956).

9. I explore Adorno in the chapter "Music as Social and Political Force," in my book *Philosophical Perspectives on Music* (New York: Oxford University Press, 1998), 304–55. Gracyk

offers a very accessible critique of Adorno's "hatchet job on popular music" (as Gracyk characterizes it), as does Middleton. See Theodore Gracyk, "Adorno, Jazz, and the Reception of Popular Music," in *Rhythm and Noise: An Aesthetics of Rock* (Durham, NC: Duke University Press, 1996); and Richard Middleton, "It's All Over Now: Popular Music and Mass Culture—Adorno's Theory," in *Studying Popular Music* 34–63.

10. Middleton, *Studying Popular Music*, 5.

11. Ibid.

12. Ibid., 7.

13. Ibid.

14. Charles Keil and Steven Feld, *Music Grooves* (Chicago: University of Chicago Press, 1994). This contrast maps itself nicely onto the controversy within jazz circles over whether jazz is an art form with, among other things, a long history to be preserved, or whether it is a fundamentally creative process. The traditionalist view, held by Wynton Marsalis, conflicts substantially with the processualist view endorsed by Keith Jarrett, Pat Metheny, and others.

15. The words of Paul Gilroy, appropriated from a decidedly different context, are far from irrelevant here. The "fantasy of a frozen culture," of "fixing communal interests" in their "most authentic and glorious" form, "reduces cultural traditions to the simple process of invariant repetition." This may help to secure comforting conservative notions of traditional identity, but these "do little justice either to the fortitude or the improvisational skills" demanded by the complexities of contemporary cultural life. Where tradition "is understood as little more than a list of rigid rules that can be applied consciously without attention or attention to particular historical traditions, it is a ready alibi for authoritarianism rather than a sign of cultural viability or ethical confidence." Paul Gilroy, *Against Race: Imagining Political Culture Beyond the Color Line* (Cambridge: Harvard University Press, 2000), 14–15.

16. By mass-mediated, I mean simply (or not so simply) that it is mass-produced and mass-disseminated by technological means, which requires its reduction from a process to a thing (a commodity). Again, contradictions spring to mind, however. People's experience of the entire musical field tends today to be mediated—even their experience of so-called classical or serious music, music that is not originally intended or generally considered to be mediated. (In North America, for instance, most listening to classical music now occurs in people's automobiles. See Audience Insight's *Classical Music Consumer Segmentation Study* [Miami, FL: John S. and James L. Knight Foundation, 2002] available at www.knightfdn.org/default.asp?story=research/cultural/consumersegmenttion/index.html.) It is, in other words, misleading to suggest that mediation, commodity character, and mass distribution are exclusive or distinguishing attributes of popular music when the same claims can now be made for the classics, jazz, and most musics that are not regarded as popular.

17. It tends, therefore, toward a simplicity uncharacteristic of notated and notation-based musical practices, though one would want to hastily add that the multidimensionality and polysemy (multiplicity of meaning) of such music would negate the possibility of simplicity.

18. These generalizations require careful qualification. Many of popular music's rituals are extraordinarily elaborate and to some extent formal, and there is in many popular music circles an extraordinary amount of concern about authenticity—most often expressed concern about whether an artist has "sold out" to commercial or other pressures. On the former point, I have in mind the relative lack of standardization in popular music endeavors: a greater latitude in the range and type of transmission practices and range of interpretive orientations deployed. On the latter point, I have in mind the degree of hybrid stylistic cross-fertilization that is generally tolerated—a degree enhanced by the relatively rapid rate at which popular music comes into and passes out of fashion.

19. For elaboration on the idea of embodiment and its potential implications for our understandings of music and music education, see Wayne Bowman, "Cognition and the Body:

Perspectives from Music Education," in *Knowing Bodies, Feeling Minds: Embodied Knowledge in Arts Education and Schooling,* ed. Liora Bresler (Dordrecht, The Netherlands: Kluwer Academic Publishers, in press).

20. Leonard Meyer designates these parameters as "primary," a move that clearly privileges musics that prioritize such formal attributes. See Wayne Bowman, "Music as Autonomous Form," in *Philosophical Perspectives on Music* for a more detailed discussion of Meyer's distinctions between primary and secondary parameters.

21. Again, I would argue that this is an important consideration in most "nonpopular" music as well.

22. I need to emphasize that a significant part of my reluctance stems from the fact that human practices admit to "definition" only in very qualified, special ways. All one can do is take a kind of tentative barometric reading at a given moment and recognize that the reading represents at best the statistical average drawn from a sample with an extraordinarily wide standard deviation.

23. Middleton, *Studying Popular Music,* 33.

24. Daniel Cavicchi, letter to the author, 20 January 2003.

25. This statement is clearly invalid if one equates popularity to relevance and in turn gauges the educational warrant of instructional practices by the extent of their appeal to a broad consumer base. That is a position with which I have little sympathy, despite its prevalence in music education.

26. On the ubiquity of music's presence and influence, see Tia DeNora, *Music in Everyday Life* (Cambridge: Cambridge University Press, 2000). See also the essay reviews of this book by Daniel Cavicchi ("From the Bottom Up"), Hildegard Froelich ("Tackling the Seemingly Obvious—a Daunting Task Indeed"), and John Shepherd ("How Music Works: Beyond the Immanent and the Arbitrary") published in *Action, Criticism, and Theory for Music Education* 1, no. 2 (2002); available at http://mas.siue.edu/ACT/index.html

27. Of course, this is one of the claims made for conventional music education. Unfortunately,

though, when the musical field is fenced off into mutually exclusive popular and serious domains, the instructional emphasis drifts toward the supposedly "intramusical" determinants of musical worth found in the latter—a move that profoundly misrepresents the unified nature of the musical field and does little to encourage critical awareness of the great majority of music that is consequently omitted. The point is not to replace the classics with the popular, but to approach the entire musical field inclusively and in a way that makes its continuity as clear as its discontinuities.

28. Although, I hasten to add, killing time is one of the pragmatic ends music has always served. I do not wish to denigrate such activity, except perhaps as an educational means or as an exclusive mode of musical engagement. I hope it goes without saying that the assumption that fans of popular music do not really listen is largely erroneous.

29. I trust that the basis for my implicit distinction between education and schooling requires no explanation. A crucial dimension of schooling that needs to be born in mind here is one that Giroux describes aptly: schooling is "a mechanism of culture and politics, embedded in competing relations of power that attempt to regulate and order how students think, act, and live." See Henry Giroux, "Doing Cultural Studies: Youth and the Challenge of Pedagogy," *Harvard Educational Review* 64, no. 3 (1994): 279.

30. Gracyk, *Rhythm and Noise.*

31. Milton Babbitt's infamous article "Who Cares if You Listen?" (*High Fidelity,* February 1958, 38–40) is one example that comes to mind. But the increasingly esoteric and specialized status of institutionalized jazz is arguably another.

32. On the other hand, some would argue—I think persuasively—that commercial interests and consumerism have become central (if covert) features of education in capitalistic societies.

33. Gracyk, *Rhythm and Noise,* 205. Despite deep personal reservations about the use (or mostly misuse) of the term "aesthetic" by music educators, I like this juxtaposition of imagery.

34. Ibid.

35. I owe this to George Odam, who expressed this profound insight almost in passing during our NUMELS meeting in June 2002.

36. George Odam commented in our NUMELS seminar that the unease attending discussions of popular music feels at times like a family discussion about how to deal with a sick child!

37. Cavicchi, "From the Ground Up," 5.

38. I take up the cognitive and educational value of ambiguity in Wayne Bowman, "Cognition and the Body."

39. Gracyk, *Rhythm and Noise,* 173.

40. I pursue what it might mean to educate musically in Wayne Bowman, "Educating Musically," in *The New Handbook of Research on Music Teaching and Learning,* ed. Richard Colwell and Carol Richardson (Oxford: Oxford University Press, 2002), 63–84.

41. Giroux, "Doing Cultural Studies," 278.

42. Middleton, *Studying Popular Music,* 293. The stage on which this struggle must be set, he continues, is "the musical mobilization of the 'new subject'—discontinuous but tentacular, locally rooted but a world citizen…"

43. This was among the provocative and challenging criticisms raised by Daniel Cavicchi in a critique of an earlier draft of this essay. I am also indebted to Randall Allsup, Roger Mantie, and Kristen Myers for comments and criticisms that helped me improve this chapter.

Wayne Bowman is professor of music education at Brandon University in Manitoba, Canada. His primary instructional responsibilities lie in the areas of music education foundations, music education research, and philosophy of music. He is widely published in matters pertaining to philosophy of music education, and in 1998 published the book *Philosophical Perspectives on Music* (Oxford University Press). An active trombonist and jazz educator, he also directs the Brandon University Jazz Ensemble.

3

Popular Music: The Very Idea of Listening to It

Theodore Gracyk

> What is unaesthetic about popular art is
> its formlessness. It does not invite or even
> permit the sustained effort necessary to
> the creation of an artistic form. But it
> provides us with an illusion of achieve-
> ment while in fact we remain passive.
> —*Abraham Kaplan*[1]

This chapter explores the intersection of
two ideas. The first is the notion that there
is a cohesive body of music identified as
"popular music." The second is the idea
that the pleasure afforded by this music is
delivered without genuine listening, or at
least without the sort of listening demanded by "serious" music.[2] I will give a qualified
endorsement to the former idea as a
springboard to challenging the latter.

The academic study of popular culture is
an interdisciplinary project that constructs
its own theoretical framework as it goes
along by drawing on cultural theory, literary
theory, sociology, anthropology, media studies, economics, and political theory. When it
comes to popular music, ethnomusicology is
often consulted. Analytical musicology has
only recently been brought to bear. My own
perspective is somewhat unusual in being

most heavily influenced by aesthetic theory
(itself an interdisciplinary affair).

Competing Notions of Popular Music

Every discussion of popular music
assumes that there is another sort of music,
music that is something other than popular.
The two most common contrasting categories are "folk" music (including most
preindustrial and non-Western music) and
"serious" music (all the music known collo-
quially as "classical" or "art" music, including music coming before and after the
classical age).[3] Nonetheless, many pieces
of folk and classical music are known and
loved by large numbers of people. Corres-
pondingly, most of what falls into the category of popular music is not very popular,
at least as measured by audience familiarity
or commercial sales. So the label "popular"
does not really describe the broad field that
it loosely designates. It is one of those
imprecise terms for which there is neither
an established definition nor a clear bound-
ary of application. Yet none of that deprives
it of utility as a category, and most individu-

als will probably agree that the Beatles, Michael Jackson, the Eagles, and Shania Twain fall squarely within the category of popular music. Haydn, Wagner, and Stravinsky do not. On most accounts, Alan Lomax's field recordings of American work songs, blues, and field hollers also do not.[4] The songs of Stephen Foster and Hank Williams are popular. Schubert's "Ave Maria" is not. Jazz used to be treated as popular music, but now it is not.[5]

I mention Foster and Williams because I want to make it clear that popular music is not synonymous with rock music. Yet for four decades, it was easier to treat popular music and rock music as interchangeable, if only because "rock" seemed to be the common thread linking hugely popular musicians like Elvis Presley, the Beatles, Madonna, and Nirvana. Until recently, journals such as *Popular Music and Society,* the *Journal of Popular Music Studies,* and *Popular Music* were largely devoted to rock music. However, the common thread turns out to be little more than the historical contingency of the taste preferences and selective interests of those constructing the analysis.[6] Their consensus on what counts as rock and as popular generally disregarded the ongoing interactions between rock and country music (treating commercial country as beneath comment) and ignored the continuing popularity of middlebrow commercial tunes (e.g., Andrew Lloyd Weber and Disney soundtracks).[7]

Distinguishing Popular Material

There are at least four distinct ways that popular material, including music, is distin-

guished from other cultural spheres.[8] First, there is what is popular in the sense of being widely liked. In this sense of the term, many critically acclaimed rock musicians are not popular; just look at Captain Beefheart and his Magic Band. Second, we can apply a traditional distinction between high and low culture, in which case the popular is whatever is low in the cultural hierarchy.[9] Once again, some rock music fails to count as popular. The Beatles are the subject of their own volume in Phaidon Press's *20th-Century Composers* series, and Elton John sang at the funeral for England's Lady Diana, Princess of Wales. Third, a work can be popular because it is liked by common people. This sphere of the popular is more or less identical with commercial culture and mass entertainment. Yet the notion of entertainment does not mean that the music is always likable and fun. A great deal of rock music is quite abrasive. What matters here is that it be commercially profitable.[10] But some rock groups, primarily punk groups, fight this expectation and adopt strategies to maintain marginality.[11] The fourth distinction restricts the popular to that which people actually produce for themselves—art "by" rather than "for" the common person. This requires either a group outside capitalist production and consumption (e.g., folk music) or consumers who transform commercial products through active consumption in which they make their own meanings from mass-mediated culture.[12] The music of Pink Floyd is suspect, but a popular use arises when Johnny Rotten scrawls "I Hate" above the band's name on a Pink Floyd shirt.

These four distinctions intersect in

complex ways. After all, they are but four facets of the original use of "popular" some five hundred years ago, meaning whatever was "of" the common people. For centuries, this included anything vulgar (i.e., the province of those with little formal education), lower class, and politically rebellious. But these different strands gradually unwound due to increasing levels of education and literacy, the rise of mass media, and a breakdown of the association of high culture with the ruling class.[13] These changes leave us with sharply competing perspectives on the popular: popular-as-mass, popular-as-folk, popular-as-counterculture.[14]

A further complication is Anahid Kassabian's warning that we unduly misrepresent popular music when we treat the "popular" as something that people *consciously* seek out. Contemporary life offers "musics that are always there, beyond our control, slipping under our thresholds of consciousness."[15] Background music known as "mood music" or "elevator music" is played in virtually every retail space and in many professional environments.[16] But there is also the sound-track music of movies, television shows, audio books, and sporting events (some of it composed as sound-track music, some of it taken intact from other sources) and the sound track playing on the midway at the county or state fair. When we telephone a business and are placed "on hold," we usually find ourselves listening to innocuous instrumental music. As I write, the most common music in the lives of many adolescents is the highly repetitive, quasi-classical sound-track music that accompanies video games. Adolescents may also encounter their own distinctive sound

track when they go to the mall. Kassabian is correct to complain that these "ubiquitous musics" are too seldom acknowledged as a substantial body of popular music.

Having provided a hasty overview of a complex topic and lacking space necessary to justify my own position, I must disclose my preferences among the competing notions of popular music. Attempting to remain true to the original idea of what is "of" the people, I endorse Kassabian's suggestion that we concentrate on "the musics heard most by the most people every day."[17] Admittedly, this approach creates as many problems as it solves. It gives us multiple popular musics by relativizing the notion to boundaries between groups of people, with different music counting as popular in Japan, North Dakota, and Mexico. At the same time, I am an American academic writing in English at the beginning of the twenty-first century, in a cultural context where the musics most people hear are created, distributed, and consumed as recorded music. Given this commercial context, most popular music will be mass art, designed to be readily understood by the average listener, who may have little or no formal music training.[18] Commercial songs will dominate this field, and rock and country music will be major categories. Rather different results might hold for the instrumental music produced as background music for everyday environments, but I hope that I will not beg too many questions in focusing on music like that of the Beatles, the Rolling Stones, and the Sex Pistols. Despite misgivings, I am going to treat rock music as a paradigm of popular music.[19]

Listening in Different Contexts

Based on these framing assumptions, what follows is a sketch of a somewhat different way of thinking about the divide between popular and serious music. Though there may be nothing common to all popular music that clearly distinguishes it from serious music, there has been a widely endorsed account of the different listening strategies employed by their respective audiences. The key idea is that there are two distinct ways to respond to music, and that the mode generally adopted for Mozart and Stravinsky differs from the mode employed in response to Chuck Berry, the Beach Boys, and U2. The attraction of this approach is that we do not have to locate any distinct features of the cultural objects in order to divide them into two groups. Instead, they can be grouped according to their distinct modes of consumption. This is highly analogous to saying that there is a difference between spicy food and bland food but that different spicy foods (or bland foods) may have nothing else in common. Some spicy food is spicy due to one set of ingredients. Some is spicy due to another set. Yet there is a real distinction between spicy and bland. The difference lies in physiological and phenomenal responses that people have when they consume it. The distinction between popular and serious music has a long history of being handled in a similar manner, by positing a difference between active and passive consumption. Historically, it has been presented as the difference between listening and hearing.

Perspectives of Hearing and Listening

> Hearing is the reception of a program heard by chance, admitted, sometimes even endured ... Listening, on the contrary, involves a search for a program, a choice and maintained attention.
> —*Georges Friedmann*[20]

Listening is usually characterized as a specifically aesthetic disinterested yet imaginative contemplation of what is heard. It is characterized as demanding informed concentration on the structural qualities of the music. Furthermore, active listening is generally regarded as an exclusive activity. Basic texts on Western music often make pronouncements of this sort:

> We have to learn to *listen,* in the literal sense: to hear accurately and acutely, to differentiate between the various pitch levels, to recognize various rhythmic patterns, melodic ideas, and so on. This is difficult and requires the greatest concentration on the part of the listener. It cannot be emphasized too strongly that it is *impossible to listen to music while doing something else.*[21]

In contrast, passive hearing is the instinctive and emotionally charged response of an infant or animal. Supposedly, their responses are to the sounds rather than to the sound structures.

I do not know when or where the distinction between active listening and passive hearing originated. Nor does it matter, given my purposes, which are less historical than metacritical. It is enough to note that the distinction plays a central part in

Eduard Hanslick's classic monograph, *On the Musically Beautiful* (1854), and in Edmund Gurney's mammoth *The Power of Sound* (1880). Succeeding generations have defended variations of Hanslick and Gurney. Let's begin with Hanslick's and Gurney's work and then explore modifications of the doctrine in David Prall, Monroe C. Beardsley, and Roger Scruton. The goal of this brief and selective summary is to show that the distinction between hearing and listening has been employed to devalue functional responses to music (e.g., responses that are primarily concerned with the music's capacity to express or manipulate emotion). Such responses are deemed irrelevant and even antithetical to listening, the mode demanded by serious music.

Hanslick quips that one "cannot help hearing the most deplorable street organ in front of our house, but not even a Mendelssohn symphony can compel us to listen."[22] He does not write like someone introducing a new distinction. Hanslick contrasts the pathological (passive) reaction of the average music enthusiast with the more valuable response of the informed, aesthetic (active) listener. For those who engage in the former, a symphony is no more significant than a good cigar or a warm bath. It lacks *musical* significance. For the fortunate minority who are capable of listening, music provides an intense aesthetic enjoyment that can only be derived from anticipations and confirmations of the music's pattern as it unfolds in performance. In order for this process to take place while listening to a performance or reading a score, one must know the conventions of the relevant musical tradition. Following

Hanslick, most theorists emphasize (and recommend) active listening in which we consciously perceive and focus on the intended organization in the heard sounds.

Hanslick proposes that most people perceive all music as "background," even in the concert hall when it is offered as the focus of attention. The listeners are passive because they do not concentrate on musical form. In the concert hall, the pathological or passive listener slips "into a fuzzy state of supersensuously sensuous agitation determined only by the general character of the piece … while what is special in every composition, namely, its artistic individuality, escapes him."[23] Hanslick complains that the most "appreciative" members of the concert audience do not follow the structure of the piece. We get precisely the same reception for similar pieces, with no discrimination as to better or worse. In today's audiences, we might point to the "moron" who yells "rock and roll!" during the quieter pieces at a concert and who responds to the beat while appraising guitar solos simply by the number of notes per second. The bulk of the audience wants to hear the hits, which suggests that they don't want to listen too actively to the music. They respond to the presence of the musician and the familiarity of the sounds more than to the unique specifics of the particular performance.

Gurney's *The Power of Sound* devotes an entire chapter to the two "ways of hearing," describing them as "definite" and "indefinite." Although he allows that an emotional response implies that some understanding is taking place, Gurney continues to defend structural apprehension as the goal of focused listening.[24] Gurney contends that while "the definite character of Music involv[es] the perception of individual melodic and harmonic combinations, the indefinite character involv[es] merely the perception of successions of agreeably-toned and harmonious sound." With indefinite hearing, auditors neither notice nor remember what is distinctive about the music. He postulates that each kind of listening offers a distinct sort of pleasure. The basic distinction is then reformulated as a distinction between two types of listeners: the "naive" or instinctive as opposed to the educated, cultivated, or trained. Yet Gurney acknowledges that most listeners can engage in both types of response, and most prefer the "definite effect" of active listening.[25] Since almost no one is exclusively an "instinctive" hearer of music, what looks like two types of listeners is really a distinction between levels of education, modes of attention, and objects of concentration.

Although Prall is not discussed much anymore, his work in aesthetics was influential through much of the twentieth century.[26] His work makes explicit what is implicit in Hanslick and Gurney. Prall agrees that aesthetic response is more than sense perception. Art appeals to the intellect because art concentrates on form, including contrasts, balance, and rhythm. Thus, successful compositions must involve formal structure if they are to afford more than an "elementary" aesthetic experience.[27] Artistic composition exploits the fact that some sensory qualities are intrinsically differentiated according to structuring relationships. Unlike tastes and smells, visuals and sound have "principles of ordered variation" that permit deliberate and comprehensible composition.[28] When intrinsically ordered elements combine, fresh properties are generated, namely structural relationships and designs. When we grasp a combination of sounds as an organized sequence in time (the horizontal axis of musical organization) or as a specific harmony (the vertical axis), we grasp melodic, rhythmic, and harmonic qualities that can then be abstracted from the specific elements embodying them. When one identifies this objective element in a combination of sounds, one has engaged in structural listening.

The experience of music is firmly rooted in knowledge of principles of relational structures. One need not learn their technical names, Prall cautions, but a listener who cannot "distinguish minor thirds from majors ... can not possibly discriminate either the melodic or the harmonic patterns that he hears." Consequently, "he does not in fact hear the actual music at all." Prall fully endorses the tradition of active listening with one's "full and active powers of attention."[29] He regards any pleasure or displeasure derived from the elements themselves as a subjective response, mere "hearing." On the surface, nothing in Prall's theory is hostile to popular music. By the time most people reach adolescence, they (and thus most popular music fans) possess all of the audiation skills listed by Prall and can experience structural and corresponding emotional change in whatever music they enjoy.[30]

Acknowledging the influence of Hanslick, Gurney, and Prall, Beardsley seeks the "phenomenally objective features" of works of art that underlie genuine aesthetic value. Like the scholars before him, Beardsley proposes that only structural qualities can account for music's semantic dimension, including the "pervasive human qualities" that we read into a work's kinetic qualities.[31] Beardsley reasons that a musical work is an auditory design arising from "intrinsic relations" among the four basic qualities of sound: duration, loudness, pitch, and timbre. Intrinsic relationships among these qualities "make it possible to combine musical tones into the larger structures that we are familiar with in music."[32] Because the essential quality that differentiates music from the other arts is the presence of "auditory movement," pitch and duration are more fundamental than timbre and loudness. Having fastened on structural relationships as the essential characteristics of musical works, Beardsley treats all expressive qualities that are objectively present in a musical work as gestalt qualities arising from musical structure. Individuals who focus on these properties listen to the phenomenally objective features of a musical work. Listeners who fail to grasp the objective patterns and kinetic qualities have not "really heard all that it is."[33] Beardsley's account is similar to that of Leonard B. Meyer, who concludes that a poorly educated listener is a passive listener who must have a much cruder and emotionally impoverished experience of music.[34]

Analyzing musical expression as a byproduct of musical structure, Scruton makes explicit two ideas that are frequently implicit in his predecessors. The first is that musical expression arises in an informed listener's "sympathetic response" to musical movements and gestures.[35] (One must understand the music to grasp its musical gesture.) The second is that listeners seek

musical patterns, and true listening is indifferent to the "actual sound events" (i.e., to the contingent material through which the music is presented in performance). Scruton thus expands on a point made by each of the other four. Melody, harmony, and rhythm are to be abstracted from the specific elements embodying them. For Scruton, the significance of this mental abstraction is that music thrusts us into an ideal world, so our sympathetic response is not to musicians and composers but rather to an ideal subject or community. If we attend to the sounds *as* sounds, we remain mired in the physical or material conditions of music production, and we are not listening to the tonal dimension that permits one tone to lead to another.

Scruton condemns most popular music for relying on mere cliches of harmony, melody, and rhythm. Offering little that demands genuine musical understanding, almost all popular music is "impoverished" and incapable of framing any interesting or sincere expression of emotion.[36] Scruton falls back on Hanslick's claim that hearing is a physiological response while listening is intellectual. Scruton claims that a taste for the music of, say, Nirvana or R.E.M. obliterates aesthetic judgment, "as though a taste in music were on a par with a taste in ice cream, [which] is precisely not to understand the power of music."[37]

How the Tradition Denigrates Popular Music

Popularity is not, as many seem to think, a specialty of strings of obvious phrases built on a simple rhythm. That music is

popular which arrests people's attention and, when heard again, compels their recognition; not that whose highest success is momentarily to tickle their ears.
—*Edmund Gurney*[38]

Although Scruton is the only one of the five authors who expresses overt scorn for popular music as something "not there to be listened to," the practical result of the hearing/listening distinction is to denigrate popular taste and dismiss much of what is interesting about popular music, particularly rock music.[39] While I am not proposing that either result was ever a goal of the distinction, they emerge in at least three ways.

First, the distinction denigrates popular music fans for failing to achieve a level of conscious knowledge about music and practice the disciplined listening that this knowledge enables.[40] But it is doubtful that the ability to note "artistic individuality" (to quote Hanslick) always requires *conscious* exercise of critical knowledge of musical form. If the fundamental criterion for listening is noticing and remembering what is distinctive about individual works, then rock fans do listen. They recognize familiar riffs and melodies when they appear in new contexts. Led Zeppelin fans will immediately recognize that Robert Plant has sampled Zeppelin's "Black Dog" and "Dazed and Confused" for the song "Tall Cool One," and almost any fan of the Rolling Stones will recognize that Neil Young directly cops the melody of their "Lady Jane" for his own "Borrowed Tune." A Beatles fan will hear the plaintive quality of the "blue notes" in the melody of "Another Girl" and will find no such quality in the Beatles' version of the Broadway standard "Till There Was

You." This awareness does not require conscious awareness of the actual blue notes in "Another Girl," yet the perceived difference arises from real differences in the tonal materials. Although the popular audience responds to more than just cliches and general effects, what is heard does not always demand attentive "listening" in the prescribed sense of an exclusive focus.[41]

Second, "listening" is treated as an activity directed at a limited aspect of the total aural experience of the music. Unfortunately, this object is the pure sound structure of the musical work, rather than the concrete performance in all its particularity.[42] But if we discount lyrics and musical embellishments, any Hindustani raga is equivalent to many others. One twelve-bar blues is remarkably like another. Musically, Bob Dylan's "Leopard-Skin Pill-Box Hat" (1966) and "High Water (for Charley Patton)" (2001) are the same as Charley Patton's "High Water Everywhere" (1929)—though only one of the Dylan songs is directly descended from Patton's. As Robert Cantrick points out, "musical composition is not the only form that music takes."[43] Any perspective that tells us that "Leopard-Skin Pill-Box Hat" is just "High Water Everywhere" is extremely parsimonious about what music is and what counts as musical activity.

Third, in directing audiences to one object within the aural experience, the traditional doctrine of listening robs popular music of much of its expressive force. Hanslick defended a strict formalism: only structural qualities matter, and they matter only for themselves. The other four authors endorse a modified formalism in which objective expressive features can be sources of genuine aesthetic satisfaction, provided that those expressive features arise from formal relations within the sound structure. Generalizing from these authors, the doctrine of "listening" asks us to ignore expressive qualities that are present for nonstructural reasons. To note a few examples in the music of the Rolling Stones, "listening" tells us to ignore the sense of anger conveyed by the fuzz tone of Keith Richards's guitar on "(I Can't Get No) Satisfaction," the forward movement that comes from the rhythm guitar and drums rather than from tonal movement in the opening seconds of "Street Fighting Man," and the extraordinarily plaintive "everyman" quality that arises from the appearance of Richards as vocalist (instead of Mick Jagger, the chief vocalist) at the beginning of "Salt of the Earth."

Expressive qualities seem equally objective when they arise from engineering and production decisions in the recording process. Think here of selective use of echo (on Elvis Presley's voice on "Mystery Train," 1955), general ambiance (Bruce Springsteen's *Nebraska* album, 1982), and instrumental texture (the effect of two to four of the same instrument playing identical parts on Phil Spector's "River Deep, Mountain High," 1966).[44] The five theorists that I have outlined here regard listeners who respond to these nonstructural qualities as naive people who are insufficiently educated and do not really listen to the music. But if fans of the music agree on the presence of these qualities and agree that they are important to the music, then why aren't these qualities objective? Is it because they are not structural? We are dealing with aesthetic qualities, and the test of objectivity

must be whether the properties are available to listeners familiar with that kind of music. Hanslick and Gurney formulated their views before the appearance of recorded music. The same is not the case with Prall, Beardsley, and Scruton, who simply ignore the implications that arise for music made, distributed, and consumed *as* recorded sound. The most important implication is that we no longer *need* to abstract from the particulars of presentation to find the music; we live in a world where the recording in all its idiosyncratic particularity *is* the musical work.

I do not mean to suggest that elitist distaste for popular music fully accounts for the continued defense of a traditional position about listening to structural properties. Those who cannot allow that the ambiance of a Phil Spector recording is as important as the song itself may have a deeper reason than cultural bias. Their reasoning may reflect a generic argument that Noël Carroll calls "the specificity thesis." The specificity thesis makes two questionable assumptions. One is that each artistic medium has some feature in which it alone excels. The other is that each art should emphasize whatever differentiates it from other arts. As such, what begins as a description of the essential qualities of the medium turns into a recommendation that we attend to those qualities alone.[45] With music, the specificity thesis moves from the insight that auditory structure is the differentiating property of music to the conclusion that music is of value for this alone. But rather than attempt to derive appropriate uses of an artistic medium from considerations of the character of the medium, we might look to the different uses of the medium in the hands of different artists. Many of the "potentials" of a medium await discovery, and "interest in art forms is to a large measure interest in how artists learn or discover new ways of using their medium."[46] Those who deny that rock music demands listening are unable to recognize the diverse ways that rock musicians use sound.

The argument in favor of exclusive, structural "listening" also rests on the principle that an activity requiring specialized or refined knowledge is superior to one that employs only basic knowledge. But this principle is without basis in fact. Specialized knowledge is required to read the *Journal of Abnormal Psychology*, but it hardly follows that I will gain greater insight into human nature by reading that journal in place of the novels of Charles Dickens and Henry James. John Fisher voices similar reservations:

> It is plausible … that the value difference implied by the high/low art distinction has been influenced in part by our tendency to grade the types of cognition and character involved in appreciating various genres of artifacts. As such, it appears to presuppose unexamined, traditional ideas about the value of various mental states and attitudes.[47]

An equally questionable presupposition holds that different grades of cognition correlate neatly with different genres, so that I employ a different and lower grade of cognition when I attend to a Grateful Dead improvisation than to Chopin's "Minute Waltz" (op. 64, no. 1).[48]

Sadly, it may be that our mental effort has a point of diminishing returns, after which the energy expended to acquire greater insight is unlikely to reward that investment with any clear gain. I speculate that, with music, most people reach this point in young adulthood, after which they receive no more music lessons or musical training. Musical tastes become less flexible, even fixed.[49] Yet if an individual's life is enriched by music, even if it is only popular music as a recreational pleasure, I cannot see any clear benefit of analytical listening.[50] Granted, analytical listening will alter the experience of music. In some cases, those who do not employ such listening will never appreciate certain music (e.g., many of the fugues of Bach's *The Well-Tempered Clavier*) as the music that it is. But applying the skills of analytical listening to a simple popular song can result in sheer boredom, for some music is just not designed for that mode of listening.

Listening in Context

As argued by Ola Stockfelt, one of the complications of contemporary musical life is that different musics and different listening situations call for distinct levels of concentration. The task is to adopt an adequate mode of listening, which involves adjusting one's listening to the context and type of music.[51] But should this surprise us? Why should music be so different from the literary and visual arts? Knowledgeable readers do not approach a short story as they would a novel. We do not attend to films the way that we attend to stage plays (one reason that good stage plays don't always lead to good movies), nor do we look at impressionist paintings by Claude Monet the way we look at Andy Warhol's pop art canvases. Conversely, when we control the selection of the music we'll hear, what we select is partially a function of how closely we plan to attend to it. Choosing music, we select a style or artist that fits the level and kind of attention we'll give the music. The music I prefer when working in my office is not the music that I prefer while driving on a long trip, neither of which is necessarily music that I'll pay to see performed live. The admission that different musics reward different modes of attention does not prove that one mode is superior to another unless, perhaps, one believes that exclusive attention is a superior activity. But are there any good reasons to suppose that listening should be an exclusive activity? Or that an exclusive activity engages a superior grade of cognition? I will now consider those premises of the doctrine of the superiority of listening.

Listening ... An Exclusive Activity?

> You have to concentrate on the music to say you heard it fully. Just because you can jump and dance don't mean you listen to the music.
>
> —*Jazz musician Charles Mingus*[52]

This section will advance two related points against the supposed distinction between hearing and listening. First, I see little to recommend the doctrine that hearing is passive (a pathological response) while listening is active, requiring conscious, exclusive attention to sound structure. Second, if both are genuinely active, then hearing differs from listening in degree but not in kind—they are points

along a continuum rather than distinct activities. The problem with recommending the "active listening" end of the continuum is that it privileges certain *uses* for music, those in which exclusive, active listening takes place. But if "active listening" turns out to be a recommendation of exclusive attention, then there is no reason to expect all music lovers to engage in this practice and to work to prefer music that rewards it.

We can start by reconsidering my earlier analogy of spicy and bland food. With bland and spicy, the difference is firmly grounded in physiological response.[53] An individual can build up a tolerance and appreciation for spiciness, but that individual is learning to appreciate what is at first independent of memory, learning, or any cognitive process. One favors bland cuisine if one does not learn to handle spiciness through repeated exposure to it. The original appeal of two modes of musical response depended on a similar story. Early theorists stressed that the response to popular music is directly pathological. In contrast, appreciation of serious music demands repeated exposure and then application of cognitive judgment to the musical object. Those who fail to acquire and exercise the requisite cognitive skills are left in the position of Nipper, the dog listening to the phonograph in the old RCA Victor logo. We hear sounds and may recognize them, but we cannot listen to the music in the sounds.

But differences between dogs and human infants should give us a reason to pause. Despite their ability to *hear* sounds that are not heard by humans, dogs can never *listen* to music. Because they do not have a human infant's instincts to listen for musical structures in the sounds, dogs cannot have the experiences and then form the memories and apply the concepts necessary for grasping music.[54] Although nonhuman primates engage in musical behavior, no primate has ever been shown to be able to follow or understand any human music. Primates "don't hear" the melodies and so cannot develop the memories and expectations required for grasping music's tonal syntax.[55]

Unlike dogs and primates, human infants can hear some of the musical properties of music, but even they do not fully listen to it. As Peter Kivy argues, the fact that a three-day-old infant "instinctively" moves to the rhythm of music does not demonstrate any talent for music, since the infant is not capable of hearing music at all. It simply does not have the requisite knowledge to "listen."[56] Instinctively preparing for language acquisition, infants listen for musical patterns in every sound in their environment. If anything counts as merely hearing music, this does, for it is not informed judgment about music.[57] Individuals require many years of acculturation with pitch-scale patterns before they "spontaneously" hear pitches in terms of the appropriate tonal frame of reference.[58]

However, if we want to contrast "listening" with the infant's instinctive response, as a label for *appropriately educated reception*, then there is no obvious reason to restrict listening to one type of music. The human language instinct leads to the development of many languages, but I hope that no one wants to say that some natural languages are more genuinely language than others!

Given the close relationship between our language instinct and music instinct,[59] we ought to allow that many musics exist and that many learned modes of hearing count as listening. Even Hanslick saw that the difference between hearing and listening is at best a matter of degree of cognitive processing, not a real difference in kind, for even the seemingly "natural" music of peasants is "artistic music through and through."[60] Our most serious mistake about listening is Hanslick's assumption that listening should be tied to pleasure taken in the most advanced *type* of music.[61] Instead of trying to isolate the unique cognitive skills called for by some music and equating listening with an educated response to *that* music, we should allow that all acquired knowledge—tacit or conscious—about musical organization makes listening something distinct from the hearing of infancy.

What puzzles me is why anyone still thinks that cases of "passive" listening are similar to the case of the infant. As with spoken language, the normal course of cognitive development rapidly takes each infant out of this naive state. Listeners do not plunge back into the instinctive state simply because the music is incorporated into other activity. The failure to distinguish the two cases stems from the claim that active listening is an exclusive activity with special cognitive demands. Ignorance accounts for the fact that the infant cannot yet follow the music's overall structure. But ignorance does not support the claim that I cannot listen to the music of Jimi Hendrix or Gustav Mahler when it blasts from my stereo while I do the dishes. Washing the dishes requires practical application of learned knowledge, yet I can wash dishes while carrying on a conversation. Why can't I listen to music while washing the dishes? Or driving a car? Or dancing with my wife? Why is listening to music so exclusive? Personally, I find that the best way to prepare for an upcoming concert of unfamiliar music is to play similar music as background music during my workday. Nonexclusive listening develops the expectations that I will need when I later engage in exclusive listening in the concert hall.

Perhaps listening is taken to be an exclusive activity because it is thought to require a distinctively aesthetic attitude. Aesthetic value has a long history of being opposed to utilitarian value. But if the lack of acquired knowledge explains why infants cannot yet listen to music, it is not for want of an aesthetic attitude or special degree of concentration. Who is engaged in disinterested perceptual satisfaction if not the infant in a crib, transfixed by the dangling mobile overhead? Conversely, there is little reason to suppose that the polite audience sitting immobile before an orchestra or ensemble is really listening. (Hanslick suspected that few were.)[62] When Charles Mingus warns that the ability to dance "don't mean you listen to the music," at least not "fully," he endorses the exclusive focus. But who displays more attention than a couple dancing to a slow popular song, their bodies moving in time to the music and who, alerted by the harmonic movement that the song is moving to closure, end their dance with the end of the song?[63] If one is dancing with the rhythm of the music, using tonality as a guide to determine when the piece is about to end, surely

one grasps the basics of its organization. One is listening to the music in the sounds and not merely hearing enjoyable sounds.

Despite these qualms, I am willing to recognize a distinction between hearing and listening. Listening is informed judgment directed to the music's particularity as the music that it is, in contrast to the mere "hearing" of infants. But if this is the right way to cast the distinction, then I am quite certain that I listen to rock music. Apart from the psychological research that shows audiences to be routinely more astute about the music that they normally listen to, I can recall a specific instance in my adolescence where a shift in my tastes revealed to me that hearing is not always listening.

Sometime in 1973, my brother brought home David Bowie's recently released album *Aladdin Sane*. I'd seen Bowie's name increasingly tossed around in the rock press, but I could not recall ever hearing him on the radio. I was curious to hear what he sounded like. The album was sitting on the turntable, so I turned it on. My immediate reaction was to recoil in distaste. Song after song struck me as sheer noise. (At the time, my own tastes favored "soft" and folk-based rock. This was several years before any of us had heard of punk, or even the New York Dolls.) There was precisely one song that I returned to, to play all the way through: "Drive in Saturday," a ballad with a languid melody.

Several years later, I had many hours of rock listening behind me, including more listening to Bowie, who'd started to make hits for American radio. I'd purchased and repeatedly listened to *Young Americans* (1975) and *Station to Station* (1976). I bought a copy of *Aladdin Sane* and now had a very different experience. The opening track, "Watch That Man," was a surreal cry of desperate, paranoid anger. Although built on an entirely different rhythmic foundation, so was "Panic in Detroit," with its Bo Diddley groove and long, arching melody line, punctuated by the syncopated cry of "panic in Detroit!" at the chorus. The title track turned out to retain a fair amount of noise, largely thanks to dissonant bursts of jazz piano instead of guitars. "Time" turned out to be a quasi-cabaret number, something that might have been at home in the decadent nightclubs of the Weimar Republic. The album's ten songs now sounded stylistically and emotionally varied. But of course they had not changed at all. I had.

One lesson here is that musical arrangements can function as noise, preventing unprepared listeners from grasping the structure of a composition, particularly its melodies. Many who dismiss rock as noise are put off by its abrasive or unfamiliar timbres. Lyrical melodies and clever modulations are often clothed in distorted guitars and nasal shouts. Beatles producer George Martin became aware of this complication when non-rock musicians covered the Beatles. "There were many people who couldn't assimilate their tunes, because they couldn't hear the music for the noise," Martin observes. But when Annunzio Mantovani and others recorded orchestrated versions of their songs "with pleasant, syrupy sounds," the same people who dismissed the Beatles as noise said, "Oh, that's a nice tune ... They do write good music, don't they?" Orchestration aside,

Martin remarks that these were "exactly the same tunes."[64]

However, Martin's comments should not be taken as evidence that rock arrangements are themselves the problem. Rock fans experience a parallel cognitive difficulty when confronted with unfamiliar varieties of rock. Wondering if I could confirm with others what I'd experienced with *Aladdin Sane,* I tried a simple experiment with forty students. I played them the Byrds' original recording of "Eight Miles High" (1966) and then the punk rock onslaught of the Hüsker Dü remake (1984). The words are nearly unintelligible on the Hüsker's version. The vocal is a hoarse shout. The tempo is faster and the instrumentation is distorted. Less than half of the students initially recognized it as the same piece of music. But after playing them the first minute of each version four times in a row, alternating between the two versions, every member of the class reported that they now heard that it was the same music. If the students had been less familiar with rock, four hearings might not have been sufficient. (In similar comparisons, the majority of my students found it difficult to hear the same melody in two different instrumental jazz arrangements even after four or five hearings.)

What I informally demonstrated to my students is a point well-known to researchers in psychology of music. Recognizing music in a stream of sound (hearing the music that it is) requires familiarity with other music in the same style.[65] Within rock music, the Byrds and Hüsker Dü are miles apart (equivalent, perhaps, to the distance between Giacomo Puccini and Béla

Bartók). Nonetheless, the Hüsker Dü arrangement of "Eight Miles High" is an instance of "Eight Miles High" and not "Why?" or "Captain Soul" (two other Byrds songs from the same period). The fact that "hard" rock music disguises or obscures harmonic and melodic movement in a flurry of distracting elements helps to explain its limited popular acceptance. It does not make the Hüsker Dü performance less musical, nor is a competent response to it any less a case of acculturated listening than is a competent response to Chopin's "Minute Waltz," music that conforms to radically different stylistic rules.

Conclusion

> The experienced listener can no more fail to understand her native music than her native tongue.
> —*Diana Raffman*[66]

Let us take stock. The traditional opposition of hearing and listening is usually married to the thesis that when we listen to nondisruptive sounds, the sounds are distinguishable into two sorts of properties, elemental or structural. Active listening focuses on essential (structural) qualities of musical works, while responses grounded in nonessential (elemental, nonstructural) aspects are denigrated as uneducated hearing. Focused attention to structural properties is the common base of "active" listening, "musicological" listening, Hanslick's "logical" listening, Beardsley's hearing "in the fullest sense," Gurney's "definite hearing," and Scruton's "aesthetic judgement." A psychological thesis about the experience of music is unsoundly derived from the assumption that musical works are sound structures. Music's qualitative elements are treated as a necessary evil, as something present only because there is no structure unless there is something to structure. Musicians who *perform* the musical work are similarly relegated to the lesser role of re-creator. Popular fandom (e.g., Beatlemania), centered on performances and the identity of the performers, is taken as evidence that the audience is not responding to music.[67]

Critics like Hanslick have defended instrumental music as the highest achievement in the art, reversing centuries of tradition that had put vocal music at the top. Philosophers and critics have emphasized a distinction between objective and subjective responses, where listening to the right features of the music legitimizes pleasure by securing it in something objective. Listening incorrectly might yield pleasure, but only of a contingent and subjective sort. Even composers of program music, otherwise at odds with the formalist defense of absolute music, have buttressed their aesthetic ideal by writing detailed programs to guard listeners against "wrong" interpretations of the music.[68] By the twentieth century, density, structural integration, and complexity were firmly entrenched as the bases of compositional success. The result? "Our culture may, in fact, be one of the most extreme in the degree to which musical participation is limited."[69] But this way of putting it already assumes that dancing in a nightclub and singing to the radio while driving are not musical participation.[70]

It would be silly to deny that objective features make different styles suitable for different uses. Punk rock at full volume tends to disrupt conversation during a dinner party, which is why I'm likely to load Django Reinhardt or some Mozart piano sonatas into the CD player before dinner guests arrive. But there are many uses of music in everyday life, all of which require some application of a listener's musical intelligence if the music is to serve its purpose. My argument has attempted to show that exclusive attention to "serious" music is merely one sort of listening, one of many ways that acculturated listeners might incorporate music into life. Rock and other forms of popular music are designed to meet the needs of large numbers of people with many different levels of musical education. Nonetheless, popular music makes cognitive demands, and its pleasures require application of rule-governed, abstract principles. We must not locate listening at one extreme of what looks to be a continuum of practices. Doing so begs too many important questions about music and its value.[71]

Notes

1. Abraham Kaplan, "The Aesthetics of the Popular Arts," *Journal of Aesthetics and Art Criticism* 34, no. 4 (1966): 355.

2. The paucity of reliable experimental data on this topic creates an environment in which absurd claims about popular taste can flourish. Most empirical studies of music are directed by assumptions about "serious" music, frequently adopting claims made by Heinrich Schenker or Leonard B. Meyer. Little has been done to determine how listeners actually hear other types of music. See David J. Hargreaves, *The Developmental Psychology of Music* (Cambridge: Cambridge University Press, 1986), 7–8.

3. Yet folk music is often treated as a branch of popular music, as in Peter Gammond, ed., *The Oxford Companion to Popular Music* (Oxford

and New York: Oxford University Press, 1991). Gammond sees "popular" as opposed to "serious" and places Charlie Parker and all other jazz musicians with popular. The same perspective informs Phil Hardy and Dave Laing, *The Faber Companion to 20th-Century Popular Music* (London and Boston: Faber and Faber, 1990).

4. For an overview of Lomax's career, see *The Alan Lomax Archive Web site*, www.alan-lomax.com.

5. For instance, jazz and the Broadway musical (e.g., *Oklahoma!*) are the only music treated as popular arts in Irving Deer and Harriet A. Deer, eds., *The Popular Arts: A Critical Reader* (New York: Scribner, 1967). In a very few years, the emphasis shifts to rock music, as in David Manning White, ed., *Pop Culture in America* (Chicago: Quadrangle Books, 1970).

6. From approximately 1954 to 1970, blues music provided a stylistic unity to a great deal of rock and roll and then rock music. But rock music was never exclusively derived from African-American sources. We should remember that from the very start, Elvis Presley was as likely to record gospel music and commercial pop songs as blues-based tunes. In addition to rock and roll, the Beatles covered a diverse mix of country music, Broadway hits, and American pop standards. For more about the diversity of styles brought together under the "rock" heading, see Allan F. Moore, *Rock: The Primary Text: Developing a Musicology of Rock,* 2nd ed. (Aldershot, England: Ashgate, 2001), 119–80.

7. Keith Negus counteracts this myopia by studying the creation, distribution, and consumption of different genres in the music industry, including country and salsa. Keith Negus, *Music Genres and Corporate Cultures* (London and New York: Routledge, 1999).

8. Raymond Williams, *Keywords: A Vocabulary of Culture and Society* (London: Fontana, 1983), 237.

9. For an informative overview of the issues involved here, see John A. Fisher, "High Art Versus Low Art," in *The Routledge Companion to Aesthetics,* ed. Berys Gaut and Dominic M. Lopes (London and New York: Routledge, 2001), 409–21.

10. Noël Carroll argues that the crucial organizing concept is not that of popular art but of

mass art. See Noël Carroll, *The Philosophy of Mass Art* (New York: Oxford University Press, 1998).

11. See Jason Middleton, "D.C. Punk and the Production of Authenticity," in *Rock Over the Edge: Transformations in Popular Culture,* ed. Roger Beebe, Denise Fulbrook, and Ben Saunders (Durham, NC, and London: Duke University Press, 2002), 335–56.

12. Charles Kiel, Reebee Garofalo, and John Fiske favor the "populist" approach to popular music. For representative texts, see Charles Keil, *Urban Blues* (Chicago: University of Chicago Press, 1966); Steve Chapple and Reebee Garofalo, *Rock 'n' Roll is Here to Pay: The History and Politics of the Music Industry* (Chicago: Nelson-Hall, 1977); and John Fiske, *Understanding Popular Culture* (Boston: Unwin Hyman, 1989).

13. For an overview of the processes that continuously redefined "popular" taste in the United States, see Lawrence W. Levine, *Highbrow/Lowbrow: The Emergence of Cultural Hierarchy in America* (Cambridge and London: Harvard University Press, 1988) and Michael Kammen, *American Culture American Tastes: Social Change and the 20th Century* (New York: Basic Books, 1999). They cover the nineteenth and twentieth centuries, respectively.

14. This formulation is based on Anahid Kassabian, "Popular," in *Key Terms in Popular Music and Culture,* ed. Bruce Horner and Thomas Swiss (Malden, MA, and Oxford: Blackwell, 1999), 113–23.

15. Ibid., 117.

16. See Joseph Lanza, *Elevator Music: A Surreal History of Muzak, Easy-Listening, and Other Moodsong* (New York: Picador, 1994), 6–66, 167–81.

17. Kassabian, "Popular," 121.

18. Carroll, *Mass Art,* 192–96; and Theodore Gracyk, *I Wanna Be Me: Rock Music and the Politics of Identity* (Philadelphia: Temple University Press, 2001), 17–26.

19. This use of "paradigm" assumes that multiple paradigms exist simultaneously within the same cultural field and is meant to reflect Thomas Kuhn's position on artistic paradigms, not scientific paradigms. See Gracyk, "You've Really Got a Hold on Me: Paradigms," in *I*

Wanna Be Me, 67–80.

20. Georges Friedmann, "Rôle et place de la musique dans une société industrielle," *Diogene,* no. 77 (1970): 30, quoted in Ivo Supicic, *Music in Society: A Guide to the Sociology of Music,* no. 4 of *Sociology of Music* (Stuyvesant, NY: Pendragon Press, 1987), 183.

21. Howard D. McKinney and W. R. Anderson, *Discovering Music,* 4th ed. (New York: American Book Company, 1962), 27–28, emphasis in original.

22. Eduard Hanslick, *On the Musically Beautiful,* trans. Geoffrey Payzant (Indianapolis: Hackett, 1986), 60.

23. Ibid., 58–59.

24. Rechristened "concatenationism," this position has been recently defended by Jerrold Levinson, *Music in the Moment* (Ithaca, NY: Cornell University Press, 1997).

25. Edmund Gurney, *The Power of Sound* (1880; reprint, New York: Basic Books, 1966), 306. For a summary and analysis of Gurney's position, see Malcolm Budd, "Sexual Motion and Ideal Motion," in *Music and the Emotions* (London and Boston: Routledge & Kegan Paul, 1985), 52–75.

26. Robert Motherwell cites Prall as "a great aesthetician," and Leonard Bernstein dedicates *The Unanswered Question* to Prall. See Robert Motherwell, "Interview with Robert Motherwell," interview by Paul Cummings, transcript of tape recording, 24 November 1971, Smithsonian Archives of American Art (available at http://artarchives.si.edu/oralhist/mother71 .htm); and Leonard Bernstein, *The Unanswered Question: Six Talks at Harvard* (Cambridge and London: Harvard University Press, 1976), 3.

27. David W. Prall, *Aesthetic Judgment* (1929; reprint, New York: Crowell, 1967), 63–68. Prall's position is reminiscent of Hanslick's idea that emotions cannot be the "content" of music because their apprehension does not depend on our knowledge of musical laws (e.g., Hanslick, *On the Musically Beautiful,* xxii).

28. For a response to Prall's position on taste and smell, see Carolyn Korsmeyer, *Making Sense of Taste: Food and Philosophy* (Ithaca, NY: Cornell University Press), 104–15.

29. Prall, *Aesthetic Judgment,* 210–11.

30. W. Jay Dowling, "The Development of Music Perception and Cognition," in *The Psychology of Music,* 2nd ed., ed. Diana Deutsch (San Diego and London: Academic Press, 1999), 603–25.

31. Monroe C. Beardsley, "The Categories of Critical Analysis," in *Aesthetics: Problems in the Philosophy of Criticism,* 2nd ed. (Indianapolis: Hackett, 1981), 75–113.

32. Ibid., 98.

33. Ibid., 337.

34. Leonard B. Meyer, *Emotion and Meaning in Music* (Chicago: University of Chicago Press, 1956), 40.

35. Roger Scruton, *The Aesthetics of Music* (Oxford: Oxford University Press, 1997), 354–59. See also Beardsley, *Aesthetics,* 321–37.

36. Scruton, *The Aesthetics of Music,* 157. The Beatles and Buddy Holly are Scruton's exceptions in rock music. Their melodies, along with those of Andrew Lloyd Weber, are in the same category as those of George Gershwin and Cole Porter (pp. 500–501).

37. Ibid., 502. The same opposition of intellectual and physical response grounds the argument against rock music in Julian Johnson, *Who Needs Classical Music? Cultural Choice and Musical Value* (New York: Oxford University Press, 2002).

38. Gurney, *The Power of Sound,* 406.

39. Scruton, *The Aesthetics of Music,* 500. To read Scruton's argument without reading the 510 pages of *The Aesthetics of Music,* and for my response to that argument, see Roger Scruton, "The Decline of Musical Culture," and Theodore Gracyk, "Music's Worldly Uses, or How I Learned to Stop Worrying and to Love Led Zeppelin," both in *Arguing about Art: Topics in Contemporary Philosophical Aesthetics,* 2nd ed., ed. Alex Neill and Aaron Ridley. (London and New York: Routledge, 2001), 119–34 and 135–47, respectively.

40. For a discussion of the contributing role of the European music concert in the eighteenth and nineteenth centuries, see David Gramit, "Performing Musical Culture: The Concert," in *Cultivating Music: The Aspirations, Interests, and Limits of German Musical Culture, 1770–1846* (Berkeley and Los Angeles: University of California Press, 2002), 125–60.

41. The argument is made that the popular music fan is attending only to trivial customizations of otherwise banal and interchangeable tunes. For my response to this claim, see Theodore Gracyk, "Adorno, Jazz, and the Aesthetics of Popular Music," *The Musical Quarterly* 76, no. 4 (1992): 526–42.

42. In Hanslick's words, "The form (as tonal structure) ... is the music itself" (Hanslick, *On the Musically Beautiful,* 60).

43. Robert Cantrick, "Commentary on Nicholas Cook," *Music Theory Online* 8, no. 2 (2002). Available at www.societymusictheory.org/mto/issues/mto.02.8.2/mto.02.8.2.cantrick.html.

44. Nonstructural properties play a major role in the impact of many rock recordings. See Theodore Gracyk, *Rhythm and Noise: An Aesthetics of Rock* (Durham, NC, and London: Duke University Press, 1996), 61–67, 99–124; and Albin J. Zak III, "Sound as Form," in *The Poetics of Rock: Cutting Tracks, Making Records* (Berkeley and Los Angeles: University of California Press, 2001), 48–96.

45. Noël Carroll, *Philosophical Problems of Classical Film Theory* (Princeton: Princeton University Press, 1988), 82–83. Carroll introduces and criticizes the specificity thesis in relation to Rudolf Arnheim's aesthetics of film. As an example of an appeal to the specificity thesis for music, consider the transitions in this argument by Edward Cone: "No musical form, no music. That is as true of improvisation as of symphonic composition, of primitive folk-songs as of Lieder, of hard rock as of dodecaphony. To be music is to have form. To hear music is to hear musical form." Edward Cone, "Music and Form," in *What is Music,* ed. Philip Alperson (New York: Haven, 1988), 134.

46. Carroll, *Philosophical Problems of Classical Film Theory,* 86.

47. Fisher, "High Art Versus Low Art," 413.

48. Those who favor analytical listening and are unfamiliar with the extended improvisations of the Grateful Dead might look at the transcriptions and analysis of one such improvisation in

Graeme M. Boone, "Tonal and Expressive Ambiguity in 'Dark Star,'" in *Understanding Rock: Essays in Musical Analysis,* ed. John Covach and Graeme M. Boone (New York and Oxford: Oxford University Press, 1997), 171–210.

49. Arlette Zenatti, "Children's Musical Cognition and Taste," in *Psychology and Music: The Understanding of Melody and Rhythm,* ed. Thomas J. Tighe and W. Jay Dowling (Hillsdale, NJ: Erlbaum, 1993), 185.

50. A prototype of this argument is Gurney, *The Power of Sound,* 403. For an extended discussion of this idea, see Theodore Gracyk, "Valuing and Evaluating Popular Music," *Journal of Aesthetics and Art Criticism* 57, no. 2 (1999): 205–20.

51. Ola Stockfelt, "Adequate Modes of Listening," in *Keeping Score: Music, Disciplinarity, Culture,* ed. David Schwarz, Anahid Kassabian, and Lawrence Siegel (Charlottesville: University Press of Virginia, 1997), 142. See also Moore, *Rock: The Primary Text,* 24–28.

52. Quoted in Tom Moon, "The Black Saint's Epitaph," *Musician,* no. 128 (1989): 122.

53. Even with food, physiology does not account for everything. Beliefs about food can contribute to phenomenal differences. Knowing which part of an animal (or even which animal) is on one's plate can have a profound effect on how it tastes.

54. What are those instincts? Above all, the instinct to notice changes in intervals and pitch levels of melodies and to notice and remember melodic contours. Evidence strongly denies any instinctive preference for diatonic or "Western" musical patterns. For a summary of the relevant recent research, see Dowling, "The Development of Music Perception and Cognition," 604–10.

55. Michael R. D'Amato, "A Search for Tonal Pattern Perception in Cebus Monkeys: Why Monkeys Can't Hum a Tune," *Music Perception* 5, no. 4 (1988): 478.

56. Peter Kivy, *Music Alone: Philosophical Reflections on the Purely Musical Experience* (Ithaca, NY: Cornell University Press, 1990), 41. As Allan Moore puts it, "until we cognize the sounds, until we have created an internal representation on the basis of their assimilation, we have no musical entity to care about, or which to give

value" (Moore, *Rock: The Primary Text,* 17, emphasis deleted).

57. Martyn Evans observes that cases of cross-cultural exposure seem to be our only genuine instances of an adult whose listening can be characterized as naive. Martyn Evans, *Listening to Music* (London: Macmillan, 1990), 11.

58. For most listeners, seven seems to be the pivotal age for grasping the syntax of the tonal system. See John A. Sloboda, "Music as a Language," in *Music and Child Development,* ed. Frank R. Wilson and Franz L. Roehmann (St. Louis: MMB Music, 1990), 28–43.

59. Some researchers have concluded that music and language begin in the same instinct to organize the aural environment into distinct events according to musical qualities. See Christoph Fassbender, "Infants' Auditory Sensitivity towards Acoustic Parameters of Speech and Music," in *Musical Beginnings: Origins and Development of Musical Competence,* ed. Irène Deliège and John Sloboda (Oxford: Oxford University Press, 1996), 56–87. See also Albert S. Bregman, *Auditory Scene Analysis* (Cambridge: MIT Press, 1990); Stephen Handel, *Listening* (Cambridge: MIT Press, 1990); Carol L. Krumhansl and Peter Jusczyk, "Infants' Perception of Phrase Structure in Music," *Psychological Science* 1, no. 1 (1990): 70–73; and Sandra Trehub, E. Glenn Schellenberg, and D. Hill, "The Origins of Music Perception and Cognition: A Developmental Perspective," in *Perception and Cognition of Music,* ed. Irène Deliège and John A. Sloboda (Hove, UK: Psychology Press, 1997), 103–28.

60. Hanslick, *On the Musically Beautiful,* 69–70. But in the same passage, he denies that a rhythm by itself is genuinely "artistic" music, that is, music beyond what is natural and instinctive.

61. Ibid., 74.

62. For examples of audience engagement at the height of the classical age, see Lydia Goehr, *The Imaginary Museum of Musical Works* (Oxford: Clarendon Press, 1992), 191–93, 236–39.

63. Listeners' expectations about when a musical segment will end are "fairly precisely synchronized" with what subsequently happens. Complex metrical structures alter those expecta-

tions in predictable ways. See Mari Riess Jones, "Attending to Musical Events," in *Cognitive Bases of Musical Communication,* ed. Mari Riess Jones and Susan Holleran (Washington, DC: American Psychological Association, 1992), 91–110.

64. George Martin, *All You Need Is Ears* (New York: St. Martin's Press, 1979), 34–35.

65. One reason is that the average listener does not construct an abstract representation of a musical work: "memory for music typically operates in terms of more precise representations of particular stimuli than has been generally thought." (Dowling, "The Development of Music Perception and Cognition," 620). It seems likely that unfamiliar styles introduce distracting stimuli that limit comparisons with remembered music.

66. Diana Raffman, "Proposal for a Musical Semantics," in *Cognitive Bases of Musical Communication,* 30.

67. Although Scruton praises the Beatles, he makes just this complaint about fans of the rock group Nirvana (Scruton, *The Aesthetics of Music,* 500).

68. See Roger Scruton, "Programme Music," *The Aesthetic Understanding* (London and New York: Methuen, 1983), 41.

69. Carol L. Krumhansl, "Internal Representations for Music Perception and Performance," *Cognitive Bases of Musical Communication,* 198.

70. To counter such assumptions, Christopher Small recommends thinking about "musicking" (a verb he coined to cover *any* activity relating to music). Christopher Small, *Music of the Common Tongue: Survival and Celebration of Afro-American Music,* (1987; reprint, Middletown, CT: Wesleyan University Press, 1998); and Christopher Small, *Musicking: The Meanings of Performing and Listening* (Middletown, CT: Wesleyan University Press, 1998).

71. I thank Magdalene Chalikia and Elizabeth Nawrot for directing me to a wealth of relevant psychological research on music perception and cognition.

Theodore Gracyk is a professor of philosophy at Minnesota State University–Moorhead. His work on aesthetic theory has appeared in such journals as *The Musical Quarterly, The Journal of Aesthetic Education, The Journal of Aesthetics and Art Criticism,* and *The British Journal of Aesthetics.* He has published two books on popular music, *Rhythm and Noise: An Aesthetics of Rock* (Duke University Press, 1996) and *I Wanna Be Me: Rock Music and the Politics of Identity* (Temple University Press, 2001).

4

None So Deaf: Toward a New Pedagogy of Popular Music

Martha Bayles

American popular music has always posed a challenge to music educators, but the shape of the challenge has changed rather drastically over the past thirty years. This chapter begins by sketching the reasons why the Afro-American idiom, which includes such forms as jazz, blues, gospel, and blues-based rock, was for many years excluded from the nation's formal musical curricula. Admittedly this is no longer the case; many institutions now gladly include jazz and other Afro-American forms. But ironically, just as Afro-American music has gained academic approval, it has ceased to be the driving force behind popular listening. Indeed, the new inclusiveness has been accompanied by a sea change in popular music—one that makes it harder than ever to connect student taste with what most educators consider music. I will describe the two major transformations that have changed popular music from a listening experience to a sort of theater in which visual stimuli and ritualized forms of audience participation matter more than sound. The obstacle this poses to music education should be obvious. I will close with a brief

counterintuitive "modest proposal" for helping young people move beyond what has become an exceedingly limited conception of music and toward a broader appreciation of their rich and varied musical heritage.

The Old Idiomatic Debate

It is remarkable how many debates over "high" versus "popular" culture avoid the topic of music. One reason may be that the participants in these debates tend to come from literary or visual-arts backgrounds. But another reason may be an awareness, however vague, that the relationship between "high" and "popular" is more problematic in music than in any other field. Helpful here is the work of Henry Pleasants, the maverick critic who, after several decades of writing about twentieth-century musical modernism, began to wonder, in the 1950s, why such modern music attracted such a minuscule audience, even among people eager to embrace highly intellectualized art. In particular, Pleasants found himself concluding that serialism after Webern was a sterile, hyper-mathematical exercise better suited to the burgeoning science of electronics than to the human ear, and that the "aleatory" music of Cage and others, despite taking the opposite path of composition through random, irrational processes, was no more listenable. These are not the sum total of musical modernism, to be sure, but during the postwar period, they staked an uncompromising claim to being the sole legitimate heirs of the Western musical tradition.

Pleasants was not the first to dispute this claim; anyone with ears can tell you that rigor in following a particular composing method or style is no excuse for musical rigor mortis. However, Pleasants was the first to argue convincingly that the twentieth century offered an alternative:

> In art and literature, the assumed "modernity" of the contemporary product may well be as bogus as I hold the "modernity" of contemporary Serious music to be. But neither in the graphic arts, nor in literature, is there a vital so-called subculture to disturb the assumptions of an Establishment.[1]

That "vital so-called subculture" is Afro-American music. For Pleasants, the essential point was that unlike the "kitsch" decried by Clement Greenberg or the literary "midcult" lambasted by Dwight MacDonald, Afro-American music is not a watered-down imitation of high culture. Unfortunately, this fact was long lost on the "serious" music establishment, which dismissed all Afro-American music as "popular," meaning artistically inferior. Writes Pleasants:

> This curious obduracy in the face of acknowledged virtues stems, I think, from the persistence of an obsolete terminology. We regard the distinction between Serious and Popular as qualitative when it is, I believe, idiomatic. We are dealing, in my view, not with two grades, the one substantial and the other trivial, but with two separate musical idioms, the one European, the other, Afro-American.[2]

The term *Afro-American* should be defined broadly, to include not only such "black" forms as jazz, blues, and gospel, but also a great portion of twentieth-century music, high and low. For Pleasants, *Afro-American* is practically a synonym for *American*. This country's ethnically and culturally diverse musics become distinctive only when they acquire the imprint, light or heavy, of the black idiom. Many would object to such a broad definition, some because they wish to downplay the Americanness of black music, others because they wish to downplay the blackness of American music. The case may look more convincing when we consider the essential characteristics of the Afro-American idiom as it evolved through the first half of the twentieth century. To do so, let me focus for a moment on jazz.

The first thing that strikes the European-trained ear about jazz is its structural brevity and simplicity. Almost all traditional jazz performances are a blend of composed, rehearsed, and improvised material built upon either the thirty-two-bar popular song or the twelve-bar traditional blues. One exception might be the longer compositions of Duke Ellington, such as *Black, Brown, and Beige.* But even these are suites, collections of the often brilliant short pieces for which Ellington is renowned.

Other jazz figures, notably Thelonious Monk, composed short works with intricate structures. By the 1950s, John Coltrane, Ornette Coleman, and Cecil Taylor were carrying free-form improvisation to heroic lengths—and proclaiming jazz's proud independence from European-derived notions of musical architecture. Hence Andre Hodeir's 1954 pronouncement, "Jazz is not constructed music."[3]

Since the elaborate structures of European art music are intimately related to its rich harmonies, it follows that jazz has suffered a disadvantage here, too. As Hodeir notes, what passes for harmonic sophistication in the songs of Broadway and Tin Pan Alley is usually watered down from a European source.[4] But jazz also relies on the blues, whose distinctive pentatonic scale creates harmonies that, Hodeir admits, have "a real beauty of their own" that "avoids banality."[5] Because of the blues, banality is rare in the harmonic explorations of Ellington in the 1920s, Coleman Hawkins and Art Tatum in the 1930s, Charlie Parker in the 1940s, and Miles Davis in the 1950s. Thus, Pleasants could write in 1969 that "those who speak disdainfully of the harmonic element in jazz are plainly unaware of what has been going on."[6] The same could be said of melody: while the melodic achievements of the great American songwriters of the 1920s, 1930s, and 1940s are in some sense borrowed from European models, the addition of blues coloration keeps this music from sounding derivative.

Indeed, jazz has a long history of borrowing musical ideas from European and American modernism. And while the modernists also borrowed from jazz, it is generally acknowledged that jazz made more creative use of modernist devices than vice versa. Throughout the early decades of the century, jazz musicians exploited with stunning speed and originality such modernist ideas as chromatic harmony, modal scales, electronic instruments, and electronically altered sound. It is tricky to take a balanced view of this process, because neither side is entirely comfortable with the exchange. Many in the "serious" music establishment dismissed jazz as a Johnny-come-lately rummaging in modernism's castoffs. At the same time, many in the jazz establishment belittled or denied the role of European ideas.[7]

From the music educator's perspective, the line between jazz and modernism is, of course, less important than the broader idiomatic differences between the Afro-American and classical traditions. Most important here is the musical element of *rhythm*. Pleasants notes that like all good things, the structural complexity and harmonic richness of classical music in the eighteenth and nineteenth centuries were achieved at a cost:

> The dramatic, reflective and recitative character of nineteenth century Serious music exacted a price in rhythmic debility ... The dynamic faculty of tempo changes, both sudden and gradual, and all the dramatic inflection inherent in various types of acceleration and retardation, while they served an "interpretive" and "expressive" purpose in European music, also contributed to the weakening of the beat as a phenomenon collectively anticipated and collectively experienced.[8]

As for the beat in serialist and aleatory music, it is most accurately described by Groucho Marx's famous line, "Either this man is dead or my watch has stopped."

All European rhythm, even the liveliest baroque beat, sounds mechanical when compared with Afro-American, and most Afro-American rhythm sounds mechanical when compared with African. Explains Gunther Schuller, "African music, including its drumming, is wholly contrapuntal and basically conceived in terms of polymetric and polyrhythmic time relationships."[9] Recognizing that "African rhythm is based on additive rather than divisive principles," Schuller notes that when first listening to African music the Western ear expects the steady "structural" beat to mark off metronomic intervals, but this does not occur in African rhythms.[10] Rather, each vocal or percussive part has a slightly different rhythm, which "crosses" the others only at strategic moments. Moreover, the structural beat is frequently implied rather than played, while the numerous other pulses surrounding it receive equal if not greater accentuation. Schuller calls this "the 'democratization' of rhythmic values."[11] The result is a thick rhythmic texture, which suggests to Leonard B. Meyer "an analogy between the role of the temporal organization in African music and the role of harmony in Western music."[12]

Rhythmic polyphony defines the essential quality known as "swing." At some point, nearly every critic tries to unpack Ellington's famous title, "It Don't Mean a Thing If It Ain't Got That Swing." But like so many other qualities in music, swing eludes verbal definition. Hodeir comes closest with his list of five elements: "infrastructure" (structural beat), "superstructure" (rhythmic counterpoint), "getting the notes and accents in the right place," "relaxation," and "vital drive." He also admits that while "the first three are technical in nature and can be understood rationally; the last two are psycho-physical, and must be grasped intuitively."[13]

Today many educators teach jazz as "America's classical music." The process by which this acceptance came about was tragically prolonged and unjust. No American art form has risen so high so fast, and yet encountered so much snobbery, as jazz. Study its history, and you will be amazed at the rigidity of those in the "serious" music establishment who dismissed it out of sheer prejudice. But consider: when the issue was decided in the years after World War II, it was decided on *musical* grounds. The important questions, those addressed by Hodeir, Pleasants, Schuller, and others, were *musical*: How does jazz work? Does it replicate something the classical European repertory already does? Or does it add something exciting and new? Clearly, it should have been easier to get jazz through the front gates of civilization. But today, listening to the rhetoric of those who would tear down those gates altogether, I feel a grudging respect for the resistance offered to jazz. Without defending the racism that distorted their judgment, I am glad that the establishment gave jazz a hard time. It made victory all the sweeter, civilization all the richer. There should always be someone guarding the gates, just as there should always be someone storming them.

The First Transformation: Primitivism

Unfortunately, the latest assaults on popular music have little to do with musical value as understood by either the classical or jazz tradition. Not surprisingly, the first of these arises out of a deeply rooted misunderstanding of the Afro-American idiom.

The resistance offered to jazz in the early twentieth century stemmed in part from the fact that for all its rhythmic power, Afro-American music is actually *less* emotional than the beloved eighteenth- and nineteenth-century repertory. For three centuries Western music had focused less on the bodily response to music than on the emotional, and with late romanticism this emotional emphasis got carried to such an extreme that the modernists wearied of it and called for a more rational, disciplined, and restrained approach to music. Interestingly, several modernists—Cocteau, Satie, Milhaud, Stravinsky—were attracted to jazz. And while their attempts to incorporate it into their own compositions were not very successful, largely because the "jazzy" bits were not performed by experienced jazz musicians, these modernists were right about one thing: a good way to flush exhausted romanticism out of people's ears was with jazz.

To accuse Afro-American music of not reaching the peaks and abysses of romantic emotion is about as appropriate as blaming football for not having home runs. Its emotional cast tends to be restrained, even stoic, as befits a music created by people who could ill afford to cultivate their passions, especially negative passions like rage and despair. Under slavery, Jim Crow, and

segregation, Wagnerian transports could get you killed. To be sure, blues and gospel achieve moments of high emotional intensity. However, these are ritual in nature, intended to help the listener get a grip, get over, and get through another day.

Because the true admirers of Afro-American music understand this and find in its most highly developed expressions the classical virtues of wit, elegance, accessibility, and naturalness, they also find galling the long-lived image of Afro-American music as crude, instinctual, and animalistic. Needless to say, this was originally a racist idea, as evident in this oft-quoted 1913 letter to the Paris editor of the *New York Herald:*

> Can it be said that America is falling prey to the collective soul of the negro through the influence of what is popularly known as "rag time" music? ... If there is any tendency toward such a national disaster, it should definitely be pointed out and extreme measures taken to inhibit the influence ... [This] music is symbolic of the primitive morality and perceptible moral limitations of the negro type.[14]

Some people still think about Afro-American music in this grotesquely insulting way. But more common (and more relevant to contemporary popular music) is an equally grotesque *compliment* based on the same assumptions. This attitude, which I call *primitivism,* perceives the same crudity but instead of deploring it *celebrates* it. Consider this rave review of Josephine Baker's 1925 debut at the Théatre des Champs Elysées:

> In the short *pas de deux* of the savages, which came as the finale of the Revue

Nègre, there was a wild splendor and magnificent animality. Certain of Miss Baker's poses, back arched, haunches protruding, arms entwined and uplifted in a phallic symbol, had the compelling potency of the finest examples of Negro sculpture. ... The frenzy of African Eros swept over the audience.[15]

Behind this lies the assumption that the rhythmic element in Afro-American music is the product not of developed art but of raw instinct. Gushed another Parisian, "Josephine moved like an animal. An animal doesn't think about how it moves, it just moves."[16] Never mind that Baker had learned how to move like that through a long apprenticeship in vaudeville or that rhythm is no more "natural" than any other musical talent and must be cultivated before blossoming as art.

This view of rhythm is still intellectually respectable. The most quotable sentence in Allan Bloom's 1987 bestseller, *The Closing of the American Mind,* was, "Young people know that rock has the beat of sexual intercourse."[17] The reading public seized upon this comment because they knew, without the aid of philosophy, that it aptly describes the simple, repetitive beat of hard rock. Indeed, Steven Tyler of the band Aerosmith seconded Bloom when he remarked of his own rhythmic style, "It's twos and fours, it's f—ing."[18]

But is this the final word on rhythm? Of course not. Rock grew out of the blues, most varieties of which have a strong backbeat. But a skilled blues band will also play other rhythmic patterns in creative tension with the backbeat. This is the African touch, known as syncopation, swing, funk,

or groove. Musically speaking, the worst thing about contemporary rock is its utter lack of any such rhythmic counterpoint. Rock ceased to swing in the 1960s, when the focus shifted away from the drums and bass and toward the lead guitar. To support the complex forward motion of such virtuoso guitarists as Eric Clapton and Jimmy Page, the rhythm section was reduced to keeping time (at top volume), and by the time Bruce Springsteen came along, it was considered a compliment to call this time keeping the "dinosaur beat."

I mustn't beg the question, though. Swing, funk, and groove may be more appealing than the dinosaur beat, but perhaps that very appeal is primitive. After all, rhythmic energy leads to toe-tapping and other forms of physical "agitation." There's an old joke about Southern Baptists disapproving of sexual intercourse because it might lead to dancing. But unless they are living under the rule of some Taliban, most people understand, as human culture always has, that bodily movements, like mental and spiritual ones, can be more or less graceful, beautiful, and virtuous.

Such subtleties were lost on the primitivists of rock. Please note that I locate the beginning of the sea change in the 1960s, not the 1950s. Culturally, 1950s rock and roll functioned much as swing had done: it was dance music, youth music, the music of (more or less) innocent good times. To quote Alan Freed, the enterprising Cleveland disc jockey who helped to introduce northern white youth to rhythm and blues, "Rock 'n' roll was merely swing with a modern name."[19] The same can be said of early-1960s Motown, soul, and the Beatles before they went psychedelic. The real transformation came a few years later, when British and American rock musicians began to bludgeon the Chicago blues.

Like all practitioners of Afro-American music, the Chicago bluesmen spanned the spectrum from sweet to salty, smooth to rough, pure to gritty, soft to loud, slow to fast. Yet they also emphasized the latter qualities—saltiness, roughness, grittiness, loudness, and speed—to the point where they lost ground among black listeners.[20] In the mid-1960s the leading Chicago bluesman, Muddy Waters, grew tired of this harsh style and returned to the mellower style of his native Mississippi Delta.[21] But for the young rock musicians of the time, the harsher the better. To be fair, the Rolling Stones did not bludgeon the blues. They sped the music up and made it more hard-edged. But compared with later developments, they treated it with respect.

Perhaps the most precipitous decline was vocal. To this day, Janis Joplin is described as a great blues singer in the mold of her self-proclaimed model, Bessie Smith, but the two were miles apart. Smith, whose vocal range barely exceeded one octave, was a stunning practitioner of blues "mixtery," shading every note and beat with rich nuance.[22] Joplin had a strong three-octave voice, but rather than develop its potential, she cauterized it with a style that consisted almost entirely of screaming. Reviewing a London show featuring B. B. King and Joplin, Pleasants compared the former's "consummate musicianship" with the latter's reliance upon "a sound that little boys of four or five produce when trying to determine just what degree of aural torture will finally drive Mommy or Daddy into giving them a smack in the teeth."[23]

Why is Joplin lionized? Because she screamed *on principle*. According to one biographer, she was a protean spirit who needed to "experience not just the blues but the original impulse that created it: the violence, eroticism, craziness and sputtering of rage before the blues had been codified and ironized."[24] In other words, forget stoicism and the hard-won craft of the blues; what matters is unfiltered passion.

Instrumental blues fared little better. Blues bands typically include several instruments: two or three guitars, acoustic bass, drums, harmonica, piano, all involved in a shifting interplay. Sixties rock, by contrast, was stripped down to lead guitar, bass guitar, and drums. To be sure, this was the lineup on the Beatles' early records. But the Beatles did not sacrifice musical interplay to extravagant virtuosity. Others did. The first "guitar heroes"—Clapton, Page, Hendrix— were deeply rooted in the blues. But while their many descendants—people like Ritchie Blackmore, Eddie Van Halen, Randy Rhoads, Yngwie Malmsteen, and Beck—are virtuosos, many with classical training and a sophisticated grasp of harmony, not to mention state-of-the-art engineering skills, the music they play is extremely limited both in expressive power and in tonal and rhythmic content. Having lost the subtlety of the blues, it is aptly named *hard* rock and *heavy* metal. Flashy, accelerated, knife-edged, it runs the gamut of emotion from A for *angst* to B for *blitzkrieg*.

So that's rock primitivism, largely the creation of whites. What about blacks during the same period? In the early 1970s, the disco craze produced some good music. But as demand rose, quality fell. The drum machine, or computerized rhythm track, was easier to record than a live rhythm section. But what about the quality? For reply, let me quote the great James Brown's classic comment about disco, with its micro-timed beat patterns spat out by computer: "I taught them everything *they* know, but not everything *I* know."[25]

The disco era was also when soul music lost its soul. When the great gospel-trained soul singers sang about love, they expressed both its erotic and spiritual side. A prime example would be Al Green, who eventually became so disillusioned with the state of secular black music that he returned to the church. In 1969 Isaac Hayes, a studio musician at the Stax label, released an album called *Hot Buttered Soul,* one of the first black attempts at a so-called concept album. Prolonged tracks of fifteen minutes or more did not sound bad when Hayes did them. They still sounded acceptable two years later when Marvin Gaye made his classic album *What's Going On.* But it wasn't long before self-indulgence took over. The intertwining of body and soul that had come from gospel was forgotten when "love men" like Barry White reduced hot butter to warm oleo. Meanwhile, on the distaff side, there arose the "disco queen," who didn't sing so much as pant, sigh, yelp, and moan on cue. Thus did the inheritors of the great soul tradition come to extract the eroticism from their art with all the efficiency and beauty of a strip-mining operation.

White primitivism on one side, black on the other. Popular music was in a sorry state in the late 1970s. Something had to give. And when it did, the energy behind it came from a place totally outside the Afro-American musical tradition.

The Second Transformation: Perverse Modernism

Perverse modernism did not begin in America. It emerged in Europe over a century ago, as one of modernism's earliest impulses. It has two sides, the second more troubling than the first. The first is a debunking of art itself, or rather of certain lofty claims made for art since the romantic period—most notably, that it embodies transcendent truth in a way that makes it a worthy successor to philosophy and religion. Stated baldly, this claim may sound extreme, but no one familiar with aesthetic philosophy since Kant can deny its persistence. Within modernism this exaltation of art led to a withdrawal from the world and into a navel-gazing obsession with art's own materials and processes. This more introverted strain of modernism includes non-representational painting after Malevich, nonreferential poetry after Breton, and serialist and aleatory music. Introverted modernism produced some brilliant works, but it also turned art into an insider's game, excluding everyone except the most knowledgeable. And it invited debunking—which was provided, soon enough, by the first generation of perverse modernists.

These perverse modernists quit making objects and began pointing to things in the world, proclaiming, "This is art because I say so." In this spirit, Marcel Duchamp placed a urinal in a New York art gallery, and (long before Cage) the Italian futurist Luigi

Russolo argued in *The Art of Noise* that music was a thing of the past. The perverse modernists also turned art into a publicity stunt, a quest not for fame in the traditional sense but for instant notoriety. Needless to say, this game is still being played.

The second, more troubling side of perverse modernism might also be called *the culture of transgression.* As we trace it back to such early modernist movements as German expressionism and Italian futurism, we see a direct link to the anarchist belief that the right outrageous gesture, made at the right moment and magnified by the media (a century ago this meant newspapers) would cause the repressive social order to implode. The literary scholar Roger Shattuck has traced this connection to late nineteenth-century Paris, where anarchists assassinated prominent citizens and exploded bombs in public places. One such figure, a young man "of illegitimate birth and hysterical disposition" named Vaillant, threw a nail bomb into the Chamber of Deputies. No one was killed, but Shattuck recalls the tribute paid to Vaillant by the literary critic Laurent Tailhade: "What do a few human lives matter, *si le geste est beau* [if the gesture is beautiful]?"[26]

This cult of aestheticized violence was dampened by two World Wars. But in the 1960s it sputtered back to life, as a new generation of artists vowed (in Marinetti's phrase) "to spit on the Altar of Art."[27] Proclaiming their hatred of commercialized culture, various 1960s art movements revived the futurist (fascist) dream of the bold, in-your-face stroke that will destroy social complacency. The Viennese "actionist" Hermann Nitsche, for example, poured the blood of freshly slaughtered animals over the nude trussed bodies of fellow performance artists. Other actionists, such as Rudolf Schwartzkogler in Austria and Gina Pane in France, took the logical next step of public self-mutilation.[28]

If this sounds esoteric, it is. But it wasn't long before these impulses were crossing over to popular music. Helped along by Andy Warhol, Yoko Ono, Malcolm McLaren, and countless other visual artists who admired the subversive popularity of rock, perverse modernism became the guiding aesthetic of punk, the hugely influential late-1970s phenomenon. Indeed, to understand the generation gap between baby boomers and their offspring, start with punk. Keep in mind that music is only a small part of punk; the rest is attitude. And the attitude comes from perverse modernism.

The salient fact about punk is that it emerged less from popular music than from the fringes of the art world. The first signs appeared in the late 1960s, when groups like Alice Cooper, Iggy Pop and the Stooges, the New York Dolls, and Frank Zappa's Mothers of Invention began giving rock concerts that were more like happenings. Indeed, the most influential band of the period, the Velvet Underground, made its name playing with Andy Warhol's happening, the *Exploding Plastic Inevitable.*

I will return to the Velvet Underground later, because their influence extends beyond punk, but for now, let me stick with the American forerunners of punk. In the early 1970s, a tiny club in downtown Manhattan called CBGB hosted an odd assortment of acts intent on turning rock into a species of performance art. Some of these acts, like the Talking Heads, were musically talented. Others, like the Ramones, were basically comedy acts. The Ramones specialized in rapid-fire songs less than two minutes long that both spoofed and exploited the memory of 1950s rock and roll.

Then, in the late 1970s, punk exploded across Britain. Some saw British punk as a working-class revolt against hard times and the conservatism of Prime Minister Margaret Thatcher. But as the British cultural theorist Simon Frith has written, punk was "the ultimate art school music movement."[29] One of punk's masterminds was Malcolm McLaren, a fashion designer who knew nothing about music but had attended six British art colleges. Inspired by the New York scene, McLaren put together a band called the Sex Pistols: four young kids who didn't know how to play an instrument or sing. They did, however, know how to scream, spit, curse— and attract media attention.

As with CBGB, some people associated with British punk went on to become accomplished and successful musicians. But even these retained for a long time what Elvis Costello called "this anti-attitude." Much as they wanted to play music straight, to express emotion, they could not shake off an air of irony, distance, and campy superiority that, when applied to the popular musicians they were emulating, was quite unjustified.[30] Only in recent years, as they relax into the role of elder statesmen, has this generation of British musicians learned the elusive art of musical sincerity.

As for the musical legacy of punk itself, the topic brings to mind what Samuel Johnson once said to a young writer, "Your work is both good and original. Unfortunately, the part that is good is not original, and the part that is original is not good." During the 1980s, the so-called new wave aped a variety of older, more listenable styles, from Jamaican reggae to Motown. This sold a lot of records for musicians like Blondie, Boy George, and the Eurythmics. But when the new wave was musical it was not punk, and when it was punk it was not musical. This is still true twenty years later. The legacy of punk remains, at bottom, antimusical.

The original champions of punk claim that it revived the rollicking energy of 1950s rock and roll. This is a notion that can only be believed by people with tin ears. The punk slogan was, "Do It Yourself"; the unspoken part was, "Don't Do It Well." For punk purists, only a few musical values are acceptable even today.

First is speed. The rhythmic basis of punk is the thrash beat pioneered by the Ramones. Punk fans credit the Ramones with playing 1950s rock and roll at 78 rpm instead of 45, and they call that more stimulating. Maybe it is to them, but not to anyone with a sense of rhythm. Like the rock beat, the thrash beat doesn't swing. The rhythmic counterpoint of authentic 1950s rock and roll gets lost, and what's left sounds like Pat Boone at 78 rpm.

Second, punk worships volume. From heavy metal it takes sweltering sheets of electronic sound. Not virtuoso guitar, mind you—that would violate the "do-it-yourself" ethic. Instead, punk revels in what former Sex Pistol John Lydon (known then as Johnny Rotten) calls "structured noise." The old perverse-modernist trick proposition that there is no difference between noise and music is worth thinking about, once or twice in your life. In the long run, however, most people conclude that yes, there is a difference between noise and music.

The third essential punk quality is a vocal style that lurches between whispery crooning and banshee shrieking. This is a cliche of the late nineteenth-century German expressionist theater, passed down through various forms of avant-garde performance and introduced into rock by none other than Yoko Ono, who studied with Cage before she married John Lennon. Yoko's singing, like her conceptual art, was (to put it mildly) derivative. Yet every postpunk singer who lurches from whispering to shrieking gets credit for being wildly original.

The Marginalization of Listening: Minimalism and Hip-Hop

Like the child brought before Solomon, the best Afro-American music is a living whole in which every dance, even the liveliest, has melody; and every song, even the tenderest, has rhythm. Popular music still possessed this wholeness back in the mid-1960s—indeed, that was when *Billboard* eliminated its color-coded charts because whites and blacks were buying the same records. But at the end of the decade, two developments conspired to dismember the living body of the music. One was the abandonment of both rhythm and melody as previously understood. The other was a musical reaction to the racial polarization of the time: a most un-Solomon-like deci-

sion to make rhythm the sole and exclusive property of black musicians, to assign melody to whites, and to abandon harmony to the cultural equivalent of foster care.

To begin with the first development, few would deny that in the last thirty years there has been a massive cultural shift away from the ear and toward the eye. Literary people complain about the conquest of print by images. A more profound complaint could be made by musicians, whose art has been almost completely absorbed by the visual media. It is beyond the scope of this essay to pin down all the forces at work in this shift, but there can be no doubt about its impact. At all levels, from the Broadway stage to the latest youth craze, listening is now distinctly subordinate to looking. In the visual feast of a culture dominated by photography, film, video, computer graphics, and high-tech stage-craft, music is rarely more than aural sauce.

Ironically, the musicians who contributed most to this change thought they were doing the opposite. In 1965, Philip Glass was inspired by Indian raga to try a new compositional approach in which the Western tendency to "take time and divide it" would be replaced with the Eastern tendency to "take very small units and add them together." He took brief, simple melodic-harmonic motives and repeated them over and over, along with "cycles of different beats, wheels within wheels, everything going at the same time and always changing."[31] Similar ideas occurred to the avant-garde jazz artist La Monte Young and composer-engineers such as Terry Riley, Steve Reich, and Mike Oldfield. Dubbed *minimalism,* the music that

emerged from these efforts was emphatically conceived not as mere background. For
Reich, the goal was to "facilitate closely
detailed listening."[32]

In the popular realm, minimalism was
an instant hit. Rock fans bought Riley's *A
Rainbow in the Curved Air* (1968) and
Oldfield's *Tubular Bells* (1973). Today
minimalism is blamed for New Age, the
easy listening mood music disparaged by
critics as "aural wallpaper" or "sonic laxa-
tive."[33] Add a shot of computerized rhythm,
and you have contemporary dance and
techno. But here, too, minimalism keeps
company with the visual. Beginning with
the passages from *Tubular Bells* used in *The
Exorcist* (1973) and continuing through
Glass's stunning scores for *Koyaanisqatsi*
(1983) and *Hamburger Hill* (1987), minimalism's slowly shifting repetitiveness—its
"wallpaper" quality, if you will—has largely
conquered the silver screen. Indeed, minimalist soundtracks often work better than
the traditional orchestral kind. What this
means, however, is that the high ambition
of minimalism's creators—that pulsing
trance-like sound would foster a new quasi-
spiritual listening—is not fulfilled. Outside
the concert hall, in the casual, secular,
technologically driven settings where most
people now listen to music, minimalist-
derived forms succeed precisely because
they do *not* demand the concentrated attention once routinely paid to shaped melodic
structures from the symphony to the
sonata, the popular song to the jazz solo.

A similar pattern can be seen in rock.
Ask any young fan of today's "alternative
rock" which 1960s band he or she admires
the most, and the answer will likely be the
Velvet Underground, the obscure New York
band that became famous in 1966 when
Andy Warhol hired them to accompany the
Exploding Plastic Inevitable. The Velvet
Underground had direct ties to minimalism. Along with songwriter Lou Reed, the
band's cofounder was John Cale, a violist
who had worked with La Monte Young.
Reed and Cale claimed to be inspired by
1950s rock and roll with its steady backbeat,
basic chord changes, and simple melodies.
Yet as Rockwell notes, "this fascination with
the basics was merely a rock extension of
the whole lower-Manhattan art world's
devotion to minimalism."[34] The Velvet
Underground did not sound like 1950s
rock and roll—or like 1960s rock, for that
matter. Rather than embellish their simple
songs with rhythmic counterpoint and
blues expression, Reed and Cale added the
ingredients of minimalism: the drone, the
unaccented 4/4 pulse, the melody shards
set against dissonant chords. Writes Charlie
Gillett, this "deliberately primitive musical
accompaniment seemed to have filtered all
the black influences out of rock 'n' roll,
leaving an amateurish, clumsy, but undeni-
ably atmospheric background."[35] This
atmospheric minimalism did not top the
charts at the time, but with the rise of MTV
and the music video over the next twenty
years, it became one of the most important
influences on rock.

Whatever else can be said about minimalism, it does not really partake either of
primitivism or of perverse modernism. But
it might not have achieved its present
salience had it not been for primitivism and
perverse modernism. Now that I have
traced both through popular music, the

reader may be wondering, Do they ever come together? Yes, I regret to say they do. They come together in gangsta rap.

I am of two minds about rap, or hip-hop, as it is more properly called. It is important to note that gangsta rap is only one strain of hip-hop. It is a highly visible and marketable strain, but in my view it is not enough simply to blame the profit motive for its prevalence. The real question is, Why is gangsta rap so marketable?

The enemies of hip-hop complain that it is musically stunted. It contains speech and rhythm, with zero harmony and only the most rudimentary melody. With the extensive use of sampling and with hip-hop artists reworking older recordings, the amount of melody has increased. There is a limit to this, however. If hip-hop becomes too melodic, it will no longer be hip-hop, because hip-hop is based on speech (indeed, it is no accident that many hip-hop stars aspire to become film actors).

To say that hip-hop is based on speech is not a criticism; it is merely a description. Hip-hop did not grow out of the musical tradition of black North Americans, it grew out of the spoken tradition of black West Indians. The first rappers were young people in New York whose parents had immigrated from Jamaica, Barbados, and elsewhere in the Caribbean. This is important because in the Caribbean, popular music was not played on the radio; radio was government-controlled and (like the pre-1960s BBC) emphasized the European classics. Nor was it played in private homes, because most people were too poor to own record players. Instead, popular music was played by travelling DJs whose large record

collections, powerful "sound systems," and colorful personalities made them regional celebrities. These DJs did not just spin platters; they also delivered a steady patter known as *toasting*. To most North Americans, *toasting* suggests a brief tribute over champagne—not the same thing. Caribbean toasting is improvised oral poetry, part of a tradition that dates back through three centuries of calypso in Trinidad to the *griots* of West Africa, who (like the bards of ancient Ireland or Yugoslavia) could recite clan histories, offer praise songs, and insult prominent people with such skill that the better ones made an excellent living just keeping their mouths shut.

As part of this oral tradition, early hip-hop stressed quick-witted improvisation. Today, of course, hip-hop is high-tech. Records and videos are assembled digitally in the studio, and live performances tend to feel canned. Still, as a blend of words with state-of-the-art sound and visual collage, the artistic potential of hip-hop is great. But without the addition of melody and harmony, its strictly musical potential will remain limited.

As for melody, it has been relegated to such "whites-only" precincts as country music, easy listening, and the new generation of singer/songwriters. I hate to be a killjoy, but none of these "melodic" genres offer anything like the melodic richness of the great standards of the past. This is, of course, a tricky judgment. Because of its deceptive simplicity, melody is one of the hardest elements in music to explain or evaluate. Aaron Copland writes, "Why a good melody should have the power to move us has thus far defied all analysis. We cannot even say, with any degree of surety, what constitutes a good melody."[36]

As Copland well knew, good melody need not be elaborate. One of the premier melodists of modern jazz, Miles Davis, had from the beginning a "penchant for minimalism," a preference for sketched understatement over embellished overstatement.[37] Like a drawing by Matisse, in which a single line suggests a full three-dimensional volume, a melodic sketch by Davis in his prime had the power to evoke larger forms. Davis's finest music involves melodic repetition, but not in the minimalist sense. As Wynton Marsalis has noted, Davis knew how to repeat a "sweet" melodic motive only as long as it took to squeeze the sweetness out, then he would drop it and hunt for another.[38] He was proud of this ability, as shown by his storied retort to John Coltrane, who complained about not knowing how to end a solo. Davis is said to have suggested, "Try taking the horn out of your mouth." Davis's squeezing of the motive was always closely related to his awareness of harmonic structure, even within the loose boundaries of modal improvisation. In his autobiography, Davis alludes to this awareness with typical bluntness: "We ain't in Africa, and we don't play just chants. There's some theory under what we do."[39]

Beginning in the 1970s and continuing into the 1980s, Davis's melodies quit suggesting larger forms and became "just chants." At the end of his career, he became a minimalist in the sense of recycling a single fragment throughout an entire performance.[40] That he found success in doing so is merely a reflection of the dismembered state of music in our time. It was no individual musician's fault that the ability to write, play, *or listen to* melodies longer than two bars seemed as forgotten as the art of the fugue. The change had come, and all someone like Davis could do was recognize it. "A lot of people ask me where music is going today," he says at the conclusion of his autobiography. "I think it's going in short phrases. If you listen, anybody with an ear can hear that."[41]

As mentioned above, various schools of hip-hop now venture more freely into musical territory. This includes gangsta rap—indeed, the celebrated producer Dr. Dre first added dribbles of melody to the choruses of his protégé Snoop Doggy Dogg. But in gangsta rap, at least, this sweetening only goes so far. The lyrics and video images are still freighted with abusive sex, casual violence, and grotesque racial stereotypes. The defenders of gangsta rap point out that some of this crude material comes from Afro-American folklore, and they're right. Like all folklore, Afro-American folklore contains a strain of gutter humor. But the question is, Why is gutter humor now considered the acme of black expression? My answer is that here, too, we are dealing with the legacy of punk. Remember, gangsta rap is "crossover" music, black music deliberately marketed to whites. And many of today's white listeners, raised on metal and punk, have a taste for in-your-face lyrics and assaultive sound, not to mention grotesque racial stereotypes providing an extra thrill.

In the context of hip-hop, the marginalization of melody is defended as a liberation from the hegemony of "white" music.

But if liberation means converting from a music based on shapely melody and sophisticated harmony to one based on mere squiggles (or, as record producers call them, "melody hooks"), then not just hip-hop but the great bulk of popular music has now been liberated, and listeners of all colors are the poorer for it.

A Brief Counterintuitive Modest Proposal for the Music Educator

Are we at the end of an epoch? Has popular music moved irrevocably away from its Afro-American base? Fortunately, it is not up to music educators to resolve the question. Not if they conceive of their job as being, at least in part, the handing down of a valuable legacy. One advantage of teaching the greatest American popular music is that it has never been "elitist" in any social or political sense, only in an *aesthetic* sense. Since the early days, the best Afro-American music has been not only an equal opportunity employer, but also a meritocracy. As Louis Armstrong remarked, back in the days when jazz venues were segregated,

> These people who make the restrictions, they don't know nothing about music. It's no crime for cats of any color to get together and blow. Race-conscious jazz musicians? Nobody could be who really knew their horns and loved the music.[42]

In broad outline, my proposal to the music educator is to engage in subterfuge to make the rich legacy of American popular music compare favorably with what is out there today. I offer it with tongue planted only halfway in cheek.

The proposal depends on reverse psychology. The first step is to enforce rigorous classroom study of the three changes described above: (1) the primitivist reduction of Afro-American music to hard rock and computerized "dance music," (2) the history and subsequent popularization of perverse modernism, and (3) the emergence of minimalism and hip-hop as music cultures oriented more toward the eye than the ear. Since most students are familiar with the these changes, the assiduous teacher should feel free to pile on the reading, particularly dry and jargon-ridden treatments of popular music drawn from the more esoteric precincts of academic cultural studies. Whether the experts you assign be doddering deconstructionists, greying Marxist/ethnic/feminist cultural theorists, or bright young pioneers in postmodern sexuality, make sure their work focuses not on musical sound but on what various forms of popular music reveal about power, social marginality, and resistance to oppression. Exclude all use of hegemonic words like *beautiful* and *good*.

I am serious. Young people have no idea where their cherished pop mythology comes from, and when it is pointed out to them how long its history is and how much reading is required to grasp that history fully, they react by loosening their proprietary grip. Some become keenly interested; others are turned off. But almost all quit identifying personally with attitudes and postures that they now see as part of history and not the exclusive property of their generation.

In the same vein, it is useful to question the generational myth. By what law of nature must parents and children loathe each other's music? For one thing, today's students don't hate the music of their parents; often they know the Beatles more intimately than their parents do! But in terms of their own "cutting-edge" music, young people still adhere to the myth that music must foment a war between the generations. Yet this myth, like so many others, originated with their parents, who, caught up in the heady atmosphere of the 1960s counterculture, tried to turn the normal tension between child and parent into a social revolution. That was a long time ago, I point out to my students. Isn't the idea (pardon the expression) getting old?

Finally, I would advise the canny teacher to position good music on the curricular menu in roughly the same place as dessert. In my literature classes, I treat poetry not as the focus of classroom discussion but as a break from it. At the end of the each seminar meeting, or of the week, I have my students read aloud poems that they have chosen and prepared. I confine their choices to an anthology, as a form of quality control, but otherwise I give them their heads. We talk briefly about how effectively each poem was read, and sometimes we read it again, or even a third time. But that's all. We do *not* analyze the poems. I find that in most cases this approach prompts a lively curiosity about poetry that was not at all evident before.

Of course, to do this the educator must overcome the assumption that the only connection between "pop music" and the classical repertory is the analytic pedagogy with which they are approached. This may be true when the "pop music" involved is inferior in quality to the traditional repertoire. But I am not suggesting this method as a way of introducing inferior music into the classroom. Again, it is vital to limit the universe of choice. It does no good to let students bring in the latest poetry-slam fare, so likewise there is no point in letting them play the same music they listen to all day. After a steady diet of primitivism, perverse modernism, and sound subordinated to visual stimuli, give them the opportunity to spoon a little real music into their ears. Again, the less didactically this is done, the better. Define the choices, include everything from Mozart to Monk, but treat the listening sessions as a break, as *fun*. And while it is likely that many students really do not know how to listen to good music, much less take pleasure in doing so, allow them the novelty of trying. No scores or lyric sheets should be open (my classes keep their books closed while listening to poems). Make them rely on their ears. Do not ask them to articulate what they hear, at least not for a while—save the verbiage for the dry, academic reading about the music they know best. Then let them encounter the real stuff wordlessly. Just sit back and play something wonderful, then turn off the stereo and send them on their way. Soon enough, they will want to hear more and learn more. And at that moment, their musical education will have begun in earnest. Why not give it a try? And if you do, please let me know how the experiment comes out!

Notes

1. Henry Pleasants, *Serious Music—and All That Jazz!* (New York: Simon and Schuster, 1969), 43.
2. Ibid., 25.

3. Andre Hodeir, *Jazz: Its Evolution and Essence* (New York: Grove Press, 1961), 139.

4. Ibid., 141.

5. Ibid., 142.

6. Pleasants, *Serious Music,* 45.

7. Modernism came later to music than to the other European arts. Literature and painting, for example, became modernist during the late nineteenth century. Music held out until World War I (perhaps because it was more deeply imbued with romanticism). Because modernism came of age with jazz, modernists from Milhaud to Copland understandably tried to include "jazz effects" in their work. The ungainliness of these efforts, typically executed (in both senses) by nonjazz musicians, convinced a generation of critics that jazz could not rise to the level of "serious" music—while ironically, the more vital borrowing was on the jazz side.

8. Pleasants, *Serious Music,* 65.

9. Gunther Schuller, *Early Jazz: Its Roots and Musical Development* (New York: Oxford University Press, 1968), 8, 11 (quotation from p. 11).

10. Ibid., 8.

11. Ibid.

12. Leonard B. Meyer, *Emotion and Meaning in Music* (Chicago: University of Chicago Press, 1990) 242.

13. Hodeir, *Jazz: Its Evolution and Essence,* 197.

14. Quoted in Neil Leonard, *Jazz: Myth and Religion* (New York: Oxford University Press, 1987), 12.

15. Quoted in Phyllis Rose, *Jazz Cleopatra: Josephine Baker in Her Time* (New York: Double-day, 1989), 31.

16. Quoted in *Chasing a Rainbow: The Life of Josephine Baker,* dir. Christopher Rolling, Csáky Ltd., 1986, documentary film.

17. Allan Bloom, *The Closing of the American Mind* (New York: Simon & Schuster, 1987), 73.

18. Quoted in *The Decline of Western Civilization, Part 2: The Metal Years,* dir. Penelope Spheeris, New Line Cinema, 1988, documentary film.

19. Quoted in Arnold Passman, *The DeeJays* (New York: Macmillan, 1971), 203.

20. Charlie Gillett, *The Sound of the City: The Rise of Rock 'n' Roll* (New York: Pantheon, 1983), 172.

21. Peter Guralnick, *Feel Like Going Home: Portraits in Blues and Rock 'n' Roll* (New York: Perennial Library, 1989), 85.

22. Henry Pleasants, *The Great American Popular Singers* (New York: Simon and Schuster, 1974), 74–75.

23. Ibid., 308.

24. David Dalton, *Piece of My Heart: The Life, Times, and Legend of Janis Joplin* (New York: St. Martin's, 1985), 38.

25. James Brown and Bruce Tucker, *James Brown: The Godfather of Soul* (New York: Macmillan, 1986), 242–43.

26. Quoted in Roger Shattuck, *The Banquet Years: The Origins of the Avant-Garde in France, 1885 to World War I* (New York: Vintage Books, 1968), 21.

27. Quoted in Caroline Tisdall and Angelo Bozzola, *Futurism* (New York: Oxford University Press, 1977), 89.

28. Rose Lee Goldberg, *Performance Art: From Futurism to the Present* (New York: Harry N. Abrams, 1988), 164–65.

29. Simon Frith and Howard Horne, *Art into Pop* (New York: Methuen, 1987), 124.

30. Quoted in Bill Flanagan, *Written in My Soul: Conversations with Rock's Greatest Songwriters* (Chicago: Contemporary, 1987), 231.

31. Quoted in Donald Clarke, ed., *The Penguin Encyclopedia of Popular Music* (New York: Viking, 1989), 467.

32. Quoted in Andy Mackay, *Electronic Music: The Instruments, The Music and The Musicians* (Minneapolis: Control Data, 1981), 107.

33. Clarke, *Penguin Encyclopedia,* 850–51.

34. John Rockwell, *All-American Music: Composition in the Late 20th Century* (New York: Alfred A. Knopf, 1983), 235.

35. Charlie Gillett, *The Sound of the City: The Rise of Rock 'n' Roll* (New York: Pantheon, 1983), 309.

36. Aaron Copland, *What to Listen for in Music* (New York: McGraw-Hill, 1957), 49–51.

37. Amiri Baraka, quoted in Gary Tomlinson, "Miles Davis, Musical Dialogician," in *A Miles Davis Reader,* ed. Bill Kirchner (Washington, DC: Smithsonian, 1997), 72.

38. Wynton Marsalis, "Miles Davis" (segment

20), in *Making the Music,* prod. Murray Horowitz and Wynton Marsalis, National Public Radio, 10 August 1998.

39. Miles Davis and Quincy Troupe, *Miles: The Autobiography* (New York: Simon and Schuster, 1989), 400.

40. Max Harrison, "Collector's Items," in *A Miles Davis Reader,* 226.

41. Davis and Troupe, *Miles,* 393.

42. Quoted in Gene Lees, *Cats of Any Color: Jazz Black and White* (New York: Da Capo Press, 1995), 2.

Martha Bayles is the author of *Hole in Our Soul: The Loss of Beauty and Meaning in American Popular Music* (University of Chicago Press, 1996). She writes about music, the arts, and cultural policy for the *New York Times,* the *Chronicle of Higher Education,* the *Wilson Quarterly,* and many other publications, and she lectures frequently at universities, arts festivals, policy conferences, and professional associations. She currently teaches humanities in the Honors Program at Boston College.

Historical Perspectives

5

Popular Music in the American Schools: What History Tells Us about the Present and Future

Jere T. Humphreys

This chapter consists of a brief overview of the development of popular music in the United States and trends in music education history that relate to the teaching of popular music. It ends with some conclusions about the past and present and some speculations about the future of popular music in American schools.

Webster's Unabridged Dictionary of the English Language gives eight definitions for adjectival uses of the word "popular." Seven of the eight definitions refer to common, ordinary people: "people in general," "of, pertaining to, or representing the people, esp. the common people," "of the people as a whole," "prevailing among the people generally," "adapted to the ordinary intelligence or taste," and "suited to the means of ordinary people." One of the seven definitions uses popular music as its example: "suited to or intended for the general masses of people: *popular music.*"[1] Interestingly, this definition does not take into account how a particular music is actually used, but instead deals with its suitability, or intended suitability, for the masses.

Popular music is defined in this chapter as music intended for wide audience appeal. It is distinguished from classical music, whose aim may be seen as transcendence, and from traditional or folk music, "a sphere ruled by a belief in continuity."[2] Not all writers on the subject agree with this categorization. I find it problematic because it relies on the apparent or assumed intentions of composers, performers, and producers, even though social conditions frequently cause some musics to shift between categories.[3]

In a 1955 survey, Gilbert Chase became the first notable historian of American music to treat popular music seriously.[4] Writing in 1961, Allen Britton explained the roots of popular as opposed to classical music among the first permanent settlers in what became the United States:

> Although they [the Puritans] were drawn from the rising mercantile classes [in England], their Calvinistic religious convictions made them critics rather than imitators of the conventions of social classes higher in status, and they never emerged as patrons, in the European sense, of music or of any other

art. Such music as they had they made themselves, fitting it into the normal religious and recreational aspects of their lives. The function of music in the society they created has ever since required that the music be understandable to the majority, a situation that has fostered the development of popular forms but that has provided little encouragement for the growth of a high art.[5]

The historical overview presented in this chapter shows that popular music has been taught continuously in American schools from the beginning, arguably more so than in other countries. However, the American music education establishment did not formally acknowledge popular music as worthy of being taught until the "Tanglewood Declaration" of 1968.[6] Before and even after that, popular music was taught for a host of "utilitarian" reasons, among them: (1) its usefulness in church; (2) its perceived role as a "hook" to bring students into music programs where they could study "serious" or "legitimate" music, or simply as a bridge toward "something better" (typically Western European and North American art music); and (3) its power to enhance school-community (public) relations. Not long after Tanglewood, leading arts education advocate Charles B. Fowler presented three reasons some music educators considered the twentieth century's leading type of popular music, rock and roll, unsuitable for the American school curriculum: "(1) Rock is aesthetically inferior, if it is music at all. (2) Rock music is damaging to youth, both physically and morally. (3) School time should not be expended teaching what is easily acquired in the vernacular."[7]

This essay deals with the fact that school syllabi in several countries mandate popular music, among them Australia, England, Scotland, and the Nordic countries of Denmark, Finland, and Sweden.[8] Given the Tanglewood mandate and the importance of popular music in the school curricula of some countries, why does it continue to play such a minor role the United States, at least in formal curricula? The question becomes more significant when we consider that much popular music in the school curricula of other nations originated in this country.

American Popular Music

According to author Robert Pattison, the commonplace (or "vulgar") in art blatantly appeared in the seventeenth-century paintings of Rembrandt, where the Dutch master depicted ordinary people with red noses, pockmarked faces, and other "common" features. Pattison believes that the sociological roots of modern popular music can be traced to the French and Industrial Revolutions, when "the vulgar mob … wrested power from its genteel rulers" and workers eventually gained some control over their work and lives.[9]

Today, many writers include the phenomenon of commercialism in their working definitions of popular music, with recording technology and mass marketing usually figuring heavily in the mix. However, commercialism in music did not begin with recording technology. Musicologist Richard Crawford credits a tune book published in 1761 as the first "to bring psalmody straight into the commercial arena."[10] Consisting of a wide variety of psalm tunes, anthems, and hymns, this book was intended for use in the church, choir, and home. William Billings, a leading composer, tune-book compiler, and singing-school master of the Revolutionary War era, also sought to appeal to a wide audience. After the Revolution, psalms and hymns by several composers became popular with the public. These works, like those of Billings and even earlier composers, bore sacred texts but functioned "more like popular music."[11]

Later, Lowell Mason employed sacred and secular music in his tune books and other instructional manuals, and the Boston Academy of Music, founded in 1832 by Mason and George J. Webb, featured instruction in and performances of both types of music. Moreover, Crawford believes that Mason may "have been the first American musician who realized capital-profit in excess of expenditures and wages—for musical work." Isaac Baker Woodbury, George Fredrick Root, and others continued the practice of combining sacred and secular works, and the latter began to write overtly popular songs during the 1850s.[12]

Throughout much of the nineteenth century, classical music, especially opera, was extremely popular in the United States. However, before the turn of the twentieth century, a rigid hierarchy of musical and other cultural forms had begun to take shape. This hierarchy manifested itself in many ways, including the founding of elite symphony orchestras in Boston, Philadelphia, Chicago, and New York. Lawrence Levine notes that "inevitably, ... the ideology of culture assumed ethnic and racial dimensions."[13]

This division of culture into a hierarchy

of ostensibly aesthetically determined spheres included the advent of Tin Pan Alley in the 1890s, a commercial venture centered in New York that sold popular songs in the form of sheet music. Ragtime, a precursor of jazz, also began in the 1890s and quickly became a "popular mania."[14]

By the 1920s, widespread use of the phonograph, followed closely by radio, was creating an unprecedented market for popular music. The technology-driven distribution of popular music coincided with what British sociologist and rock music critic Simon Frith sees as the roots of an American mass youth market, and for more than just music: "it is from the 1920s that we can date a consumer culture [in the United States] in which continuous purchase is encouraged with the suggestion that you are buying something that makes and keeps you young."[15] Thus, the music industry as we know it today began in the 1920s, due in large part to the presence of new recording technologies and a mass youth culture and market.

This period also saw the advent of the blues, country music, many types of popular songs, and jazz in various forms, swing band music among them. Along the way, country music, a white folk tradition, became a popular commercial force. Paralleling the development of country music was the emergence of rhythm and blues, a form of black popular commercial music with roots in the blues (not jazz, as is commonly thought).

These two forms of music, country and rhythm and blues, merged to form rock and roll. A few bands, some black and some white, produced what they later claimed were rock music recordings in the 1940s, and a deejay in Cleveland named Alan Freed began to play recordings of black tunes for his white teenage audience in 1952. However, when Elvis Presley, a nineteen-year-old white singer born in Tupelo, Mississippi, made his first professional record in Memphis on July 6, 1954, the two genres fused to create the rock and roll sensation. This first recording took place just six weeks after the U.S. Supreme Court handed down its *Brown v. Board of Education* decision that outlawed racial segregation in schools. Presley's initial recordings and the music that followed changed people's attitudes toward the mixing of the races and their musics. They may have been "a more accurate reflection of the current sweeping across America" than the High Court's ruling.[16]

The fusion of black rhythm and blues and white country music into rock and roll was facilitated by the historic romantic myth of black people as "Noble Savages," and by white people's perceptions of themselves as "overeducated and undersexed, unnatural and inauthentic. … In a word, … boring."[17] Rock and roll began in the American South, a region with strong, but romantic, democratic ideals and certain attitudes that emerged from its slaveholding past. The American South, along with its eventual British counterpart in the rock and roll revolution, the North of England, was a "cultural backwater" outside the mainstream of high culture.[18]

Rock became the most popular musical genre of the second half of the twentieth century, not only in the United States and Great Britain, but in much of the rest of the world as well. It was propelled beyond its working-class youth roots and into other strata of society (especially in the United States) by the Beatles, who made their debut in 1960, and was popularized even more widely by another famous British rock group, the Rolling Stones, who debuted in 1962.[19] However, despite its appeal to people of different social classes and ages, rock retained its ideological image as a representation of a single, albeit lower, social class.[20]

Rock was a product not only of the mixing of the races, but also of the primacy of feelings over the intellect and of commercial power made possible by increasingly sophisticated recording technology and mass production and distribution systems. Much like jazz, rock traveled north from the Mississippi Delta to the Midwest. It was also a music through which relatively economically and socially disenfranchised adolescents could express themselves, and with which they could identify. Some began to see rock as the music of, by, and for the American capitalist system.[21] Its wide range of messages and broad appeal led Pattison to call rock "the dazzling progeny of American's democratic premises."[22]

Popular Music in Schools

The most influential founders of the modern American society, the Puritans of Massachusetts Bay (Boston), founded a public high school only five years after their arrival in the New World. The purpose of their Boston Latin School (1635) was to prepare students for Harvard College, which was founded the following year primarily to train future clergymen. These early colonial leaders eschewed music as a school subject, preferring instead to leave music instruction to the church.

The elitism practiced by early colonial Puritan educational institutions paved the way for a more egalitarian form of education in the eighteenth and nineteenth centuries—private evening schools. One type evolved to meet societal needs for better singing in churches because the quality of congregational singing had deteriorated as settlers became further removed from the music instruction enjoyed by British and other European citizens. These singing schools also provided participants opportunities for social encounters.[23]

Singing masters taught hymn tunes, anthems, and other musical forms used in colonial churches, as well as some watered-down versions of European art music that Allen Britton dubbed "polite," "genteel," "parlor" music that was "bland" and "unexciting."[24] To the extent that singing schools promoted the reading of notation, the traditional, more popular improvisatory styles of singing psalms "continued … under a social stigma which made its whole-hearted enjoyment difficult." This resulted in "popular and learned styles" influencing each other less than in some European countries.[25] During the Revolutionary War period, singing masters taught some American folk and composed music by William Billings and other indigenous composers. Hitchcock wrote that "if there was ever a popular music, the singing-school music of the New Englanders was popular; it was accessible to all and enjoyed by all; it was a plainspoken music for plain people. Here lay its downfall, at least in the cities that had created it."[26]

A more democratic form of government evolved during the first few decades of the young nation's history, a shift that culminated during the Andrew Jackson presidential administration (1828–36). These egalitarian societal and political currents included calls for the implementation of universal education—to be delivered through a widespread system of "common schools."

The common school movement that began in the 1820s was accompanied by efforts to add music as a new curricular "branch." School music promoters like William Woodbridge and Lowell Mason used European school music education systems as models. Because Mason and most other early school music teachers were singing-school masters, they tended to teach music similar to that featured in the singing schools. In other words, much of the music they taught came from the repertoire of watered-down European "parlor" music and British folk music, in addition to some church music.[27]

Much like nineteenth-century general music, the large music ensembles still found in American schools today entered the schools during a period of change, only this time the changes were more social, economic, and educational than political. By the end of the ninteenth century, the United States had become an industrial power, which resulted in major population shifts from rural areas to cities and significant lifestyle changes for millions of Americans. The Industrial Revolution and certain new trends in educational and psychological thinking led to the progressive education movement in Western Europe and North America. Educational progressives built on the work of the child-study movement, whose advocates had begun to examine, "scientifically," the nature of children's lives, their interests, and the extent of their knowledge of various subjects, among other things.[28]

Progressive education leaders sought to enlarge the role of schools in society by making them more responsive to individual interests and needs, including preparing people for the increasing amounts of leisure time they were expected to gain as a result of the industrialized economy. Perhaps most importantly, progressives wanted to make schools "levers of social reform." Over the next few decades, American education changed a great deal from the days of the "three R's," one-room schools, lightly qualified teachers, short school days and years, and precious little in the way of funding or even the respect of society. The changing philosophy of schools, manifested robustly in an expanding curriculum, provided opportunities for widespread adoption of three types of musical ensembles that were already well established in American society—band, choir, and orchestra. Later, jazz ensembles made their way into the schools in much the same fashion.[29]

Much like school music ensembles, general music instruction in the twentieth century also had its roots in progressivism, with changes propelled forward by the invention and use of the player piano, and then the phonograph. During the first decade of the twentieth century, general music began to shift from its historic practice of focusing mainly on sight-singing to the more eclectic approaches used today.

Again, common musical practices already in society were adopted, in this case music listening (appreciation) and the learning of instruments.[30]

The training of music teachers began informally with the earliest group of music educators, the singing masters of colonial and postcolonial America. It is likely that most of these individuals were self-taught or received their training in other singing schools. Later, school music teachers received some training in church choirs and singing conventions, and later still in summer institutes sponsored by music textbook publishing companies, which played an important role in the training of late nineteenth-century American music teachers and supervisors. Paralleling the singing conventions and institutes were normal schools. Due to their relatively high responsiveness to societal needs (as opposed to the more elite, insular universities), most public and many private normal schools provided music instruction from the beginning.[31] It appears that the early music conventions, publishing company institutes, and normal schools provided training in various types of musics, some of them popular forms.

Music in universities got off to a very slow start due to the Boston Puritans' exclusion of music from the university curriculum. When large numbers of collegiate music departments and schools began more than three centuries later, in the second half of the nineteenth century, many of the leading ones developed through an amalgamation of three European institutions: the classical medieval university, the conservatory, and the normal school.

American universities began to train general teachers at about the time they developed music departments, assuming the responsibility previously held by normal schools in Europe and various institutions in the United States.

The conservatory model tended to dominate the new university departments and schools of music, at least in terms of numbers of faculty members. Because the performance and music theory (and eventually music history) faculties, and thus the curriculum, focused almost entirely on classical art music, students training to become music teachers became steeped in that musical tradition and no other. Thus, when the role of the conventions, institutes, and normal schools was assumed by the nation's teachers' colleges and universities in the early twentieth century, the types of music taught decreased and, in most cases, were focused more toward the perceived needs of the departments themselves than the needs of the schools for which these institutions ostensibly were training teachers.

Why Not Pop?

It is time to attempt to answer the question of why popular music, especially rock and its various offshoots and derivatives, does not occupy a more formal place in the American school curriculum. Below I set forth eight reasons why this is so, not as absolutes and certainly not as the last words on the subject, but hopefully as points to consider that will generate future thinking and discussion.

Desire to Reform Tastes. One reason popular music has not taken a more formal place in the school curriculum has to do

with American music teachers' collective desire to reform the nation's musical tastes. Devotion to this ideal can be traced to the reformist practices of some Calvinist church leaders in colonial America, and even today it continues to lie like a shroud over the school music teaching profession:

> The atmosphere of reform has permeated American music education as it has all other aspects of American culture. From the musical standpoint, because of the essentially popular nature of the singing school and the system of music education derived from it, the reforms sought have always been comparatively simple in nature—an improvement in such things as voice quality, sight-reading ability, and more importantly, but in ways more difficult to understand, in the quality of music used.[32]

Later, after the nation's university music departments and schools assumed responsibility for music teacher education, teachers in training developed similar attitudes due to the music philosophies and practices encountered in those institutions. Specifically, these institutions fostered a belief in the superiority of Western European and North American art music. Like their predecessors, the early singing masters, future music educators became indoctrinated into the belief that they must assume the mantle of carrying the message about "something better" to American society. Tens of thousands of music students became convinced that their most important task was to improve their students' musical tastes, which in turn would improve the tastes of the general public.[33]

Sadly, the abject failure of music teachers

to lead the American public to develop a deep appreciation for art music has been paralleled by an equally dismal failure to satisfy students in the realm of popular music instruction. The profession's ambivalence over goals and expectations, both popular and artistic, has led to myriad problems for music teachers, including burnout due to constant striving to achieve unachievable goals and worry that their work is not being valued by society.[34]

Cultural Bias. Another reason for popular music's relative lack of standing in the curriculum is the continuing bias against American culture that also began with the Pilgrims. This attitude includes a prejudice against American popular music in almost every form. Britton wrote:

> Throughout the 19th century and too well into the 20th, compilers of school singing books have found better music to be almost anything song-like so long as it possessed no indigenous flavor, excepting only a few patriotic airs and the most popular tunes of Stephen Foster.[35]

The content of school music series textbooks improved considerably during the twentieth century, but the same attitudes are still manifested in the music education profession's lack of full acceptance of indigenous popular music.

Association with Youth Culture. The youth culture that began to develop as an economic and social force during the 1950s evolved into a powerful political force in the 1960s. As one of the central elements of youth culture, rock music became a driving force in the proyouth, profreedom (in sex,

drugs, and other realms), antiestablishment, and antiwar cultures of the 1960s. These associations did not endear popular music to the art music, education, and other professional and cultural establishments.[36]

Bias toward Cognitive Training. There remains a bias in the Western educational world in favor of cognitive training in schools and against subjects more related to the affective and psychomotor domains. This attitude dates back at least to the writings of Plato, when schools were supposed to train future leaders only.[37]

Local Control. The United States government exercises relatively little control over the nation's schools, education being the constitutional responsibility of the individual states. The federal government has increased its authority through certain financial and judicial means, but its degree of control over education remains small compared to that exercised by most other national governments. Moreover, states delegate much authority over schools to local school boards, which tend to be populated by lay members of the communities. This system of state and local control generally results in highly conservative school systems in the United States. It appears that this country's relatively large middle class can more easily control education through local schools than the middle classes of other countries with federal ministries of education that exercise nearly complete authority over education.[38]

The purveyance of middle-class values through local school boards partially explains the entry of ensembles into schools a century ago, especially the ubiquitous American school band, which sprang from the middle-class upheavals of the French Revolution and continued in military and town band traditions. Today, bands retain their "squeaky-clean" and "motherhood and apple pie" image, and as such, unlike rock, they represent conservative, middle-class values.[39]

Lack of Demand. The conservative nature of the schools results in subjects generally not being offered until there is "an unequivocal social demand for instruction in such subjects." Music did not enter the schools for more than a century after the beginning of singing schools and the publication of the first two American tune books in 1721. Bands, choirs, and orchestras were pervasive in American society for many decades before they entered the schools. Similarly, jazz made its way into a number of schools in the 1950s, but it was not until the 1960s and beyond that formal jazz programs became commonplace in schools and colleges. Thus, "in the history of American education as a whole, subjects other than the traditional humanities have been introduced in the public (tax-supported) schools only after having been taught for extended periods in private classes."[40] Despite rock's spectacular popularity, amateur participation in rock music performance has never reached the proportional levels achieved by singing schools, town and municipal bands, church choirs, or choral societies.

Social-Class Associations. There is a tendency for Americans to de-emphasize, and sometimes even deny, social stratification in this country. It is fashionable for virtually every citizen to claim membership in the middle class. Perhaps the emergence and phenomenal success of rock and roll is one manifestation of this idealized classless society because the image of rock is also that of a single class. However, herein lies a discrepancy in values and image: schools are seen as a product and tool of the middle class, while rock consciously associates itself with the lower or working classes.[41] Just as many in "polite" society opposed jazz and jazz education due to its lower-class African-American and poor white Southern cultural roots, opposition to rock as a potential official school subject and otherwise socially acceptable art form may stem partly from the fact that it shares with jazz nearly identical social class and regional roots, as well as the black half of its racial ancestry.

Structure of School Music. Still another reason has to do with the structure and values of the schools as they relate to music instruction. Historical trends seem to suggest that rock and perhaps country music "ensembles should enter the schools …, just as vocal classes followed singing schools, and school bands, orchestras, and jazz ensembles followed their nonschool counterparts." However, these three types of music ensembles that made their way into schools do not employ instruments and voices together, "generally do not deal with controversial material," and involve large numbers of students simultaneously. Not all popular music genres have been become part of school music, including various types of popular songs and minstrel shows. Among other things, instruction in rock would have to demonstrate some social utility.[42]

Pop in the Future Curriculum

It is paradoxical that American music teachers, so steeped in a reformist tradition, have not sought to radically reform their own profession in terms of the types of musics taught but have been driven instead by a missionary-like zeal to reform society's musical tastes. In so doing, the profession has lost countless opportunities to participate in the culture of American music as it was and is, as opposed to how the profession wants it to be. "One result has been that music education, although created and nurtured by a popular love of music, has nevertheless always operated at a certain distance from the well-springs of American musical life, both popular and artistic."[43]

Given all the traditions and in the absence of a national curriculum in the United States, the best hope for significant inclusion of popular music in the formal music curriculum may lie in reforming music teacher training programs. Today, even if conditions in the schools were ripe for inclusion of popular music, the vast majority of music teachers are inadequately trained for the task.[44] However, revamping the music teacher education curriculum to train music educators to teach popular music in the schools would require programs to go against historical trends because universities usually do not offer specific training until a need for it arises in public schools.[45]

Music teacher education in popular music could be informed by models found in other countries. For example, "a new university department of musicology with a clear sociological profile" was founded at the University of Göteborg in Sweden in 1968, followed by the founding of a music teacher education program there that "included various forms of popular music

as an important part of the curriculum." Moreover, between 1979 and 1989, the musicology department at Göteborg granted twelve doctoral degrees that were "chiefly devoted to the scholarly study of popular music." It is thought that "Sweden's lack of high-cultural historical ballast in relation to other nations" and its lack of "big historical names of high culture on which to focus bourgeois national identity" mean that "the institutionalisation of high culture was therefore less substantial and less powerful than elsewhere."[46]

Sibelius Academy, a high-profile conservatory in Helsinki, Finland, requires a two-semester music education course in which students learn composition and arranging in rock styles, and students present a public performance of their own music in which they rotate as performers on the guitar, keyboard, bass, and trap set. Also in Finland, at the University of Oulu, students study acoustic and electric guitar for two years, perform for three years in small combos similar to those at the Sibelius Academy, and develop keyboard skills for three years. Popular Afro-American and Afro-Cuban music is approached through work in "sound production and reproduction technology," improvisation, and songwriting.[47]

Interestingly, Göteborg, Oulu, and the English city of Liverpool, not to mention the American South, were all far from the musical and cultural mainstreams in their respective countries. This suggests that teacher education programs that truly emphasize popular music may first emerge in areas and institutions not considered in the forefront of "high" culture, much like North Texas State College in Denton, which became the first American institution to offer a degree in jazz.[48]

On the other hand, the best hope for bringing popular music into schools may not lie with teacher education, because, to date, all watersheds in American school-based music education have occurred in conjunction with major changes in society and the educational system itself, with universities then following suit, usually belatedly. Singing schools arose largely to fulfill a perceived need for improved congregational singing in Calvinist churches, and when music entered the Boston schools on a permanent basis in 1838, it did so as part of the common-school movement then sweeping the country. When ensembles entered the schools in the early twentieth century, the schools were beginning the next major change in their history: the powerful progressive education movement. Similarly, general music as a multimodal form of teaching with multiple purposes (as opposed to single-purpose sight-singing instruction) emerged in schools in the early twentieth century, also fueled by the new goals of progressivism and new technology that made feasible the teaching of music appreciation.[49]

We are currently experiencing a period in which the American economy has already shifted from its manufacturing base to its new knowledge base. Just as the schools were slow to change from one-room structures to factory-like models when the economy became industrialized and the population urban, we are still trying to make the old Industrial Revolution–era schools function well in the new economy. I believe that schools of the future will

provide flexibility to students beyond anything we can imagine. Students will be able to choose which types of schools to attend (including much online instruction) and, for the most part, what to study. They will be able to choose between many alternatives geared not only toward different student goals, but also toward different learning styles and abilities.[50] Surely significant, meaningful participation in learning popular music will become an option in the new order of schooling.

Some problems will have to be addressed with regard to popular music education in the schools. One is whether popular music instruction should be delivered through the medium of general music (i.e., for general students), elective performance ensembles, or a combination of the two. Another has to do with rock music's associations with youth and its sometimes antiestablishment image. Still another problem is that current popular music, the rock culture in particular, is characterized by male chauvinism that manifests itself in countless pervasive ways, including the scarcity of female rock stars and frequent images of women as sex objects.[51]

Other than changing teacher education to facilitate the teaching of popular music, the biggest problem facing the profession may be the issue of authenticity, a problem made particularly acute by the transitory nature of modern popular music. It is true that "music always is of a time and of a place,"[52] but in the case of rock and other currently popular genres, the issue of currency is especially problematic:

> Top Forty radio rests on one of the central paradoxes of the record industry: radio programming policy is determined

by record popularity as measured by sales, ... so that ... the greatest number of listeners can be attracted by playing the currently best-selling records as often as possible.[53]

A Finnish academic popular music specialist, Lauri Vakeva, recently described problems associated with "keeping up with the rapidly changing contemporary Popular/Afro-American music scene, ... while at the same time trying to keep up the quality of the work," so that "you find yourself as a pop historian before you know it!"[54] Realistically, it is unlikely that popular music will ever be taught authentically in the schools because, more so than most, it is music intended to be experienced in the "here and now." On the other hand, authenticity in rock music education is a problem only of degree, as the issue continues to surface in discussions on schooling of all types.

Problems aside, popular music should be taught in schools because it is the music of our time. Rock, in particular, is about needs and wants, not the intellect. It coexists with the capitalist commercial system because it is part of the system. Despite what some may think, rock does not try to change the system, because it is the system. It is "the ubiquitous ingredient of American popular culture," and it is "first, last, and always a musical return to the primitive." For better or worse, rock is the music of the American democracy, and its appeal has spread far beyond this nation's borders, undoubtedly for that very reason.[55]

To change the current situation, the music education profession, and perhaps society and its schools as well, would have to reconsider the traditional musical canon and admit that it too is a social construction, and then acknowledge that "we have indulged in the process of inventing tradition and have become the prisoners of our own constructs."[56] To justify the inclusion of popular music in the schools, Frith recommends that we "reverse the usual academic argument: the question is not how a piece of music, a text, 'reflects' popular values, but how in performance it produces them."[57]

Notes

1. *Webster's Unabridged Dictionary of the English Language* (New York: Random House, 2001), 1505.

2. Richard Crawford, *A History: America's Musical Life* (New York and London: Norton, 2001), x.

3. That musics and other cultural "products" can and do change functions as a result of social conditions is one of the main arguments in Lawrence W. Levine's *Highbrow/Lowbrow: The Emergence of Cultural Hierarchy in America* (Cambridge and London: Harvard University Press, 1988). For a more thorough treatment of categorizations of types of music in relation to music education (in the United Kingdom) see Lucy Green, *Music on Deaf Ears: Musical Meaning, Ideology, Education* (Manchester, UK, and New York: Manchester University Press, 1988). The Levine and Green books were published in the same year.

4. Gilbert Chase, *America's Music: From the Pilgrims to the Present* (New York: McGraw-Hill, 1955). Crawford (*A History,* xi) also notes that H. Wiley Hitchcock was among the first to propose a musical categorization scheme based on attitudes toward the music rather than the music itself, in the first edition of Hitchcock's *Music in the United States: An Historical Introduction* (Englewood Cliffs, NJ: Prentice Hall, 1969). Simon Frith provided a ground-breaking treatment of rock music in his *The Sociology of Rock* (London: Constable, 1978).

5. Allen P. Britton, "Music Education: An American Specialty," in *One Hundred Years of Music in America,* ed. Paul Henry Lang (New York: Grosset & Dunlap, 1961), 212–13.

6. Robert A. Choate, ed., *Documentary Report of the Tanglewood Symposium* (Washington, DC: Music Educators National Conference, 1968), 122.

7. Charles B. Fowler, "The Case Against Rock: A Reply," *Music Educators Journal* 57, no. 1 (1970): 30; quoted in David G. Herbert and Patricia Shehan Campbell, "Rock Music in American Schools: Positions and Practices Since the 1960s," *International Journal of Music Education,* no. 36 (2000): 14.

8. Lauri Vakeva, e-mail correspondence to MayDay Group (via J. Terry Gates), 19 November 2002; Peter Dunbar-Hall, "Creative Music Making as Music Learning: Composition in Music Education from an Australian Perspective," *Journal of Historical Research in Music Education* 23, no. 2 (2002): 94–105; Peter Dunbar-Hall and Kathryn Wemyss, "The Effects of the Study of Popular Music on Music Education," *International Journal of Music Education,* no. 36 (2000): 23–34; Börje Stålhammar, "The Spaces of Music and Its Foundation of Values—Music Teaching and Young People's Own Music Experience," *International Journal of Music Education,* no. 36 (2000): 35–45; and Charles Byrne and Mark Sheridan, "The Long and Winding Road: The Story of Rock Music in Scottish Schools, *International Journal of Music Education,* no. 36 (2000): 46–57. Many of these programs have been in place since the 1970s.

9. Robert Pattison, *The Triumph of Vulgarity: Rock Music in the Mirror of Romanticism* (New York and Oxford: Oxford University Press, 1987), 13, 15 (quotation from p. 13).

10. Crawford, *A History,* 37. The tune book was *Urania, or A Choice Collection of Psalm-Tunes, Anthems, and Hymns,* compiled by James Lyon, a Presbyterian and recent Princeton graduate. Designed for broad appeal, *Urania* was much larger and more diverse in content than earlier tune books.

11. Ibid., 37–38, 45–46 (quotation from p. 46).

12. Ibid., 140, 149–55 (quotation from p. 149).

13. Levine, *HighBrow/LowBrow,* 116–38, 219 (quotation from p. 219).

14. H. Wiley Hitchcock, *Music in the United States: A Historical Introduction,* 3rd ed. (Englewood Cliffs, NJ: Prentice Hall, 1988), 201. The American sheet music business began more than a century earlier, in the 1780s: Crawford, *A History,* 90.

15. Simon Frith, *Sound Effects: Youth, Leisure, and the Politics of Rock 'n' Roll* (New York: Pantheon Books, 1981), 192.

16. Pattison, *The Triumph of Vulgarity,* 32, 63, 84 (quotation from p. 32).

17. Ibid., 74.

18. Ibid., 82.

19. Frith, *Sound Effects,* 97–98.

20. Pattison, *The Triumph of Vulgarity,* 154. Popular music was only one aspect of the Americanization of European popular culture that began in the 1920s and 1930s with motion pictures, clothing fashions, and many other things.

21. Frith, *Sound Effects,* 272.

22. Pattison, *The Triumph of Vulgarity,* 212.

23. Allen P. Britton, "The Singing School Movement in the United States," in *International Musicological Society, Report of the 8th Congress,* vol. I, (Kassel: Bärenreiter, 1966), 90–91; and H. Wiley Hitchcock, "William Billings and the Yankee Tunesmiths," *HiFi/Stereo Review* 16, no. 2 (1966): 56.

24. Britton, "Music Education: An American Specialty," 215; and Allen P. Britton, "Music in Early American Public Education: A Historical Critique," in *Basic Concepts in Music Education, The Fifty-seventh Yearbook of the National Society for the Study of Education,* part 1, ed. Nelson B. Henry (Chicago: National Society for the Study of Education, 1958), 205.

25. Britton, "Music in Early American Public Education," 202–203 (quotation from p. 202).

26. Hitchcock, "William Billings," 61.

27. For information on some specific European influences on Lowell Mason, see Carol A. Pemberton, *Lowell Mason: His Life and Work* (Ann Arbor, MI: UMI Research Press, 1985), 97–112, 139–50; and Wilfried Gruhn, "European 'Methods' for American Nineteenth-

Century Singing Instruction: A Cross-Cultural Perspective on Historical Research," *Journal of Historical Research in Music Education* 23, no. 1 (2001): 3–18. For information on German, Swiss, and English influences on William Bradbury in the late 1840s, see Juanita Karpf, "'Would that it were so in America!': William Bradbury's Observations of European Music Educators, 1847–49," *Journal of Historical Research in Music Education* 24, no. 1 (2002): 5–38.

28. Jere T. Humphreys, "The Child-Study Movement and Public School Music Education," *Journal of Research in Music Education* 33, no. 2 (1985): 82; and Jere T. Humphreys, "Instrumental Music in American Education: In Service of Many Masters," *Journal of Band Research* 30, no. 2 (1995): 41. The latter was originally published in *The Ithaca Conference on American Music Education: Centennial Profiles,* ed. Mark Fonder (Ithaca, NY: Ithaca College, 1992).

29. Jere T. Humphreys, "Applications of Science: The Age of Standardization and Efficiency in Music Education," *The Bulletin of Historical Research in Music Education* 9, no. 1 (1988): 7; Humphreys, "Instrumental Music," 43–45, 47, 50; and Jere T. Humphreys, "Some Notions, Stories, and Tales about Music Education in Society: The Coin's Other Side," *Journal of Historical Research in Music Education* 23, no. 2 (2002): 147–48.

30. Humphreys, "Instrumental Music," 44, 46, 48–49. The shift in general music approaches was in large part complete by the beginning of World War II.

31. Britton, "The Singing School Movement," 94. For an overview of American music teacher education and specific information about the first state-supported normal school in the United States, see George N. Heller and Jere T. Humphreys, "Music Teacher Education in America (1753–1840): A Look at One of Its Three Sources," *College Music Symposium,* no. 31 (1991): 49–58.

32. Britton, "Music Education: An American Specialty," 214.

33. North American universities have added a plethora of popular music courses during recent decades, but most of these are aimed toward non music majors. See Paul Théberge, "The Project Ahead: Some Thoughts on Developing a Popular Music Curriculum," *Canadian University Music Review* 21, no. 1 (2000): 28–39.

34. Humphreys, "Applications of Science," 18–19; and Humphreys, "Some Notions, Stories, and Tales," 138–41.

35. Britton, "Music Education: An American Specialty," 214–15.

36. Even in the 1990s, one musicologist characterized rock as "a major supplier of messages that helped to fuel a national crisis": Richard Crawford, *The American Musical Landscape* (Berkeley: University of California Press, 1993), 105. A less biased argument would be that the Vietnam War *was* the crisis, not the protests against it and certainly not rock music, although unquestionably rock helped galvanize the antiwar protest movement.

37. Humphreys, "Some Stories, Notions, and Tales," 142–43.

38. Jere T. Humphreys "Music Education in the U.S.A.: An Overview," *Moysike Ekiiaideyse (Music Education;* The Journal of the Greek Society for Music Education) 1, no. 3 (1998): 63 (English abstract). Australia, Canada, and Germany also have relatively decentralized systems of education.

39. Humphreys, "Instrumental Music," 39, 45; and Jere T. Humphreys, "Strike Up the Band: The Legacy of Patrick S. Gilmore," *Music Educators Journal* 74, no. 2 (1987): 26.

40. Britton, "The Singing School Movement," 90.

41. Pattison, *The Triumph of Vulgarity,* 154. For examples of writing on rock and its links to social structure and class, see John Shepherd, "Toward a Sociology of Musical Styles," *Canadian University Music Review,* no. 2 (1981): 114–37; and Graham Vulliamy and John Shepherd, "The Application of a Critical Sociology to Music Education," *British Journal of Music Education* 1, no. 3 (1984): 247–66. For an opposing view, see Keith Swanwick, "Problems of a Sociological Approach to Pop Music in Schools," *British Journal of Sociology of Education* 5 , no. 1 (1984): 49–56.

42. Humphreys, "Instrumental Music," 62–63 (quotations from p. 62).

43. Britton, "Music Education: An American Speciality," 215.

44. Herbert and Campbell, "Rock Music in American Schools," 14. The National Standards for Arts Education are not a curriculum, but curriculum guidelines: Humphreys, "Some Notions, Stories, and Tales," 149.

45. Britton, "The Singing School Movement," 90.

46. Phillip Tagg, "The Göteborg Connection: Lessons in the History and Politics of Popular Music Education and Research," *Popular Music* 17, no. 2 (1998): 219–20.

47. Thomas Regelski, e-mail correspondence to MayDay Group (via J. Terry Gates), 17 November 2002; and Vakeva, e-mail correspondence to MayDay Group. During a trip to Finland in April 2002, I witnessed snippets of popular music instruction and saw facilities and equipment for the same in three Finnish universities, including Sibelius (with Regelski), Oulu (with Vakeva), and the University of Jyvärkylä (with Jukka Louhivuori).

48. Humphreys, "Instrumental Music," 53. This degree was in "dance band." The Berklee College of Music, founded in Boston in 1945 as the Schillinger House of Music, granted its first bachelor's degrees in popular music performance in 1966. The institution does not offer a teacher preparation program.

49. Jere T. Humphreys, "On Teaching Pigs to Sing," online document (n.p.: MayDay Group, 1999[cited 14 January 2003]); available at www.nyu.edu/education/music/mayday/maydaygroup/papers/humphreys3d.htm# Technological inventions that facilitated music appreciation instruction included the player piano (1890s), then the phonograph (1910s), and then the radio (1920s).

50. Ibid.; and Humphreys, "Some Notions, Stories, and Tales," 149–57.

51. Frith, *The Sociology of Rock,* 74–75.

52. Britton, "Music in Early American Public Education," 199.

53. Frith, *The Sociology of Rock,* 124–25.

54. Vakeva, e-mail correspondence to MayDay Group.

55. Pattison, *The Triumph of Vulgarity,* 9, 36, 95, 154, 174.

56. Levine, *HighBrow/LowBrow,* 241.

57. Simon Frith, *Performing Rites: On the Value of Popular Music* (Oxford and New York: Oxford University Press, 1996), 270.

Jere Humphreys is a professor of music (education) at Arizona State University. A scholar with diverse interests, he lectures, teaches, and publishes throughout much of the world.

6

Teaching the Historical Context of Popular Music: A View

William R. Lee

Context is the set of circumstances that influence the meaning or the effect of something. Every discipline seems to have its own interpretation of "context." In educational research, it may mean anything from conditions that affect the work of teachers[1] to the events or circumstances that help reveal the meaning of a historical event, literary work, or musical composition. Ironically, a more precise meaning is elusive because the meaning of the term "context" is itself dependent on the circumstances in which it is used. Yet the idea is essential to thinking and teaching. This chapter examines the idea of historical context with respect to learning popular music and explores how music is related to cognition. Further, it examines the implications of historical context for teaching popular music in the schools.

Psychologists and educators recognize the peculiar importance of popular music in the lives of youths, and increasingly adults.[2] Popular American music is deeply embedded in the larger U.S. culture and enjoys nearly universal approbation. Abroad, popular music is phenomenally influential. It constitutes a growing part of formal music education, particularly in English-speaking countries, in Scandinavia, and to some extent in Germany.[3] American music educators are beginning to realize that popular music cannot be ignored.[4]

With the passage of the Goals 2000 Educate America Act, the influential legislation that led to more explicit national educational standards, music has been recognized for the first time as a fundamental academic subject. Historical context is listed in the National Standards for Music Education. Among the nine content standards, two are particularly relevant to historical context: Standard 8, "Understanding relationships between music, the other arts, and disciplines outside the arts," and Standard 9, "Understanding music in relation to history and culture."[5]

The implementation of these two standards has been problematic for music educators. Before their adoption, verbally oriented content, like historical or cultural context, generally took a backseat to more traditional music-class content: skill-centered performance, composing, or listening.[6] Traditionally, music educators have not spent class time on topics outside performance, performance-skill learning, and listening. Teachers may have some historical knowledge and a fundamental grasp of historical ideas and processes, but usually they have not given much thought to teaching historical context in a music classroom. The larger profession has paid little attention, either philosophically or otherwise, to the problem.[7]

This is further complicated by the fact that the discipline of history has its own claims as a distinct form of inquiry and way of knowing.[8] History has professional organizations, recognized teaching strategies, and national standards.[9] These are little known in music education. Some attention was given to history in the Comprehensive Musicianship Project,[10] but it related history mainly to the manipulation of formal elements in composition. Though there were a few "how-to" articles published at the time of the adoption of the National Standards,[11] history has been given little attention. The effect of teaching historical context on music learning has not been researched, though very positive effects of teaching historical context have been noted in visual-arts education.[12]

Content theorists, philosophers, and others in music education have contributed to the sharp divisions made between content taught "about" music and the direct experience of musical sound as performer or listener. The distance between the cognitive and the musical remains wide. American schools have overwhelmingly continued to value the verbally oriented cognitive aspects of learning. On the other hand, fear of diminishing the unique value of music as an aural art in an instructional setting seems to remain strong among music educators.[13]

The dichotomy between the cognitive and the emotional/feelingful is not new among theorists and philosophers,[14] and the relationship between the cognitive and the emotional/feelingful in a school setting, between the historical and the artistic/ aural, largely remains distant. This is unfortunate, for it has shackled the musical experience and excluded music from the understanding and sensing of the historical.

History educators declare that history has a special role in education because our understanding of the past can be distorted, sometimes unintentionally, but also intentionally, for material or political gain.[15] Popular music has often been at the center of political, religious, and social movements, and it can play a role in a more nuanced understanding of the past. In the German Reformation, popular music often was used as religious propaganda, and today popular music is at the center of political "culture wars" and the ideologies that circumscribe them.[16]

This chapter, however, focuses more narrowly on context and how it relates to experience with popular music. The historical context of popular music is defined as a set of circumstances that influence our understanding and feeling of the music. As we shall see, historical meaning, either of the formal or informal kind, plays a special role in the experience of popular music. Context is essential to history. History as a discipline relies entirely on context for meaning, and it is context that distinguishes history from other disciplines. The facts that make a historical concept can only have meaning "within an ensemble of other meanings."[17] Music, too, only has meaning "within an ensemble of other meanings." Historical or musical works are embedded in the mind in a complex array of ideas, images, and feelings; context plays a special role in our understanding and sensing of them.

Historical Context Informs the Musical Experience

The view that historical context is important in the arts has become widespread only in the last two decades. Unlike visual-arts educators, music educators have been slow to teach historical context. As Reimer has pointed out, music education philosophy formerly emphasized almost exclusively the universal aspects of music, the embodied or inherent, to the exclusion of the cultural or contextual aspects.[18] According to the older view, instruction is best when a work is experienced and enjoyed on a purely inherent or formal level without reference to its context or knowledge of it as a social or historical product. In such a view, attention in the classroom is given primarily to the formal elements (melody, timbre, etc.).

This view is changing in music education. Interest in the cultural and historical context, in teaching styles more authentically, in understanding the cultural milieu, is growing. This shift seem to have come mostly from a group of educators interested in multiculturalism in music,[19] and likely it has been influenced by the postmodern mind set in academia that puts great emphasis on the historical and the cultural. When teachers ignore designative meaning (i.e., meaning learned and imposed upon works by their social and cultural milieu), very human aspects of musical works, which become part of the experiencing of the work itself, are ignored. One may experience a work without knowing very much about it, with attention largely to its formal aspects, but such an experience would be different, perhaps vastly different, from the original context or intended context. Such a "contextless" approach may not be appropriate in an educational setting, because it is so incomplete.

Because people learn both formally and informally, a new consensus is building about the larger contextual nature of learning. In psychology, there are calls for a "second psychology" that looks at context-dependent factors that direct the way humans learn. Culturally created mediators, such as physical tools, social conventions, and language, guide learning and encourage groups to think and approach problems in a similar way. This idea recognizes the deep influence of groups to which one belongs and the importance of both formal and informal learning. The influence of Mead and Vygotsky is evident in this understanding of learning as something socially mediated.[20]

Experiencing music in its totality can be very complex. Musical experience is not usually just the result of attention to formal musical elements. Cultural and societal factors are very important to the actual feel of the piece. The minstrel tune "Dixie" has a 150-year history of changing meanings, some innocent, others hateful and injurious. "Dixie" has a simple triadic and scalar melody, but it is difficult to hear it ahistorically. Prior to the 1980s, many high school bands in the southern U.S. played "Dixie" for its excitement and entertainment value, just as Sousa played it in the early 1900s.[21] Since acquiring new meanings in a later volatile social and racial climate, the tune is now almost never heard without controversy.[22] For music educators and listeners today, the fluid historical context—the designative meaning—of "Dixie," the most popular piece of music in America in 1909,[23] is inescapable. As the designative meaning of a piece changes, the felt sense of the music changes, too, and the listeners'experience is not solely the result of triads and scales.

Context is particularly important in popular music because its meanings are so closely associated with the written word and the music's situatedness—historical, psychological, or otherwise. This does not diminish the need to consider the formal elements. According to Theodore Gracyk, one can grasp the patterns, the formal aspects of the music, in isolation, but one must hear them within a certain cultural framework in order to derive substantive meaning; learned cultural expectations are essential to this process. Music is more than perceived patterns; music is human. Music "has meaning through its roles in the ongoing life of a society."[24] It might be possible, through education or training, to suppress aspects of feeling in a work, but it takes a considerable investment to do so.

Gracyk does not suggest that either understanding or feeling should be an exclusive goal, but he thinks it likely that the average popular music listener aims for the visceral "felt phenomena." It is clear

that Gracyk does not regard verbal learning as information learned solely to achieve better understanding of music, though that is possible. Rather, it is an essential part of the feeling or experience of the music. One's learning, even when contextual, becomes part and parcel of the musical experience as sound.[25] It is not separate. One feels the music as a wholeness, a unity or blend.

County musician Peter Rowan's "Trail of Tears"[26] might seem on first hearing to be a crude attempt to exploit the tragic Cherokee removal from North Carolina in the 1830s. Yet it also laments the modern smug sense of discontinuity with the past. The song strives for transcendent sensitivity as it depicts a soul on an odyssey through the American landscape, with all its delights and temptations. The tune opens evocatively with a dobro solo, an instrument invented by five Czechoslovakian brothers and adapted into Southern string bands in the 1920s.[27] A listener who knows the historical context of the song never quite hears and feels it in the same way as before.

For the listener, music is an odyssey, too, and the listener's investment in the formal and contextual elements of the piece governs the quality of the experience. Differences among listeners will depend on the extent of their investment, especially in the context,[28] though likely some fundamental reactions to the formal aspects of the music remain constant among most listeners. Popular music may be even more portable from culture to culture than art music, since its formal elements are simpler and require less investment by the listener.[29] Other aspects may be much less portable. Popular music based on Native American themes might feel more immediate, for example, for Native Americans than for others.

The listener must grasp the conventions before the expressive character of the music can emerge. Listeners can relate works to the time and place of their origin—the historical context—and feel them as the complex experiences they are. Gracyk cites as an example Jimi Hendrix's "distorted" playing of the "Star-Spangled Banner" at Woodstock in 1969. It is certainly easy enough to grasp the formal elements or inherent meaning of the musical sounds, but it requires an understanding of political conditions in 1969 to best experience the work. Of course, context changes, and one's personal opinions about the political events of 1969 influence one's sense of Hendrix's music. We do not automatically feel the music in some magical way that is disconnected from what we already know and feel.[30]

Reimer agrees that context is important. But in Reimer's view, context stands apart from and is secondary to musical experience. For Reimer, such understandings *serve* the musical experience and make it deeper. Verbal instruction, of which historical context would be a part, is a means to a better musical experience.[31] This is in contrast to others, such as Grayck, who seem to view such learnings as more significant parts of the musical experience itself.

Though philosophers and theorists may disagree on some of the details, there are growing areas of agreement. One is that music has inherent and embodied meanings. Perceptions of music, especially popular music, are infused with an unavoidable cognitive element. We can only properly value musical qualities if educated to do so, and we then choose to invest our time in it. People feel according to what they bring to the experience, by accident or design. They come to the music with a particular perceptual set that affects their felt experience. That perceptual set can be in some measure historically based.

Informing and Being Informed by the Historical Context

It is useful to look at historical context from the standpoint of cognitive psychology, for the cognitive and the feelingful are a two-way street. If the cognitive affects the feelings, it is possible that the feelings may inform the cognitive. Cognitive theories of emotion emphasize that emotions are the by-products of cognition. In the case of Rowan's tune, which alludes to an event in Cherokee history, knowledge of the historical context can affect listeners' feelings about the music. The sense of the music may, in turn, strongly affect listeners' sense of that context. Many historians think that the felt sense of history is an important condition in students.[32]

Looking at concept formation can reveal how the cognitive and the musical relate.[33] Concepts are clusters of ideas with logical relationships and connections that help us manage the sensory world. They are mental constructs, often unfocused and changing, but very useful. Once concepts are formed, they help guide thinking, and they can become the basis for, or contribute to, newer concepts. Related concepts generally work as ensembles, called schema.[34]

Ideas about how concepts work have

changed within the last decade. They are regarded as fuzzier, more complex, and more dynamic than previously. Traditionally, discussion in the research literature usually focused on sorting words into categories and trying to see how these categories could be manipulated to produce understanding of similar categories. Now concepts are seen in a larger sense, as interconnected bits of perceptual information, such as ideas, images, feelings, sounds, even smells and tastes—any relevant kind of imagery or sense. These blends change, if only in small ways, as we accumulate new experiences or forget old ones.[35]

Thus, concepts have a felt component in addition to a cognitive function. In a sense, their mechanisms are multisensory. An example is the word "family," which has meaning for almost everyone. Our concept of family is similar enough for us to communicate with each other about the word "family" and the relationships it evokes. On an individual level, "family" may have significant differences in patterns, feelings, logical connections, imagery, perhaps even sounds and smells—depending on a person's life experiences and culture. A person's perceptual set may be similar to others, but it also may be different in important particulars.

The felt sense of the concept "gospel music" would vary tremendously depending on the prior experience (conceptual set) of the listener, though the sense of the formal aspects may be similar among people, whatever their cognitive achievements or investment. The conceptual sense of gospel itself does not have separate components but is felt as a unity with patterns used to understand other music. The "feel" or affective

sense of the concept "gospel music" would be different for those who learned it in a rural religious setting as opposed to those who learned solely by listening to a recording. The total sense—sight, sounds, smells, room ambience, and knowledge—would be different. In either case, one may have developed the concept partially through language, an abstraction of ideas, which may contribute to feeling of the pattern. In such a circumstance, the cognitive and feelingful aspects of music meet head-on and become one.

We do not usually learn alone, and both formal and informal education affect our concepts of music. Sociohistorical theory may eventually help explain how such complex concepts are learned in communities. This may be especially useful for understanding how people learn and share popular music. Clues about how people obtain knowledge are found in the community (or communities) to which people belong; in the community's peculiar tools, concepts, and symbol systems; and in its social, linguistic, and material histories. Cultural activities enable people to internalize their community's tools for thinking. The social nature of this view derives, at least partly, from the work of Vygotsky and Mead[36] and shares similar intellectual roots with the postmodernism mindset. Social learning is especially relevant to popular music because its composition and performance are very group oriented.[37]

Role of "History" in the Learning of Popular Music

The role of history in popular music performance can be seen in the interviews of Lucy Green. Green investigated how popular musicians learn by interviewing fifteen British popular musicians over time. According to Green, young musicians learn music informally; they "pick up" skills with the encouragement of peers and family, by watching, listening, and imitating other musicians.[38] Their chief learning activities are copying and making reference recordings. These informal music-learning practices differ from formal music education. Formal music learning emphasizes technique, regular practice, large groups, and teacher-directed study. Informal music learning emphasizes learning pieces the student likes, practice directed at immediate performance or pleasure, small groups, and student-directed study. Students practice irregularly, sometimes for long hours, sometimes not for days.[39]

Green does not address popular musicians' use of history, but she does note the group-mediated and formal-informal characteristics of their learning, and she provides long quotes that give some sense of how they use popular music history. The interviewees often demonstrated substantive knowledge of the history of popular music, at least of those styles they knew and wanted to perform. With exceptions, this knowledge seems directly related to performance. The musicians did not seem to learn aspects of popular music history systematically but as an outcome of their interest in performance. What they knew of history—musicians, technical approaches, groups, subcategories of popular music, eras—was directly connected with particular styles. With the exception of one interviewee, their historical knowledge seemed to lack breadth, but they often demonstrated depth and enthusiasm for the particular styles they did know. Since sound is an immediate and core part of their informal learning practices, they relate the bits of acquired history directly to the sounds studied.[40]

Their knowledge seemed essential to learning their instruments or vocal parts. Because their overriding learning strategy was careful listening and copying, they developed a wide range of knowledge that related to styles, trends, personalities, and works in time—a decidedly historical approach, though Green did not call it such. They were very knowledgeable about the styles they played, as the style, or "feel," of the music concerned them regularly as they played in cover and theme bands. Further, it seems that interviewees had great respect for "classical music."[41]

The more experienced musicians Green interviewed could speak in depth about the history of popular music. Bass guitarist Rob had an encyclopedic knowledge of bass guitar styles, outstanding players of the bass, and aspects of the development of his particular instrument. Others seemed to know what was happening within the context of their particular interests, though perhaps more narrowly. They seemed to have substantial historical knowledge, especially if they played in tribute bands, sessions, cover, or function bands. Another interviewee, Bernie, was a fan of a certain jazz pianist (he was not a pianist himself) and had immersed himself in the pianist's music. Brent knew several styles and personalities and could place styles and personalities in the correct decades.[42]

It is clear that these popular musicians saw themselves as part of a continuing and significant musical tradition, and their accounts have a sense of historical immediacy and continuity. Interviewees built a past from facts and memory and added themselves to the center of it. They saw themselves as sharing a past with an artistic tradition that they felt very strongly about and with which they identified.[43] They constructed a useful memory made of history and myth.

National Standards in History and Music Education

There has been an increase in the attention given to history education over the past two decades. Prominent historians and influential organizations have begun to see history as having great importance in understanding and supporting other fields.[44] There is active speculation about how history plays a role in life, how it gives nuance and feeling to life, and how it informs decision making and judgment. This renewed interest has been accompanied by an increased interest in popular culture in academic circles, much of the interest influenced by a postmodern mindset. Postmodernists see culture and history as central to their opinions. They disdain hierarchies, such as "high and low art," as manifestations of political hegemony, and they have contributed to a revival of interest in popular culture.[45]

At no time in U.S. history has history itself been such an ardent part of public discourse. Since the late 1980s, there has been a strong reform movement to improve history instruction in the schools through such agencies as the Bradley Commission, and popular history has received a boost

from a cable station devoted to history. Several books on historical subjects have reached the best-seller lists. National interest in historical documentaries, including one on jazz by Ken Burns, has been extraordinary.[46]

When the national standards for history were published, there was an angry public outcry against them. There was a gulf between what historians in universities and what the American public thought was important. A largely avant-garde academy wanted to move away from the memorization of facts and base the curriculum on big thematic concepts. As things settled down in the 1990s, history educators have eschewed extremes. Dates, names, and events, many have come to believe, form a secure scaffolding on which to practice interpretation and analysis. There is, too, a strong desire to teach students evaluation and interpretation so they can be flexible, critical, and insightful. The view of the past is fluid, and it changes as we gain new insights or reexamine old evidence. Documents or books cannot represent *the* history of popular music, but only *a* history.[47] Especially for popular music, each generation of students has to learn history anew in light of its own experiences.

Historical context is the set of circumstances that influence the meaning or understanding of historical events. The idea of historical context is useful and self-limiting. One of the great problems of teaching—one that thinkers from Herbert Spencer to Walter Pater have addressed—is choosing what to know and learn, what to teach, when to teach it, and how to teach it. One chooses only those aspects of popular music history that help students perceive the meaning of the music, enhance their experience of it, or help them understand its situatedness and connectedness to humanity.

Connecting music to history, as outlined in Standards 8 and 9, is difficult, partly because scholarship making the connections has been so infrequent. Richard Crawford, a prominent musicologist, notes that, as late as the 1970s, American historians rarely included music in their books, despite the relevance of music to their work. They have not been at home with musical data.[48] On the other hand, music history has been dominated by musicologists whose focus has been the composers and works of the concert hall. This artificial divide has begun to erode, and a few works have appeared that more closely tie music to general history. Among these are Lawrence W. Levine's works, including his important *Highbrow/Lowbrow: The Emergence of Cultural Hierarchy in America.*[49]

But what aspects of historical context should be taught? One approach that has developed among history educators is not only to teach the necessary bits and pieces—facts, dates, and places—but also to try to identify several larger concepts or themes that might be useful in scaffolding ideas and developing critical skills. The development of themes has happened periodically in history education. The Bradley Commission on History in the Schools developed a set of "vital themes and narratives" that decidedly influenced state adoption of history standards in the early 1990s.[50]

Similar principles or themes could be developed for the historical context of popular music. With these themes in mind, it is possible to scaffold the bits and pieces of remembered sound, facts, dates, and names. A set of themes might include the following:

- *Change.* How have institutions, conditions, values, and performers affected popular music? What are the origins of individual styles, and how did they spread? How can popular musics be grouped, and what criteria can be used to group them?
- *Multiple causes.* Events in popular music history have multiple causes. Why did rock music come about? Was it through the agency of a few strong leaders? Was it related to economic conditions?
- *Evidence.* What is the evidence for the causes of change in popular music? Though documents and histories might provide a view, the actual music would be very important.
- *Choices.* What important choices and decisions have affected popular music?
- *Origins.* Where does popular music come from, and who supports it?
- *Material context.* How have technological, political, geographical, cultural, and economic developments affected popular music, nationally and internationally? What are the stages of technological and industrial development?
- *Social patterns.* What patterns of social and political interaction have affected its sound? What is the role of immigration, migration, social mobility, censorship or lack of it, and racial and gender structures?[51]

For an effective teaching of the context

of popular music, teachers have to answer several standard questions about curriculum:

- What are the goals and objectives of the class?
- What specific content will be taught to meet those goals and objectives?
- How will the content be taught?
- How will the results be appraised?

As this chapter proposes, the teaching of historical context informs the music experience and gives experiences that are systematic and useful and otherwise meet the National Standards for Music Education. Teaching should take into account teaching principles followed in music education and in the field of history. Strategies should be based on the experience of sound, with student listening, playing, or creating at the center of instruction. There should be a clear balance between facts, dates, places, and big ideas or themes in the development of popular music.

What Content Should Be Taught and How?

Music educators should take into account the nature of music and history, their traditional modes of teaching, societal influences and factors, and the changing view of how to teach and learn in music and history. In the last decade, history teachers have advocated balancing fact-based, bits-and-pieces learning with larger themes and principles. With its emphasis on social history, the belief that common people can affect events, the history of minorities and women, and the process of interpretation, history teaching has taken a new direction.

The postmodern mindset that emphasizes the importance of history and culture, especially the popular, over larger traditional issues has influenced this shift.[52]

In this context, Green's work can be useful. Green's interviews give some clues about how popular musicians use the historical. First, the musicians learned what they learned largely for direct practical application. For popular music taught in more formal circumstances, it is reasonable to give priority to material directly related to playing, feeling, or understanding the music. Research in other content areas supports this practice. Students generally value what they learn when it can be shown to have an immediate use.[53]

Clearly, when Green's popular musicians were talking about history, they were talking about style, about how certain music characteristically sounds and feels. So, as in the larger field, music educators should maintain, or find an equivalent substitute for, the common practice of looking at the basic style characteristics. Concepts can become "silent knowing," without a verbal base. Nontraditional organizational terms or means to help students understand style may work.[54]

Dates and chronology are still emphasized in the larger field of history education. Music educators should consider other ways of assisting students in organizing their thoughts about popular music. Green's musicians usually talked about style in reference to particular performers, rarely by dates or periods.[55] It is probably more important to associate style with performers, or possibly with standard popular music labels —rap, grunge, disco—as the larger population is accustomed to thinking that way.

Selecting what music students may like is very important and not unknown in music education. This does not necessarily mean that educators should exploit students' personal preferences. Research has noted that students' popular music preferences are often very personal, that they are reluctant to reveal them, that they are very partisan about them, and that they sometimes view questions about them as an intrusion. They may be more open to styles that are more distantly related to their favorite music.[56] Popular music from another era, distant from them but related to their experience, might be appropriate, depending on the type of music class and its objectives. Students tend to understand best when they can relate examples to prior knowledge.[57]

One does not teach the whole of popular music history, but delimited aspects of it. The teacher should not feel pressure to cover everything. Research in history has shown that students do best where there are a limited number of topics for lessons, substantive coherence and continuity, thought-provoking tasks, and good teacher modeling of thoughtfulness.[58] Robert Garofalo, who has suggested teaching at least one band work per year in great depth, follows this pattern.[59] Narrower "posthole" techniques, the intense studying of a limited slice of history, were used in the larger field of history right after World War II and rejected.[60] Music educators, however, might consider this technique. It may be important for students to have deep knowledge of one group of styles if such an approach leaves them with a sense of wonder and interest in music.

The idea of historical context is especially helpful in making judgments about what to teach. Teachers should choose only those aspects of popular music history that help students perceive the meaning of music, that enhance their experiences of it—say, through learning a performance technique—that help them understand its situatedness and connectedness, or that help them focus on its formal elements. Music educators generally should not teach popular music history that goes beyond these bounds.

Parents sometimes will object to certain lyrics, jacket covers, or the music of groups whose lifestyles are not to their liking. They rarely object to the music directly. In choosing musical examples, teachers should adhere to state and local guidelines. Traditionally, music educators have not taught about the lifestyles of composers or performers of any era or discussed salacious lyrics, even those encoded in Renaissance madrigals. Teacher should be aware of the issues.[61]

In teaching the context of the country tune "Maple's Lament," sung by Laurie Lewis, it may be necessary to explain that the tune and its antecedents are Celtic, associating the sound of Lewis's keening fiddle with the traditions of Ireland and particular style patterns and sound combinations—its formal elements. The singer sings the piece in high tessitura and with a bright voice quality (the "high lonesome" sound of so many folk cultures, and of older country music). It may or may not be useful to explain the word Celtic, associate Irish history with the music, or tell about the geography of Irish settlement. The music teacher works outward from the sound of the piece and connects and elaborates only for sound instructional reasons. For students who live in Boston, the Irish Canal section in New Orleans, or Appalachia or who have a consciousness of Ireland, deeper explanation may be useful. When music teachers move too far from the history as it relates to the sound, they are moving out of the field of music, away from the historical context, and into another subject area. The teacher's judgment with respect to both content and time spent is paramount, and music teachers should err toward experiencing the art as sound.

Learning musical skills and performing are the main activities in large ensembles in middle and secondary schools. They present problems for teaching historical context because the time is largely spent on skill acquisition. Choral and instrumental ensembles usually perform a variety of music, including popular music. Popular pieces are often arrangements, which may not be authentic. Yet the historical context has importance and needs to be taught. Long lectures about a piece may not fit the purposes of the class. In music education, there always has been tension between the aural and the verbal. Though historical context may contribute to the musical experience, it is largely verbal material that takes class time to present. This may limit the students' direct experience of music as performers, makers, or listeners. Again, the experiencing of the sound is fundamental to music education.[62]

If the teacher intends to teach without expending too much time and yet move beyond mere factual assertions, anecdotal teaching may be effective. Anecdotes— short, factual, incisive ministories, a minute or two long—can be an effective mode of presentation, especially if connected directly to what is being taught. Anecdotes are not merely amusing asides, shallow in content and purpose, but short stories that present the essence of understanding.[63]

There are other alternatives, and many of these are traditional ways of teaching often ignored in music classes. Large-ensemble situations might also include student-made bulletin boards, small-group or individual reports derived from Internet or library resources, outside players or speakers, or critiques, including comparing movies based on popular music to actual historical events. Teaching should always be related to sound; it should occur when students listen to or play the piece. The music should be connected to the styles or personalities known to the students, insofar as it is possible.

Student- or teacher-led discussions are possible, though much less so in ensembles. Socratic dialogue is helpful in peeling back and understanding the meaning in popular music history. Students should know how to use Socratic questioning and reasoning. Teachers should avoid herding the students toward specific "answers." Some questions are best left open-ended. Much in popular music and much historical content are not facts, but judgments of what is known. Historical interpretation is often tentative. Students must not be left with the idea that everything is a fact or that everything must have a "correct" answer.

One corrective to this attitude would be to use a suppositional teaching style. The teacher models uncertainty about historical facts by using words like "maybe," "perhaps," and "possibly" and encourages students to challenge historical concepts and musical interpretations. Students will begin to see knowledge as fluid, tentative, and open. The object is to develop an atmosphere of questioning and searching that continues outside the classroom and into adult life. This teaching style is characteristic of outstanding teachers.[64] Such a style would help build the critical attitude historians see as essential in learning historical thinking.[65] History is highly interpretative, qualified, and contingent.[66]

Much of the content taught, especially in ensembles, is contingent. It happens, unplanned, because of the musical situation and teacher intuition, not because of teacher planning. Historical content taught in such situations can be taught well if the teacher knows the history thoroughly and is able to act at the right moment. Such improvisational teaching may be given some control by keeping a list of what was taught and how it was taught. The teacher can then "cycle in" complementary topics and strategies as needed to meet pre-planned goals. Such instructional improvisation is closer in spirit to the more informal, more sporadic, less structured, but effective, approach Green's popular musicians took in their general learning.[67]

If teachers seek to find a model of learning closer to the informal, they might consider teaching students to find out about popular music history for themselves. The Internet, its word and audio resources, books and magazine print media, tapes, videos, and information and audiovisual resources found in the library are useful. Books sold in retail bookstores are devoted to popular music figures and genres and are written for popular consumption. There are growing numbers of institutions devoted to popular music, and many have educational programs. Among these are the Rock and Roll Hall of Fame (Cleveland) the Georgia Music Hall of Fame (Macon), Alabama Music Hall of Fame (Tuscumbia), Mississippi Musicians Hall of Fame (Clinton), the Country Music Foundation (Nashville), Australian Country Music Foundation (Tamworth), and Texas Heritage Music Foundation (Kerrville). Most U.S. organizations are in the southern United States. Many are new and at least partially supported by state government.

With respect to evaluation, traditional testing may be in order. But testing must reflect the goals and objectives of the class. In most music education classes, popular music plays a minor part; thus, testing of historical context would not be extensive. Green suggests that in circumstances related to popular music, testing could actually be harmful, or at least inaccurate. Students may have what she refers to as tacit knowledge.[68] When the historical context blends with the felt sense of the piece, that aspect may not be testable at all. Formative evaluation, evaluation done in the process of teaching, "on the fly," may be sufficient.

Levels of Historical Learning of Popular Music

Children learn formally in school or informally outside school. One of the obvious goals of formal education should be to provide circumstances where they can learn better than on the street or on their own. To facilitate learning, I tentatively propose five categories of formal and informal learning of historical context. These categories may overlap.

Fandom. Fandom can be described as enthusiastic, extreme, uncritical, and slavishly devoted acquisition of information about a popular musical group or figure. Fans will (a) focus primarily on individuals or groups, (b) know much detailed, sometimes trivial, information, (c) be highly uncritical, and (d) deliberately and enthusiastically acquire new material. The movie *Rockstar* (2001), set in Pittsburgh in the early 1980s, provides an example. The lead character, Rob, is an intelligent, talented, blue-collar youth who is the front for a tribute band devoted to a group called Blood Pollution. Rob knows every detail about Blood Pollution. He works hard at it. He knows all the band's music and insists on authenticity in the copying that his tribute band does. When the pet dog of a member of Blood Pollution dies, he sends flowers. He is awed by a historical display of Blood Pollution's musical accoutrements at their recording studio. Rob's uncritical acceptance of information about Blood Pollution is at the heart of the story. His efforts are deliberate and thorough, but narrow and uncritical; he blocks out the negative. This level of understanding is likely common. Fandom should not be regarded always as a bad thing, unless of course the same pathology is applied in every circumstance.

Historical Acculturation. This refers to the learning of historical context of music without deliberate effort. It is usually the result of simple socialization, what one draws from one's social and cultural surroundings. It is most often uncritical and unsystematic and happens with little real effort.

Buffdom. Buffs know many facts and often have some idea of the critical process. They tend to focus on larger issues and can be quite knowledgeable. They work hard to learn, but their learning is idiosyncratic and narrow. They may have little knowledge of the larger historical context, and their rawly formed, idiosyncratic ideas have been little subjected to the polish of critical examination.

Naive Study of Popular Music History. It is formal and school based, but it is unsuccessful study, with little attention to the critical nature of history, or often even the aural nature of music. It is dates-and-facts learning.

Ideal Study. Students will have substantive knowledge of names and dates, styles, personalities, and groups. They can scaffold much of their learning on larger trends, ideas, styles, and movements. They have a good idea about popular music in historical context. They can question the veracity of evidence and will welcome a critique of their conclusions. They can use their knowledge in listening or for performance or composition.

Fandom, buffdom, and historical acculturation usually happen outside school. Naive study and ideal study are usually found in schools. It is possible for these categories to overlap, and some individuals may fit more than one category, depending on the subject. It is also possible to move to ideal study without formal study, say, from buffdom, when a buff learns context, is able to exercise critical thinking, and subjects ideas to a critical process.

Coda

Popular music is a fantastically successful phenomenon. It is learned and enjoyed internationally with a high degree of enthusiasm and devotion. Even more conservative elements in American society, who have in the past decried offensive lyrics or the lifestyles of popular musicians, are embracing popular styles at an astonishing rate and for various purposes.[69] In universities and colleges, its study is accepted more readily, possibly as a result of the positive fallout from the postmodernist mindset, which does not readily accept a dichotomy between "high" and "low" art. Yet popular music does not appear to be given institutional attention and resources in proportion with its importance in society.

Considering its prominence in American society and in the lives of students, it is astonishing that popular music has been so rarely and unsystematically addressed in music teacher education. When it is taught in higher education, it appears in listening-focused, nontechnical courses for the general college population. Rarely is it treated as a worthy practice in music education or as an object of determined scholarship.

Popular music is something music teachers must address, but they cannot do it with a desultory education. When the day comes that it is addressed more substantively, the understanding of historical context will likely play a part. Popular music is deeply embedded in the societies that produce it, and there will be a great need to understand its history, psychology, sociology, and aesthetics. Teachers will need to have a clearer idea of how historical context shapes learning and what place it has in teaching. They need to know popular music history to the level of ideal study.

As Gracyk notes, knowing about popular music is central to understanding and experiencing it. If popular music is to be represented seriously in the curriculum, as Reimer says it should,[70] then historical context must be addressed, formally or informally. Without knowing and teaching the historical context, music teachers risk a debilitating amnesia about one of the most powerful musical movements in our time.

Notes

1. Joan E. Talbert, Milbrey W. McLaughlin, and Brian Rowan, "Understanding Context Effects on Secondary School Teaching," *Teachers College Record* 95, no. 1 (1993): 45–46.

2. Peter G. Christenson and Donald F. Roberts, *It's Not Only Rock and Roll: Popular Music in the Lives of Adolescents* (Cresskill, NJ: Hampton Press, 1998), 41–71.

3. Richard Jakoby, *Musical Life in Germany* (Bonn: Inter Nationes, 1997), 20, 50.

4. Bennett Reimer, "The Contextual Dimension of Musical Experience," in *A Philosophy of Music Education: Advancing the Vision*, 3rd ed. (Upper Saddle River, NJ: Prentice Hall, 2003), 168–98.

5. Consortium of National Arts Education Associations, *National Standards for Arts Education* (Reston, VA: Music Educators National Conference, 1994), 62–63.

6. Reimer, "The Meaning Dimension of Musical Experience," in *A Philosophy of Music Education*, 141–42, 146.

7. Ibid.; Robert Garofalo, *A Guide to Teaching Comprehensive Musicianship through School Band Performance* (Ft. Lauderdale FL: Meredith Music Publications, 1976), vi–vii.

8. Harvey J. Graff, "Teaching [and] Historical Understanding: Disciplining Historical Imagination with Historical Context," *Interchange* 30, no. 2 (1999): 150.

9. Paul Gagnon and the Bradley Commission

on History in Schools, eds., *Historical Literacy: The Case for History in American Education* (New York: Macmillan, 1989), passim.

10. Michael L. Mark and Charles L. Gary, *A History of American Music Education* (New York: Schirmer Books, 1992), 348–50, 361–62.

11. For example, see Elizabeth Hoffman, "Illuminate the Music," *Teaching Music* 2, no. 4 (1995): 28–30; and Evonne Nolan, "Orchestrating Meaningful Performance," *Teaching Music* 2, no. 4 (1995): 36–37.

12. Lynn Galbraith, "Research in Visual Art Education: Implications for Music," in *The New Handbook of Research on Music Teaching and Learning,* ed. Richard Colwell and Carol Richardson (Oxford: Oxford University Press, 2002), 966.

13. Reimer, *A Philosophy of Music Education,* 141–42, 146. The literature that addresses this question is extensive and growing.

14. Alan Ryan, *John Dewey and the High Tide of American Liberalism* (New York: Norton, 1995), 254; also discussed in Reimer, *A Philosophy of Music Education,* especially Chapter 3; and Iris M. Yob, "The Cognitive Emotions and Emotional Cognitions," in *Reason and Intellect: Essays in Honor of Israel Scheffler,* ed. Harvey Siegel (Dordrecht, The Netherlands: Kluwer, 1997), 43–44.

15. Graff, "Teaching [and] Historical Understanding," 148.

16. Rebecca Wagner Oettinger, *Music as Propaganda in the German Reformation* (Aldershot, England: Ashgate, 2001), 36; Eric Nuzum, "Freedom of Speech: An Overview of Music Censorship," in *Parental Advisory: Music Censorship in America* (New York: HarperCollins, 2001), 3–12.

17. Graff, "Teaching [and] Historical Understanding," 153.

18. Reimer, "The Contextual Dimension of Musical Experience," in *A Philosophy of Music Education,* 168–98. See especially page 169.

19. Terese M. Volk, "Multiculturalism: Dynamic Creativity for Music Education," in *World Musics and Music Education: Facing the Issues,* ed. Bennett Reimer (Reston, VA: MENC, 2002), 18.

20. Bruce Torff, "Comparative Review of Human Ability Theory: Context, Structure, and Development," in *The New Handbook of Research,* 510–11.

21. John Philip Sousa, *Marching Along: Recollections of Men, Women, and Music* (Boston: Hale, Cushman, and Flint, 1928), 112–15.

22. E. Lawrence Abel, *Singing the New Nation: How Music Shaped the Confederacy, 1861–1865* (Mechanicsburg, PA: Stackpole Books, 2000), 51.

23. Ibid, 47.

24. Theodore Gracyk, *I Wanna Be Me: Rock Music and the Politics of Identity* (Philadelphia: Temple University Press, 2001), 133.

25. Theodore Gracyk, *Rhythm and Noise: An Aesthetics of Rock* (Durham, NC: Duke University Press, 1996), 215.

26. From Peter Rowan, *New Moon Rising,* Sugar Hill Records SHR 3762, 1988.

27. Cecelia Tichi, *High Lonesome: The American Culture of Country Music* (Chapel Hill: The University of North Carolina Press, 1994), 181–83, 206–10.

28. Theodore Gracyk, e-mail to author, 13 January 2003. I am indebted to Professor Gracyk for clarifying this point for me. Cognitive theories of emotion vary primarily with respect to what role physiological arousal plays in the sequence of events. See Lester M. Sdorow, *Psychology,* 3rd ed., (Dubuque, IA: Wm. C. Brown Communications, 1995), 444–46.

29. Gracyk, *I Wanna Be Me,* 216–17.

30. Grayck, *Rhythm and Noise,* 132–39.

31. Reimer, *A Philosophy of Music Education,* 197.

32. The Bradley Commission on History in Schools, *Building a History Curriculum* (Washington, DC: Education Excellence Network, 1988), 10–11; Richard Crawford, "A Historian's Introduction to Early American Music," *Proceedings of the American Antiquarian Society* 89, no. 2 (1979): 261–98. I am using "feelings" and "emotions" interchangeably.

33. There are vast differences among theorists on the origins and nature of concepts. See Robert W. Howard, *Concepts and Schemata: An Introduction* (London: Cassell, 1987), especially Chapters 1 and 9.

34. Howard, *Concepts and Schemata,* 4–5, 51–52. Some theorists make no distinctions

between the terms "schemata" and "concept"; for others, a schemata is a cluster of concepts.

35. Ibid., 4–5, 172–73.

36. Wilfried Gruhn and Frances Rauscher, "The Neurobiology of Music Cognition and Learning," in *The New Handbook of Research,* 446.

37. Lucy Green, *How Popular Musicians Learn: A Way Ahead for Music Education* (Aldershot, UK: Ashgate, 2002), 5.

38. Ibid., 76–83.

39. Ibid., 86–93, 186. Also see especially Chapter 4.

40. Ibid., 21, 28, 30–35, 40, 44.

41. Ibid., 121–25.

42 Ibid., 30–31, 33–35.

43. I owe my pattern of analysis of this to Susan Engel, *Context is Everything* (New York: W.H. Freeman and Co., 1999). See especially pages 110–11 and 158–59.

44. John J. Patrick and Charles S. White, "Social Studies Education, Secondary Schools," in *Encyclopedia of Educational Research,* 6th ed. (New York: Macmillan, 1992), 1239.

45. Keith Winschuttle, *The Killing of History* (San Francisco: Encounter Books, 1996), 25. I have adopted Reimer's term "mindset" as appropriate.

46. Michael Kammen, "Introduction" and "Historians and the Problem of Popular Culture in Recent Times," in *American Culture American Tastes: Social Change and the 20th Century* (New York: Alfred A. Knopf, 1999), xiii–xix, 219–41.

47. Diane Ravitch, *Left Back: A Century of Failed School Reforms* (New York: Simon and Schuster, 2000), 433–37, 450; and John D. Bransford, Ann L. Brown, and Rodney R. Cocking, eds., *How People Learn: Brain, Mind, Experience, and School* (Washington, DC: National Academy Press, 1999), 147.

48. Crawford, "A Historian's Introduction," 261–62.

49. Lawrence W. Levine, *Highbrow/Lowbrow: The Emergence of Cultural Hierarchy in America* (Cambridge: Harvard University Press, 1988).

50. The Bradley Commission on History in Schools, *Building a History Curriculum,* 10–11.

51. Ibid, 51. I have used the Bradley themes as a general basis.

52. David Hackett Fischer, *Albion's Seed: Four British Folkways in America* (New York: Oxford University Press, 1989), vii–xi.

53. Glenn Tetterton-Opheim, "History, Science, and Literature: Integrating Knowledge and Involving Students in American High Schools," in *Learning History in America: Schools, Cultures, and Politics,* ed. Lloyd Kramer, Donald Reid, and William L. Barney (Minneapolis: University of Minnesota Press, 1994), 78.

54. Robert Cutietta has proposed what he believes is a more effective alternative. See his "The Musical Elements: Who Said They're Right?" *Music Educators Journal* 79, no. 3 (1993): 48–53.

55. Green, *How Popular Musicians Learn,* 30.

56. Ibid., 200.

57. M. C. Whitrock, "Students' Thought Processes," in *Handbook of Research on Teaching,* 3rd. ed., (New York: Macmillan, 1986), 297–314.

58. Graff, "Teaching [and] Historical Understanding," 145, 150–51, 157.

59. Elizabeth Hoffman, "Understanding Improves Performance," *Teaching Music* 2, no. 4 (1995): 34–35.

60. R. De Keyser, "History: Educational Programs," in *The International Encyclopedia of Education,* 2nd ed., ed. Torsten Husen and T. Neville Postlewaite (Pergamon, NY: Elsevier Science, 1994), 2621.

61. Books such as Nuzum's *Parental Advisory* are useful.

62. Reimer, "The Contextual Dimension of the Musical Experience," in *A Philosophy of Music Education,* 169–70.

63. Robert Eric Frykenberg, *History and Belief* (Grand Rapids, MI: Wm. B. Eerdman's, 1996), 96.

64. Joseph O. Milner, "Suppositional Style and Teacher Evaluation," *Phi Delta Kappan* 72, no. 6 (1991): 464–67.

65. Gagnon, *Historical Literacy,* 271–73.

66. Suzanne M. Wilson and Gary Sykes, "Toward Better Teacher Preparation and Certification" in *Historical Literacy,* 269.

67. Green, *How Popular Musicians Learn,* 197.

68. Ibid., 97.

69. Popular music has been a feature of smaller evangelical Protestant churches, with

rock music at the center of many services. In the southern U.S., the "praise band," a group consisting mostly of keyboards, guitars, and drums, is finding acceptance in large numbers of mainline Protestant churches, and traditional choirs and services are being pushed aside. Some evangelical Protestant groups are aggressively using popular music in their missionary efforts in Central and South America with a high rate of success.

70. Reimer, *A Philosophy of Music Education*, 168.

William R. Lee is professor of music at the University of Tennessee at Chattanooga where he teaches graduate and undergraduate music education and brass and conducts an ensemble. He has published more than fifty articles and book reviews, mostly in the history of music education and has published several arrangements and compositions. He is a member of the editorial boards of the *Journal of Research in Music Education* and the *Journal of Historical Research in Music Education*.

International Perspectives

7

Music Education in the Aquarian Age: A Transatlantic Perspective
(or "How Do You Make Horses Thirsty?")

George Odam

When the Moon is in the Seventh House,
And Jupiter aligns with Mars,
Then peace shall guide the planets,
And love will steer the stars.
This is the dawning of the Age of
Aquarius.

When Gerome Ragni and James Rado wrote those words for their musical *Hair* in 1967 they were probably unaware of the set of essays titled *Moving into Aquarius* that English composer Michael Tippett wrote in 1959. I have chosen to use the term again some forty or so years later, having been moved and impressed by Tippett's writing when it first came out and finding it still fresh and relevant today.

Tippett used the zodiacal term partly for devilment, knowing it would tend to upset the academic community and partly, as he said, because "our present prolonged catastrophe (moving into Aquarius) has more analogies to the changes before and after the year One (moving into Pisces) than to the birth pangs of the Renaissance."[1] He described Victorianism as a medieval hangover present in the postwar period. He detected "a refusal of something, a pressing

something down."[2] I choose to reuse Tippett's terminology partly for his reasons, partly because the Age of Aquarius has become a symbol for the beginning of the pop music scene, and also to avoid the use in my title of the terms "popular music" or "postmodern." Both terms appear to me to defy analysis and raise serious questions about boundaries and experience that are presently best avoided.

In 1965, American writer Alvin Toffler wrote *Future Shock,* a seminal text that proved prophetic if, as we can now observe, somewhat understated.[3] He defined schooling as an industrial process and diagnosed that the midcentury population of the developed world was suffering from "future shock," which he described as a mass disorientation, an inability to look to and plan for the premature arrival of the future, placing an emphasis on the personal and social costs of change.

There is no doubt that fear of change leads to suspicion of things that are transient by nature, promoting an undue reverence and nostalgia for the past. Mistrust of change means that any art form for which transience is a fundamental element (such as popular music) is likely to be given a hard time by academics and educators who revere the past and whose business is describing it and producing hierarchies and analyses.

The exponential development of microtechnology spurred on by the invention and rapid development of the microprocessor (not yet invented when Toffler wrote *Future Shock*) was hardly predicted in the 1970s. A decade later, Toffler predicted the rise of the information age and the Internet in *The Third Wave*.[4] The end of the Piscean age of the book and the onset of the Aquarian age of the computer has brought with it the burden of preserving everything. We are all more aware of our history than at any time in human development, yet we have never more needed the ability to look forward and not over our shoulders.

Coupled with this obsession with preservation is the need to learn to predict. Essential skills are those of imagination, creativity, and replenishment. The old hierarchical methods, strongly founded on traditional methodologies, have been found wanting in societies worldwide. While guarding against throwing out babies with bathwater (and this is a huge issue in education, one that cannot be addressed here), most education systems, with the exception of those based on religious fundamentalism, are being challenged to place these nontraditional qualities at their center.

Fear of transience and the burden of preserving everything are at the heart of the knotty problems teachers face in welcoming popular music into their curriculums when there has, so far, been no such tradition. Learning to value art that many music educators have only covertly been engaged in as listeners, composers, and performers is a new thing. At the fourth Northwestern University Music Education Leadership Seminar (NUMELS-IV), a former student admitted that she lied at her postgraduate audition when asked what music she listened to, listing only the classical music that she thought would be expected. Some have suggested that conductors of choirs, orchestras, and bands in U.S. schools fear a loss of face and status if they engage with popular culture. Others note that many such individuals are already doing so informally without such a danger and with great success in schools across the country. There is evidence, for example, that large segments of the Christian church in the U.S. are already espousing the musical language and outward vestiges of pop with great success, and choir directors in both churches and schools are often the same people.

A Transatlantic Perspective

Roger Scruton's most recent book, *The Aesthetics of Music*, states that recent popular music is hardly fit to be granted the status of music and clearly appears to be part of the ongoing struggle left over from the Piscean age that Tippett refers to.[5] Scruton's prolonged attack (both in the press and in a specially formed pressure group) on the proposed national curriculum for music in the U.K. in the early 1990s was a clear sign of an attitude toward hierarchies in art (and in life) that persists in some areas of British culture. Scruton called, unsuccessfully, for exclusive concentration on the study of Western classical traditions in the classroom. His attitude toward the two populist concerts, one "classical" and one "popular," in the gardens of Buckingham Palace at the recent 2002 Golden Jubilee celebrations may be speculated and no doubt is documented elsewhere.

In a recent article in the "Urbanities" section of *City Journal,* Scruton described his apprenticeship in popular music as being versed in the sentimental longing for a golden time, as in the music of Billy Mayerl, Horatio Nicholls, and Albert Ketelbey. This music, he writes, "was part of the family, played and sung with intense nostalgia on wedding anniversaries, birthdays, Christmases, and family visits. Every piece had an extramusical meaning, a nimbus of memory and idle tears."[6]

His dismay about popular culture at the end of the twentieth century, by contrast, is acute: "It is this very order that is threatened by the monsters of popular culture. Much modern pop is cheerless, and meant to be cheerless. But much of it is also a kind of negation of music, a dehumanizing of the spirit of song."[7] He accuses it of being "sentimental and idolatrous."[8] His answer is to return us all to the concert hall where "those with ears must guard them from the white noise of modern life; and exercise them only in private, or among those like minded listeners whom they encounter in the concert hall."[9] Scruton bewails the democratizing of society, which allows the freedom to buy and sell to all, and he presents a nostalgic view similar to that expressed in his strong opposition to the details of the music national curriculum.

His arguments there were for the enforced teaching of classical music, which he expressed as a canon based on the history of Western music including (if I remember it correctly) *The Ring* and Wagner's use of leitmotif for those pupils in grades 7 to 9.

Scruton's is not the transatlantic perspective upon which I wish to draw, since, in music education, as in other things, his views express that of a small elite. The development of music in our state schools has been, however, very different from what Scruton and others like him prefer. Enshrined in our national curriculum for music (and other subjects) is a philosophy of education that differs strongly from that of the independent schools with their strong links to the universities of Cambridge and Oxford, where Scruton now teaches.

Janet Hoskyns identifies three models of current European curriculum philosophy: the encyclopedic, the humanistic, and the naturalistic.[10] The first largely affects the way that education takes place in France and Italy, the second in Germany and in the independent schools of the U.K., and the third in U.K. state schools, Scandinavia, and the Low Countries. The three philosophies may be crudely summarized as based individually on knowledge, tradition, and process, respectively. The process (i.e., naturalistic) model arises from the work of Pestalozzi, Montessori, Froebel, Dewey, Vygotsky, and Bruner and underpins much of the current thinking of the English and Welsh national curriculums for music, which emphasize the direct experience of the student with facilitation and support from the teacher.

The curriculum in the U.S., including

music, in my observation, subscribes not to this third model but more nearly to the humanistic, tradition-based model. Early childhood education in the U.S., however, has recently shown strong signs of using a more naturalistic approach that emphasizes pupils making decisions and taking some responsibility for their own learning. Early childhood teachers are using High Scope and, more recently, Head Start methods to allow this to happen. In my observation, tradition is as strong in American middle and senior high schools music as it was in the Russian village of Stein and Bock's *Fiddler on the Roof* or Sondheim's Japan at the opening (but not the close) of *Pacific Overtures*. Band, chorus, and orchestra dominate, making the so-called "general music" courses unpopular with both pupils and teachers. My experience of this strong commitment in the U.S., enhanced as it has been by my attendance at the NUMELS-IV seminar, was founded some twenty-five years ago when I became the first British author to write for Silver Burdett and eventually became the principal coauthor of the unique Silver Burdett British Edition.

My observation is that the music education tradition in the U.S. continues the nineteenth-century practice of separating the composer from the performer. It tends to define musicality mainly in terms of performance and finds it difficult to handle notions of musicality outside musical practice on traditional instruments. Despite the U.S. being a cradle and home of Western popular culture in the twentieth century, electric guitars and drum kits (both American inventions) and electronic keyboards still do not largely figure in music

courses in U.S. higher education, especially those courses where teachers are trained. What has become clear to me in the recent discussions at the NUMELS-IV seminar is how much easier it appears to have been to develop and change things in the U.K. At the heart of this apparent ease lies the commitment to process as opposed to tradition. This may seem surprising coming from a monarchist country where we are all subjects and where our monarch occasionally drives around in an ancient gilded carriage.

Key International Issues in Aquarian Music Education

In *The Third Wave*, Toffler identified the nineteenth-century development of music in terms of factory development, proposing that the building of concert halls and the orchestras and bands they contained reflected the principles of the industrial development of bureaucratic offices divided into departments and coordinated by a managing director.[11] Music education was focused on standardization and testing devices, based on industrial models, in a variety of areas. These areas included instrumental performance, listening, and what was defined as "musical intelligence." By 1979, the personal computer was born, and the exponential changes that came with it are still happening today, a matter of considerable adjustment for many people. Life today is, however, dependent upon computers and their industrial big brothers, as technical and medical sciences venture into areas that were unthinkable only thirty years ago.

Home- and workplace-centered technology has fundamentally altered all our lives.

Access to knowledge, lifelong learning, and the tools of creativity is only just beginning to make a mark. More than ever before, the fact that schooling is only the first staging post in the life journey has come sharply into focus. New learning and the ability to adapt and change our skills throughout our lives is now paramount. Few of the younger readers of this chapter will be able to rely for the rest of their lives on maintaining those skills learned in their schooling in the same way that many of those of us of an older generation can.

These developments affect music education as much as they do any discipline. What rock musician Peter Gabriel has called the "juicy bits of music" are now readily available to anyone with an inquiring mind, a thirst for knowledge, and the ability and motivation to learn, relearn, and use a computer. As a discipline, music education is not confined to schools but extends to universities and conservatories, teacher training, adult education, the home, and increasingly into recreational and third-age (i.e., postretirement) learning.

Coming to terms with computer technology is a duty the government has laid on all teachers in the U.K., and there are now stringent requirements for trainee teachers to successfully acquire skills in information and communication technology. Indeed, the demand is enormous, and changes in statutory teacher-training courses have been draconian. In my last year as a teacher trainer, I was expected to put into force nearly five hundred new tests of competency in information and communications technology—and the requirement was first given in full only six months before the

completion of the training course! No exception is made for music specialist teachers. Students in many U.K. conservatories are currently expected to present their written work as word-processed files. Composers are expected to be fluent in the use of notation programs, and many must be conversant with sequencing and sound-generation software.

The job of a musician is rapidly changing in British society, and I also suspect in the U.S. and other countries. A new model of the new musician who needs diverse skills is emerging. It requires performers who function well in the recording studio and understand studio techniques but who also can communicate from the platform and work in education and the community. In addition, it has been estimated that 95 percent of all performers become teachers at some point in their career, whether they train for it or not. The ability to function in diverse musical styles and to work from nontraditional notations and by ear are now becoming essential professional skills for practicing musicians who want to continue to work in the media and do session work. Even live performance in certain circumstances now requires multitasking. There are currently signs that improvisation and creativity are returning to the conservatory performance curriculum, having been almost lost in most instrumental disciplines for about 150 years. A new emphasis on musical diversity has entered the field of musicology. In a recent book called *Music: A Very Short Introduction,* Nicholas Cook, a university professor of music with a high reputation for established practice in musicology, writes, "We have inherited from the past a way of thinking about music that can-not do justice to the diversity of practices and experiences which that small word 'music,' signifies in today's world."[12]

The demands of new technology have very much affected the new musician. One large effect of the rise of personal comput-er–based techniques in music is the switch from high-level skills in notation reading and interpretation to aurally based skills of memory and discrimination. Notation is rapidly becoming just one method of music preservation that produces certain results in certain types of music and has no func-tion in others. The computer is also giving rise to the "third-wave musician" who has no traditional musical instrument perform-ance skills, neither reads nor writes musical notation, but can invent and perform new music that communicates directly with its audience through recorded or live presen-tation. Traditional musical instruments themselves are, after all, merely older tech-nology. The skills such music-technology-based musicians need are only just begin-ning to be quantified by forward-looking higher-education academics in the U.K., such as Norton York at Westminster University (www.wmin.ac.uk) and Geoff Smith at Bath Spa University College (g.smith@bathspa.ac.uk).

U.K. Experience in Teaching through Vernacular Musics

Teaching through vernacular musics in U.K. schools is not an issue. We have done it for years, and it appears to be reasonably successful. I found myself at the Innsbruck ISME Conference in 1986 with a high school rock band in tow—its members were ready,

able, and willing to invent music before a live audience and play the results by the end of the week. I document this experience in my article "Music As I See It."[13]

There has been a long history in the U.K. of textbooks and research papers on teach-ing music through popular music. These include the work of Keith Swanwick, John Farmer, James Vulliamy, Edward Lee, and many others. Rock School was founded in the 1980s (www.rockchallenge.co.uk and www.rockschool.co.uk), and the national curriculum clearly gives guidance for the inclusion of popular music in the classroom at all ages and stages. This has been spelled out as practice in such texts as Pratt and Stephens' *Teaching Music in the National Curriculum.*[14] Lucy Green's recent work, *How Popular Musicians Learn,*[15] was featured as one of the three recent seminar presenta-tions at NUMELS-IV in Evanston. Since all classroom music in our state schools would be defined as "general music" in U.S. schools, including popular musics is just not a problem for us now. However, what I learned when I was trained as a teacher in the early 1960s, and what I passed on to my trainees for many years, was an attitude that said that while the Beatles and all that are interesting and fun, there is too much seri-ous work to be done to spend time on that in school. At the time, I could not see this as an inherent problem of elitism but could only express myself through that which I had inherited and fought for in an educa-tional climate in the early 1950s that did not provide much in the way of music education for me. As a young teacher, I found it hard to accept that both Western classical and popular music mattered and were different faces of a multifaceted art form that interconnected in a way that even professors of music like Wilfred Mellers at York University were explaining to my then deaf ears.

However, I am of the generation mentioned by Scruton: a product of the time before the pop explosion. For my generation, the sentimental "Down in the Glen" and "Slow Boat to China" rubbed up against Glenn Miller's masterful "In the Mood" and "Moonlight Serenade," the characterful "Ghost Riders in the Sky" and "Wild Goose," and the more proletariat "I've Got a Luvverly Bunch of Coconuts" or "Close the Door, They're Coming through the Window!" By the time Lonnie Donnegan, Tommy Steele, and Cliff Richards came on the scene and the first imported wave of Bill Haley and Elvis records became central to the emergent youth culture, I had already committed to the classical tradition. Indeed, I fought in my corner for years, and many teachers my age will have had something of the same experience. Jazz was fashionable in student quarters in the late 1950s, especially in Oxbridge, but it was considered an alternative art form and is still not what we now define as pop music. Such students became the teachers of the postwar generation, and we worked with pupils of secondary age who were hearing the Beatles for the first time. Our students took the full brunt of the pop-culture explosion, and it took a while for things to change. My conversion took place through my children and through meeting and observing Peter Gabriel at work, a privilege that fundamentally changed my attitudes and forced me to learn many new things and relearn many others.

However, a debate soon started that is well-documented in histories of music education in the U.K.[16] Gradually, the practice of mixing pop with classical music as musical examples and the basis for classroom performance became common. A few teachers took a radical position of using nearly all pop music, defining "popular" in its broadest sense—to include light music and what is now defined as easy listening. However, two things accelerated this practice. First, the introduction of and delight in the use of examples from traditional musics all over the world in the 1970s and 1980s brought about a return to an emphasis on orally/aurally transmitted music. Secondly, the growth of the practice of composing in the classroom and the introduction of computers and MIDI-based software in the 1980s and 1990s finally made teaching the processes of music in the classroom a reality.

There were problems in using popular music, none greater than the issue of a mature person trying to identify with a new art form that was specifically aimed at and consumed by a young generation—one that is getting younger every year. However, we have been at the game now for forty years, and this is becoming less of a problem since the teenagers at whom the first pop music was aimed have now become respected teachers, carrying the music of their youth with them. It does, however, bring a further problem of teachers imagining that curriculums based on music of their youth will be appropriate to the classrooms of today. Fortunately, the U.K. has largely avoided the "histories-of" approach except where history is heavily built into the art form, as with the blues. Avoiding the listings and the invention of a canon that the "histories-of" approach inevitably spawns is something the teachers in the U.S. might consider.

There are two more serious problems that have to be addressed and for which there are no easy answers. Philosopher Ted Gracyk, in his talk given at the NUMELS-IV seminar, stated:

> There is a real danger in a curriculum on popular culture. Because of the identity and living function of the music it is very difficult to decide on the choices you make. Not the problem of a canon but more—unless they are extremely provocative choices—of finding a common level of experience. Next, the more contemporary a piece you choose, the more you create a problem of identity investment, and this polarizes the students you are trying to engage.[17]

Subcultures and lifestyles can vary enormously within a classroom, indeed just within families of teenagers and young adults. The pull of these identities is so strong that it can become difficult for the teacher to separate them from musical issues. For this reason, I used to encourage student teachers to avoid using current music, except when there was a clear musical purpose. Even then, half the class can "switch off" and become disruptive merely as an automatic reaction.

Using music of more than three years ago avoids the problem but sidesteps the issue of providing an education that helps students evaluate their own world and look to the future. But as soon as the processes of music become central to the curriculum and teachers become both comfortable with and competent at the teaching of composing, things begin to change. Although a certain amount of modeling and pastiche can be helpful in teaching composing, there soon comes a point where pupils must choose the style and the type of expression through which to express themselves. Inevitably, many students choose current vernacular styles, although our experience in the U.K. is that they actually choose quite a wide variety of areas. This is especially true when they are lucky enough to have a good teacher who is able to respond to and encourage their individuality and provide dynamic input. Even the pop world itself is becoming increasingly diverse and splintered.

Sooner or later the issue of appropriateness and morality will raise itself. The tag "sex, drugs, and rock and roll" certainly applies to pop music. Teachers are now faced with difficult issues of what to censor and what to encourage, what to ban outright and what to tolerate. This is a serious issue but not an issue that is unapparent throughout all teaching in schools today. In the past, music teachers have been able to bypass some of the heavier proscriptions for social education that other subjects in the U.K. curriculum, such as religious and moral education, must carry. Drama teachers have to tackle the issues of drugs, for instance, head-on, since their methods often include improvisation, drawing on their pupils' experiences and highlighting contemporary issues, and there has to be a school policy to which teachers adhere. Music teaching now must deal with these kinds of issues as it incorporates music that helps it more strongly make connections with the street that music education has sorely lacked in the past.

A New Curriculum Philosophy?

The approach to the curriculum identified as "naturalistic" or, in my terms, "process-based" is evolving rapidly as teachers become more experienced and a new, more complex model is emerging in the best U.K. classrooms. At the center of this new approach is process. But process is the driver rather than the goal. It is easy to recognize that process alone is not enough to provide motivation. Further, it is very difficult actually to teach process itself since the focus is entirely on the individual pupil, though our classrooms regularly have two dozen or more pupils. Not that this is impossible—ask any early childhood specialist or any good art teacher and they will soon show you how to care for and cater to twenty to thirty individuals in a common classroom environment. The genesis of music technology has enhanced these possibilities enormously. Of course, band teachers in the U.S. can also do this, and they use similar techniques, except that the individual's development is more tightly channeled along set instrumental and vocal pathways.

Knowledge, experience of traditional models, and technical information all have their place in our classrooms. None have been thrown out in the acceptance of process at the heart of our curriculums. The trick is to know when to apply which and to understand what techniques or methods will best achieve goals without losing sight of the overall driving need of process. It is human to need the spur of a goal and the pride from a product created and shared. The tension between process and product generates positive energy. Indeed, if process is all pupils experience and there is no identifiable payoff, they soon opt out. Our educational system demands both social and academic payoffs. Parents need to be able to applaud their talented children at concerts, and pupils need to feel good about themselves and gain formal academic credit for their work. So any work, including popular musics, must be able to be part of both of these systems, as it is in the current examination system in our schools.

Key Principles in Teaching Music through Popular Musics in England

The following advice was presented to trainee students studying through the Open University by using distance learning materials, including television and radio, as well as printed materials. Gary Spruce, Director of the Post Graduate Certificate of Education (Secondary Music) program for the Open University, recently wrote the following excellent guidelines on using popular musics in secondary schools:

- It (popular musics) should be considered as a vital part of the music curriculum to which *all* children have access and with which all children are encouraged to learn.
- It should be fully integrated into the music curriculum and not isolated into modules or units on which it appears unrelated to other musics.
- Negative messages about its relative value *vis-à-vis* other musics should not be articulated, either overtly or subliminally.

- It should be part of a range of music of different styles and cultures which children develop an awareness of, through performing, composing, listening and appraising.
- Children should be taught *through* the use of popular musics and not simply *about* popular musics.
- Children should be enabled to develop specific and particular criteria that might be employed in evaluating pop music.
- Children need to develop an awareness of the distinction between musical and extra-musical criteria, how these impact upon each other, and how they specifically relate to pop music.[18]

I believe that this summary will demonstrate most clearly to U.S. readers the difference between our attitudes and systems. Such a set of principles would be difficult to put into practice in a band, orchestra, or choir. Schools in the U.K. commonly have orchestras, bands of many descriptions—including swing bands, big bands, steel bands, samba bands—and a multiplicity of choirs—show choirs, madrigal groups, and so on. The majority of this work goes on within the school but outside the classroom. As an important adjunct to this work, each local education authority provides its own music services that function in liaison with the schools providing instrumental tuition in schools as well as regular large and small instrumental and vocal ensemble work within the community. These so-called county youth bands, choirs, and orchestras achieve startling standards and regularly give concerts at premium venues, such as the Festival Hall and Royal Albert Hall in London, Symphony Hall in Birmingham, and the Bridgewater Hall in Manchester. There are also privately run national paral-

lel groups that achieve broadcast standards and tour nationally and internationally.

Although few teachers would recognize or admit it, since complaining to each other about ourselves is a national pastime (Australians will always describe the English as "whingin' Poms"!), music teachers in England most likely have some of the best opportunities for achieving the educational aims set out above while achieving high musical standards. Through my knowledge and observation of schools over many years in the U.K. and other countries, I stand by this claim in the face of recent research programs that have suggested that current practice is less than ideal. Our instrumental music services that employ instrumental music teachers who provide tuition in schools have recently had a renaissance and are becoming very aware of the basics of music education and the ways that such instrumental music teachers can best connect with the classroom and its curriculum. Currently the development of special focus schools, many of them featuring the arts, is of interest as well as some concern as to their effect on music education in schools that do not specialize in the arts.

To demonstrate more clearly to teachers outside the U.K. exactly how music teaching works in the U.K., I will present some extracts from official documents currently in use. The overall national curriculum document for music, which carries statutory status in our schools, includes the following statement about secondary school music:

> During key stage 3 [ages 11 to 14] pupils deepen and extend their own musical interests and skills. They perform and compose music in different styles with

increasing understanding of musical devices, processes and contextual influences. They work individually and in groups of different sizes and become increasingly aware of different roles and contributions of each member of the group. They actively explore specific genres, styles and traditions from different times and cultures with increasing ability to discriminate, think critically and make connections between different areas of knowledge.[19]

There is no mention here of either popular or classical music. Indeed, throughout most of the published materials, popular music is only obliquely mentioned and never as a special issue. So, for instance, under "Knowledge, Skills, and Understanding," it is recommended that pupils be taught music through

> a. a range of musical activities that integrate performing, composing and appraising
> b. responding to a range of musical and nonmusical starting points
> c. working on their own, in groups of different sizes and as a class
> d. using ICT to create, manipulate and refine sounds
> e. a range of live and recorded music from different times and cultures including music from the British Isles, the "Western classical" tradition, folk, jazz and popular genres, and by well-known composers and performers.[20]

At the National Standards Web site, teachers can find examples of classroom units of work. The following is for Year 8:

Hooks & Riffs (Exploring riffs, hooks and grounds and the use of music technology)

This unit develops pupils' ability to iden-

tify, explore and make creative use of given musical devices to create an intended effect.

During this unit, pupils recognise and understand how composers use repeated melodic and rhythmic devices called riffs, hooks and grounds. They explore riffs, hooks and grounds through performing and composing, and consider the effect of using these in popular music. Pupils also learn how hooks and riffs can be created and manipulated using music technology, particularly through the use of sequencers.[21]

This example for Year 9 is on Music and Media (exploring how music is used):

> *Exploration: what effects can music create*
> • Ask pupils to brainstorm ideas in response to the question *Where do you hear music?* Answers will include a variety of media and places, *e.g. television, radio, films, shops, aeroplanes.* Explore the purpose of such music through questions, *e.g. Why is it there? What is it trying to achieve? How does it make you feel? How does it affect your interpretation of a linked visual image/situation? Does the music ever conflict with the image?*
> • Sing a range of songs used in the media and discuss why they have been chosen.[22]

How Do You Make Horses Thirsty?

A thirst for knowledge is the greatest outcome of any curriculum and teaching process. Since education is a lifelong process, we need to be able to engage in self-education throughout life. I believe that music educators (maybe all educators) tend to overestimate the role they play in their students' development. School is just one part of life for students, however essential.

The principle of students taking charge of their own learning process has never been more important to the development of our societies than it is right now. Whether it is learning how to use a new piece of information-technology-based equipment through reading the manual (a challenge to all but the best learners) or learning a new language, new workplace skills, or new leisure interests, the learning process far outweighs the teaching process in importance. We have to believe in the enormous capacity of the human psyche to develop and take on more tasks, often at the same time. This applies to students and teachers alike. Multitasking is a contemporary phenomenon and will increase in necessity in our lives. Teaching music as a process while assuring technical competence, knowledge, and experience of traditional models is a highly complex multitasking technique. Never in the short history of mass music education have teachers been required to do so many things at once.

Music specialists can, however, devise the most tightly packed curriculums that are full of good things, only to find them rejected by their pupils. The greatest problem for teachers is to get their student "horses" to drink at the educational fountains they have provided. A member of the NUMELS-IV seminar commented, "If we taught sex education like we teach music education, there would be no need for birth control." If the net result of all that instrumental, vocal, and classroom teaching is that the students put away such childish things, never open up their instrument cases after their early teenage years, and listen all the time to "aural candyfloss," then questions

must be asked and research is called for.

Learning is a messy business, and teaching always tries to impose order on it. What has gone before is much easier to frame and present than what is, but the bridge from the academy to the street allows two-way traffic. What we are learning through music is something about ourselves and how we relate to others. We observe and, to some extent, experience similarity and difference, value and worthlessness through our chosen study, which is founded in sound and our perception of sound patterns in time and their meanings.

If we must order information into histories (and we do) then perhaps we might consider Nicholas Cook's vision that we might "replace the orderly chronologies of the textbooks with an elaborate criss-crossing of influences and reminiscences as music leapfrogs from one era to another, from one corner of the globe to the opposite, or from 'high' art to 'low' art and back again."[23] This description eloquently describes an aspect of the best kind of process teaching that we are currently trying to encourage through our national curriculum. Its postmodern position is obvious.

Cook points out elsewhere in his book that the national curriculum for music doesn't really go far enough and tends to end up "perpetuating the very distinctions it was designed to erase."[24] We music educators in the U.K. have certainly not gotten it all right by any means. I am nowhere near convinced of our overall success in music education in the U.K. nor do I have any proof that the system we use in the U.K. is any more effective in the long run than that of any other country. Peace hardly guides our planet, nor love our stars. Criticisms abound, and teachers find it hard to live up to the demands of their tasks with shrinking human resources and ever-growing expectations. I am certain that we face the problem of short-term rejection of their education by many of our pupils as much as teachers do in any country, although a recent survey suggested that 53 percent of students selecting music as their specialist study at age sixteen and up compose music for pleasure outside school. I see that as a significant gain. However, I do know that the issue of how we should introduce popular music into our curriculum is not really an issue with us, and this was the focus of the stimulating seminar in Evanston in June 2002.

Notes

1. Michael Tippett, *Moving Into Aquarius* (London: Routledge and Paul, 1959), 35.
2. Ibid., 36.
3. Alvin Toffler, *Future Shock* (New York: Random House, 1970).
4. Alvin Toffler, *The Third Wave* (New York: Morrow, 1980).
5. Roger Scruton, *The Aesthetics of Music* (Oxford: Oxford University Press, 1997).
6. Roger Scruton, "Kitsch and the Modern Predicament" *City Journal* 9, no. 1 (1999): 82.
7. Scruton, *The Aesthetics of Music*, 504.
8. Ibid, 506.
9. Ibid, 470.
10. Janet Hoskyns, "Music Education in a European Dimension," in *Teaching Music,* ed. Gary Spruce (London: Routledge, 1996), 144–51.
11. Toffler, *The Third Wave.*
12. Nicholas Cook, *Music: A Very Short Intro-duction* (Oxford: Oxford University Press, 1998), 14.
13. George Odam, "Music As I See It," in *Teaching Music,* 185–87.
14. George Pratt and John Stephens, eds.,

Teaching Music in the National Curriculum (Oxford: Heinemann, 1995).
15. Lucy Green, *How Popular Musicians Learn* (Aldershot, UK: Ashgate, 2002).
16. See, for example, Charles Plummeridge, *Music Education in Theory and Practice* (London: Falmer, 1991).
17. Theodore Gracyk, "Three Myths and Six Truths about Popular Music" (presentation at the 2002 Northwestern University Music Education Leadership Seminar, Evanston, IL, June 2002).
18. Gary Spruce, Flexible ITT Course Materials (Music) (Milton Keynes, UK: Open University, 2002).
19. *The National Curriculum Online.* (London: Qualifications and Curriulum Authority, n.d.[cited September 2002]); available at www.nc.uk.net
20. Ibid.
21. Department of Education and Skills, *The Standards Site* (Norwich, England: 1997–2003 [cited September 2002]), quoting Qualifications and Curriculum Authority, "Schemes of Work" (London: QCA, n.d.); available at www.standards.dfes.gov.uk/schemes2/secondary_music/mus10/
22. Ibid.; available at www.standards.dfes.gov.uk/schemes2/secondary_music/mus13/13q2?view=get
23. Nicholas Cook, *Music: A Very Short Introduction,* 79.
24. Ibid.

Currently research fellow in teaching and learning at Guildhall School of Music and Drama in London, **George Odam** was previously professor of music education at Bath Spa University College. A composer, writer, and lecturer, his published programs of material for school music are used extensively in the U.K.

8

Reciprocity and Exchange: Popular Music in Australian Secondary Schools

Kathryn L. Wemyss

The relationship between popular music and the social context from which it springs has been the source of much discussion.[1] Eyerman and Jamison highlight the reciprocal nature of this relationship not only by acknowledging popular music's tendency to reflect and comment on social movements but also by ascribing to it the ability to galvanize and mobilize such events. They have described social movements as simultaneously "providing a broader political and historical context for cultural expression, and offering, in turn, the resources of culture—traditions, music, artistic expression—to the action repertoires of political struggle."[2] Perhaps two of the most obvious examples of this hail from the peace and Civil Rights movements of the 1960s in the U.S. The antiwar commentary of Bob Dylan and the use of reinvented spirituals and popular songs during race-related protests and sit-ins not only were influenced by social concerns in terms of their lyrical content but also became collective experiences and motivators of social action.

Similarly, the relationship between popular music and systemic education is one of interface and interaction. Confrontation between the two cultural contexts, education and popular music, necessitates transformation as the school becomes a site of reciprocal exchange. Popular music, by its nature, may not be immediately compatible with the existing structures that are based on Western educational and art-music tradition. As such, it challenges the philosophical bases of classroom practice and necessitates adaptation in a wide variety of pedagogical areas, such as the priority of particular content, the nature of learning outcomes pursued, and the types of methodologies adopted. There has been some recognition of the benefits of using learning strategies of popular music culture in systemic education.[3] However, the very act of including popular music content necessitates change.[4]

Comte states that "curricular development can initiate or originate from school practice."[5] Such is the case when considering the place of popular music within Australian education. Since the 1970s when popular music was first included in the music curricula of secondary schools, there has been reciprocal exchange between the two cultures. Not only have Western educational and art-music structures sought to deepen understanding of popular music repertoire, but methods and content inherent to popular music practice have permeated Western educational structures and helped broaden understanding of a broad palate of music.

The Structure of Music Education in Australia

In order to understand the current use of popular music in Australian schools, it is necessary to examine pertinent music curriculum and policy documents. This is not an altogether straightforward task because, while the federal government oversees Australian education,[6] the individual state and territory governments control curricular development and the management of staff and resources. Australia consists of six federated states (Queensland, New South Wales, Victoria, Tasmania, South Australia, and Western Australia) and two territories (Australian Capital Territory and Northern Territory), each having a distinct education system with diverse school entry and exit levels, conceptualizations of music and music education, and accompanying syllabus documents.

Generally speaking, after what is variously named a "kindergarten," "preschool," or "transition" year, students enter their primary (elementary) schooling at the age of five or six for a duration of approximately six years. At around the age of twelve, students begin three or four years of compulsory secondary school (junior high)

education, after which there is an optional two years of senior secondary schooling ending at approximately age eighteen.

As far as music is concerned, classroom-based music lessons are mandatory throughout primary schooling and through at least part, and sometimes all, of the junior secondary years. In the junior secondary school, there is also the opportunity to study music at a deeper level (as an "elective" or "extension"). Students may pursue these elective options after completing or along with the mandatory classes, depending on the state and territory policy and, often, the desire and resources of individual schools. In the senior secondary years, students may continue with more specialized musical study as an elective. At this level, there is a great deal of choice of the type of course available. Many schools, both at primary and secondary level, offer the opportunity to participate in band, orchestra, chorus, and an instrumental program. These, by and large, however, operate as extracurricular or cocurricular programs rather than as the heart of the music program and the basis of academic credit, as is the case in many other parts of the world, such as the U.S.

A Historical Perspective

As a result of colonial history, early Australian education was modeled on the British system.[7] From the 1850s, singing classes were held in schools specializing in Hullah's fixed-*do* and later Curwen's movable-*do* systems.[8] In fact, up until the 1950s, music in school was virtually restricted to singing. It was both "on the periphery of school curricula" and "neglected in a majority of schools."[9]

It is interesting that during this early period of music education history, the first evidence of the use of popular music of the day functioned as a barometer of social class. Weiss notes that around the turn of the twentieth century popular songs such as "Old Folks at Home," "Daisy Darling," "Welcome to the Morning," and "Laughing is Contagious" were used in South Australia, where eight public schools participated in the "Public Schools Floral and Decoration Society Concerts." This content was "designed to inculcate fairly positive qualities in working class students and presumably to appeal to their uncultivated tastes."[10] In contrast, the repertoire of the 1870 concert of St. Peter's Boys College, an exclusive private boys school in Adelaide, consisted entirely of "classical works except for the closing item, the School Song."[11]

In analyzing more recent history of arts education in Australia, Comte has suggested that the arts have been chronologically conceptualized in three ways: as "literature," "reproduction," and "composition."[12] From the mid-1950s, music became increasingly important in secondary schools and was approached as *literature*. As such, classroom lessons provided for singing, history, and appreciation by focusing exclusively on Western art music and historical events and composers. A greater importance was placed upon the acquisition of vocal and instrumental skills in the mid-1960s, which resulted in performance becoming the dominant educative vehicle. During this time, music was viewed primarily as *reproduction*. Bartle's 1967 survey of music education in Australian government schools notes that general music courses of that

time emphasized practical participation through singing and the use of instruments such as recorders, rhythmic percussion, and other instruments played or made by students. Creative activities were limited, the majority being formulaic or theoretically driven workbook exercises "tackled by relatively few teachers."[13] One recommendation arising from the survey was for teachers to "examine the vast possibilities in creative music making ... and that they devise means of allowing this to assume a much more prominent position in class work."[14] As a result, the role of creativity was gradually given more credence in Australian music, leading to an era where music was viewed as *composition*.[15]

There is some evidence of the use of popular music repertoire and ensembles at the time of Bartle's survey. Not only were "songs with popular appeal"[16] listed as part of the classroom repertoire that teachers were adopting but "folk-singing groups"[17] and guitar groups under the banner of "Light Music"[18] were also among the extracurricular group activities reported in schools. That the "folk-singing groups were organized by staff members or, more often, by students themselves"[19] led Bartle to be "struck by the numbers of children who organise their own small music groups. Most schools have their groups of guitar players and singers which have come into existence quite independently of any organizing authority."[20]

Bartle acknowledged the power of "the 'pop singer' or folk-song group" to motivate the participation of the students and indicates that perhaps early use of popular music in Australian schools originated from the students themselves:

Interest in music of this type is phenomenal as may be seen from the millions of recordings sold annually, by the jump in sales of record playing equipment and by the number of transistor radios that may be heard dispensing such music wherever young people are gathered. In this respect music is unique among the arts. Interest in architecture, sculpture, drama, literature or art may be on the increase but none of these has the power to be able to dictate the fashion and tastes of thousands of young folk.[21]

In 1977, the Australian Schools Commission conducted a study and concluded that "music in schools was not always relevant to the needs of the children"—a conclusion Lepherd explains with this comment:

It is probable that this criticism arose because of a tendency of music teachers to emphasise traditional art music to the exclusion of more modern music, ethnic musics and folk musics, much of which is arguably artistic and more relevant to the interests of modern children.[22]

As a result of the 1977 study, syllabi at this time began to include the study of popular music, reflecting the growing pervasiveness and availability of popular music in society and its relevance to students' tastes and interests. For instance, the New South Wales *School Certificate Syllabus in Non-Elective Music* stipulated that "class song repertoire may include: folk, traditional and popular songs from any countries; songs by classical and contemporary composers; songs for special occasions, such as assemblies; original songs composed in class creative activity"[23] and indicated that "contemporary pop music" and "music in

every day life"[24] may be appropriate topics for study. It was during this time, too, that many schools purchased guitars and other popular music instruments for use in the classroom, a practice that continues today.

The 1980s brought a time of reflection on the state of arts education in Australia, and there was some effort "to free secondary education from the stranglehold of the external examination system" allowing for more "flexible and 'relevant' arts curricula."[25] In this way, the needs and interests of individual students could be more easily satisfied and equity of access ensured. The New South Wales *Syllabus in Music Elective* states that music education must be characterized by the following:

Relevant, balanced and broadly based music programs which cater for the needs, interests and abilities of the students. Because music education is for all students and not just the chosen few, considerable program flexibility should be available. Programs must cater for students with particular needs and interests to pursue more specialised skills.[26]

The flexibility of this syllabus was obvious in two ways. First, it became more student-centered in allowing students to choose repertoire and instruments. And second, it afforded teachers greater flexibility in the topics that they could teach. While a wide range of topics were specified as appropriate, including "Pop Music" and "Music in the 20th Century," teachers were "free to add to the list" depending on the needs and interests of the students.[27]

The 1980s also allowed school music to be viewed as part of a wider educative and arts context. Since this time, music has been grouped with dance, drama, media, and visual arts under the heading the "arts" as one of the eight key learning areas to be adopted in schools nationally.[28] This legitimizes the "arts" as essential to the development of the student by placing it on equal footing with what may be considered the more "academic" subjects such as mathematics, science, and English. It also locks together the disciplines of dance, drama, media, music, and visual arts. While recognizing that these disciplines may perform similar functions, it acknowledges the unique character of each, allowing variety in the avenues of artistic expression and greater possibilities for cross curricular and "real-life" applications. For instance, it may be possible not only to compose, perform, and record popular music but also to design CD artwork and choreograph and film a video to accompany it. Thus, it enables a more holistic approach and positions music firmly within a wider context.

Current Music Education Trends in Australia

Currently, at both junior and senior secondary education levels, choice is a characteristic of Australian music syllabi, with freedom afforded "in topic selection, repertoires for study, methods of teaching and learning and combinations of types of assessment."[29] In this way, music education caters to the different needs, interests, and cultural backgrounds of students in the diverse society of twenty-first century Australia. Popular music courses and topics, repertoire, and instruments are featured as valid choices alongside a myriad of other

types of music and instruments, including those of more "traditional" Western art music. This is particularly important at the junior secondary level as all students must participate in a music class, and their interest level, musical skills, experiences, and capabilities may traverse a broad range.

Junior secondary music education is generally viewed as a direct continuation of that offered in the primary school.[30] Students pursue similar core content and are encouraged to achieve a greater understanding of the musical concepts or elements and acquire musical skills through active participation. This continuity between education levels is obvious in the framework-like structures recently adopted by most education departments. The syllabus in Victoria, for instance, provides the framework of learning for students from the preparatory year to year ten, the extent of compulsory schooling.[31] Similarly, the Western Australian document provides for arts experiences from kindergarten to year twelve.[32] In this way, there are clearly delineated overarching common features that allow for increasingly sophisticated understanding as students progress.

The framework approach to arts education is based upon student learning outcomes that are not directly associated with the chronological school years and so allow flexibility in assessment and planning. In the arts, they are stipulated by national government policy to be organized into three strands: "Creating, making and presenting," "Arts criticism and aesthetics," and "Past and present contexts."[33] Each of these "are interrelated and inform one another."[34] These strands are interpreted more specifically for music at state and territory level, using a variety of terminology. In Victoria, for instance, outcomes are placed in the categories "Arts practice—ideas, skills, techniques and processes" and "Responding to the arts—criticism, aesthetics and contexts."[35] In contrast, the syllabus in New South Wales groups outcomes under the headings "Performing," "Composing," "Listening: Past and Present Contexts," and "Listening: Arts Criticism and Aesthetics."[36] It describes the course as "study of the concepts of music through the learning experiences of performing, composing and listening within the context of a range of styles, periods and genres."[37]

What is immediately obvious in current junior secondary music education syllabi is that skills, processes, activities, and responses are emphasized over knowledge that is based on particular repertoire. This shift from a canonic approach, or "music as product," to one of "process" allows freedom to apply a variety of repertoire. In fact, variety of repertoire is a major focus of the junior syllabi, and there is concerted commitment to the study of contemporary and popular music. This supports the idea of popular music as part of a greater repertoire and of life and has served to break down the "unnecessary division between 'serious' and popular music."[38] The Tasmanian Junior Music Syllabus states that "music in education should reflect the ways music is used in society" and that "school is a microcosm of society, and if music is to offer something to all students, it is necessary to recognise music as it is in society, with all its genres, styles and purposes."[39]

At the junior secondary level, not only is popular music one of many repertoires through which students experience music, acquire skills and knowledge, and develop values, it may also form the basis of discrete topics of study. While mandatory courses allow for some study of specific topics, topic-based approaches are particularly common in the elective or extension streams of music study. Again, however, variety of repertoire is important. For example, the New South Wales Year 7–10 Additional Study Course stipulates that Australian music is a compulsory topic and one that may be continually revisited in various ways, whether it be through Australian Indigenous music, Australian popular music, or Australian art music.[40] There are also three categories of topics from which students must study equally. One category contains art-music topics based around the three major art-music periods (baroque, classical, and romantic). A second category offers such topics as "Traditional Music of a Culture" and lesser-known art music, such as "Medieval Music." The third offers "Popular Music," "Jazz," "Music for Radio Film and Television," and "Music for the Theatre after 1900." The draft version of the New South Wales syllabus currently in development for 2004 lists an even greater variety of topics allowing for popular music study: "Popular Music," "Rock Music," "Music and Technology," "World Music," and "Music for Small Ensembles."[41]

In the senior school years, music is offered as an elective, and it is at this level that external examination processes take place in many states and territories. As at the junior level, music courses require participation in a variety of musical activities in order to develop skills, aesthetic response, and conceptual and contextual understanding. At the senior level, however, a greater depth of contextual understanding is generally promoted, and students may be given the opportunity to specialize in performance, composition, or musicology. Popular music content may be incorporated as topics in existing flexible curriculum structures, as the basis of specialist courses, or through the study of instruments associated with popular music.

In incorporating popular music into existing senior secondary school curricula, many states and territories allow for elective topics such as popular music, rock music, and contemporary music. Existing courses have also been modified to allow study of popular music. Such is the case in New South Wales, where the New 2 Unit A Music Course was first implemented in 1978. The rationale stated that "the present structure of Music courses in the senior school pre-supposes a firm foundation of musical literacy and does not allow for a later development of interest in or aptitude for music."[42] This course forms the basis of what today is known as Music 1, a course where study of selected topics such as "An instrument and its repertoire," "Popular music," "Rock music," "Technology and its influence on music," "Music of the 20th and 21st centuries," and "Music for radio, film, television and multimedia" is possible.[43] As indicated in the syllabus, Music 1 allows students at the senior level with minimal music literacy and prior musical study to begin music study:

> The course provides students with
> opportunities to engage in a range of

musical styles, including contemporary popular music, and for many, it will serve as a pathway for further training and employment in the music industry or in contemporary music fields ... the curriculum structure is adaptable enough to meet the needs and interests of students with varying degrees of prior formal and informal learning in music.[44]

The course, therefore, gives students who approach music aurally or who have been self-taught greater access to music courses. Students who have interest in non-notated musics, such as popular music, frequent this course. These students previously would not necessarily be deemed appropriate for higher study in music.

In some states, senior school music curricula are modular in design, allowing for a great variety of courses to be offered and for students to tailor their courses individually. Such is the case in Tasmania, where students may select from a plethora of courses in popular music and related industries. Some of these are "Contemporary Music," "Audio Design," "Sound Reinforcement," and "Music Industry Studies."[45] Similarly, Queensland is currently piloting an "Arts in Practice" course that has a number of arts-related strands, including the Certificate in Music Industry. This course provides an opportunity for students to develop musical skills and knowledge while acquiring vocational certification. Core content for this course allows students to "develop and update music industry knowledge," "develop music knowledge and listening skills," "follow health, safety and security procedures in the music industry," and "work with others."[46] Through the Music Studies component course, there is also the opportunity to study in the areas of "Performance," "Music Management," "Sound Technology," and "Music Creation."[47] Essentially, the Arts in Practice syllabus "provides schools with the flexibility to cater not only for students with interests in the more technical aspects of the arts, but also for those with interests in the more performance-based and creative-based aspects."[48] Again, flexibility of course construction is of ultimate importance and is illustrated in the capacity to combine various components and arts strands in order to individualize pathways of study.

In most states or territories, performance may be the focus of study at the senior level, and this may include the study of instruments associated with popular music. The New South Wales Course 1 allows freedom of choice of instrument and repertoire as long as it is directly linked to the topics chosen for study. In contrast, the system in Queensland prescribes repertoire but allows for study of a variety of instruments. It lists drum kit, electric bass, synthesizer, contemporary popular keyboards, and contemporary popular guitar (electric and/or acoustic) alongside orchestral instruments as appropriate for study.[49] The repertoire suggested for contemporary popular guitar includes works by Lennon and McCartney, Joe Satriani, Tommy Emmanual, Eric Clapton, and the Red Hot Chilli Peppers.[50] Students may also select repertoire to examine, although this is subject to approval.

Issues Arising from Popular Music in Australian Secondary Schools

Since its introduction into Australian

secondary schools in the late 1970s, popular music repertoire has been included in syllabi in an ever widening variety of ways. In introducing this content, teachers have transformed the methods they use in their classroom practice. As noted by Dunbar-Hall, the problem is that "unlike art music, a developed and accepted teaching model for popular music does not exist."[51] Teachers have had to respond to the nature of popular music and develop strategies that are both appropriate to the genre and efficacious pedagogically. These new practices appear to encourage a broader concept of musicality while providing a much wider palate of teaching methodologies and ways of understanding music of all types in Australian schools.

The first challenge for teachers has been in incorporating more integrated learning experiences. While there is an obvious delineation of labor between the composer and performer in art music, popular music nullifies this division, as in many instances the performer also does the creating. Furthermore, as popular music usually exists in a hands-on, *in situ* format, listening, performance, and/or creative experiences tend to happen concurrently as the activity progresses. Learning, then, occurs contextually and meaningfully as students employ the problem-solving strategies that the repertoire itself demands. The resulting effects of these attributes on classroom practice have been varied. Popular musicians' more holistic approach to music means that teachers generally place less emphasis on workbook-type exercises, which isolate aspects of theoretical knowledge. Instead, they favor an integrated and constructivist approach, which promotes learning that progresses from the repertoire toward theory, rather than vice versa. Furthermore, the common practice of dividing lessons into separate compartments of "listening," "practical" or "performance," and "composition" activities makes less sense, and teachers tend to organize their lessons so that listening, creativity, and performance can occur simultaneously.

Another issue that teachers have had to consider since the introduction of popular music into the curriculum has been the use of creativity, as popular music has challenged more traditional ideas of what creativity is, how creative processes may occur, and who may be involved. The very nature of creativity and its resultant manifestations have been contested by popular music. As stated by Spencer, "the European tradition has tended to equate creativity with the specialised art of composition."[52] While composition plays an important role in popular music, particularly through the art of songwriting, the scope of what is considered creative activity has broadened considerably. For instance, popular music encourages a greater emphasis on both improvisation, a result of the common use of semi-improvised and improvised forms, and arrangement, an important creative skill in such tasks as generating stylistically unique cover versions. These activities, while present in the art-music tradition, assume a much larger and intrinsic role in popular music, and teachers are adopting these more often as a mode of learning in the classroom.

It is interesting to note that the broadening of the scope of creativity has had far-reaching effects, notably on syllabi development and in teacher training. In comparing the New South Wales *Music Years 7–10: Draft Syllabus*,[53] due for implementation in 2004, with the document it superseded,[54] improvisation plays a much greater role. While the earlier document merely lists improvisation as one of the creative activities to be developed, the later document singles it out as an area for greater explanation, stressing its importance "as a tool for developing knowledge, skills and understanding of a variety of aspects of music."[55] Teacher-training institutions, too, are responding to these changes. For example, the Sydney Conservatorium of Music, traditionally an art-music-focused institution, now incorporates improvisation training in its courses for prospective teachers.

Composition in popular music is most often represented in the art of songwriting, and many teachers incorporate this as an integral part of their music programs. In the classroom, songwriting may be approached in a variety of ways, ranging from a relatively free and individualized approach to a more structured cumulative group activity where one aspect is developed at a time (such as lyrics, chord progressions, bass lines, or guitar riffs), and a song is gradually "assembled." What is notable, however, is that popular songwriting seems to have little in common with traditional "pen-and-paper" approaches, and teachers have had to develop more appropriate strategies. Generally speaking, popular music seems to emphasize experimentation and so encourages teaching and learning strategies based on trial and error rather than more formulaic approaches driven by Western tonal harmonic systems. While more formulaic approaches tend to focus, at least initially, primarily on rhythmic and pitch elements, popular music provides earlier opportunities to focus on elements that are traditionally considered the domain of the more musically experienced, such as tone color and texture.

Technological advances have certainly enhanced these sonic possibilities. Students now have access to wider palates of sound than ever before. Using samples and MIDI technology, students can hear and manipulate a wide variety of sound sources they may not have had access to formerly. Technology has also given students the ability to edit and re-edit, layer sounds, perform in virtual time and listen in real time, subdivide, speed up and slow down their pieces, and notate their work. The individual ear and musical aesthetic sense drives the creative urge without being restricted by the need for substantial theoretical knowledge and instrumental and, most obviously, notational skills.

Unlike art music, then, where certain academic knowledge and skills have traditionally been regarded as prerequisites to composition, popular music more readily allows creative participation as it has been largely liberated from such knowledge and skills. The aural nature of popular music means that creative activity is more accessible to a greater number of students. Many popular music structures and forms, which are generally shorter, relatively "user-friendly," and not driven by complex Western harmonic tradition, also enhance popular music's accessibility. Whether it is the use of small cells of created material in a layering of textures in techno style, the creation of

ostinati as bass lines, the improvisation of a pentatonic pop melody, or the use of more complex popular song forms, popular music allows a greater number of students to participate in this important outlet of expression rather than being "the preserve of the gifted few."[56] Interestingly, this has been obvious in syllabus development. The first music syllabus published in New South Wales in 1956 regarded composition exclusively as the domain of "gifted students."[57] Current syllabi, however, require that all students compose; and assessment structures reflect this. In the junior secondary syllabus, for example, assessment in each of the learning experiences (listening, performing, and creating) is to be "evenly weighted."[58] In the senior school, all students, regardless of their area of specialization, submit compositions that contribute to at least part of their assessment.[59]

Another major challenge has come to teachers in the predominance of the aural experience in popular music, in contrast to Western art music, which essentially has a literate or notated tradition. Popular musicians appear to use their ears much more readily than their eyes, and much learning occurs through listening and copying, whether it be through using CDs to work out what particular artists have done in performance or in composition or through playing in the rehearsal room with their peers. This certainly is not to discount the value of notation to all types of music. It is a valuable skill for popular musicians and art musicians alike, and transcription is particularly useful for popular musicians. It does, however, indicate a swing in emphasis; the "sound before symbol" ideology is necessitated, as popular music source material often exists only in recorded form. Notably, popular music has encouraged a greater diversification in how notation or documentation may occur: aurally on CDs, DAT tapes, and computers and in alternative written notation systems such as chord charts, lead sheets, and guitar tablature. Again, technology has done much to advance this cause, not least in the development of notation software. The result for teachers has been a move to more aural approaches in study of all genres of music and an increased variety of documentation strategies.

Popular music also appears to have had some impact on the variety of learning structures used within the classroom. In addition to whole-class activities, there has been extensive use of small groups, collaborative strategies, and peer teaching, particularly when students emulate popular music ensembles or bands. In this format, decisions need to be made regarding who plays, parts need to be generated, and arrangements must be constructed following the typical pattern of how a band in the real world may rehearse. Students learn from each other as well as from the teacher. In contrast to this, highly individualized strategies may be used, particularly in composition, as students work on their own computer, at their own pace, on their own particular music project.

Popular music has also influenced the musical vocabulary used in classrooms. This has been felt in specific structural descriptions, such as in terminology of "riffs" and "hooks." More significantly, there has been increased attention to essential popular music concepts such as "feel" and "groove,"

and students and teachers communicate using associated appropriate vocabularies.

Perhaps the most fundamental challenges teachers have faced with the use of popular music in the curriculum originate in the underlying philosophical arena. The use of popular music has brought many questions in terms of the nature of the aesthetics of the art itself. It has questioned canonism and suggested alternate ways of understanding and knowing music. It has contested the idea of music as merely a product, suggesting that music is also the process behind it, a vehicle intrinsic to deeper understanding of music and a valuable avenue of self-expression. This focus on process has had great effect on classroom procedure and produced considerable challenges, particularly in developing appropriate teaching methods and modes of assessment. In assessing students, teachers apply a variety of strategies so that they can consider both product and process in gauging student progress. Process diaries, work samples, and peer and self assessment, all strategies intrinsic to popular music, now feature among assessment strategies teachers use, regardless of the genre of music.

In terms of the student, the use of popular music has challenged the notion of who is musical by questioning the inherent qualities of what constitutes a musical person and opening up a much wider range of possibilities. It has opened the way for a diverse range of manifestations of musical talent and, as a result, has necessarily led to a more flexible and student-centered, rather than content-centered, approach to teaching.

The incorporation of popular music has also challenged the role of the teacher. The vast range of skills and knowledge and the idea of the student as "expert" relegates the teacher to the role of facilitator, a fellow learner rather than a keeper of knowledge. Such education seeks to equip students with metacognitive skills to enable musical understanding. In the words of Small, this education reveals "to the pupils the quite simple fact that learning is not a preparation for life but a basic experience of life itself, and giving them confidence in their ability to learn whatever it is they wish to learn."[60] In this way it is anticipated that students will adapt their learning to a myriad of preferred repertoires and engage with music as a lifelong pursuit. Indeed, the use of popular music in schools appears to be having the desired effect. The external music examining body, the Australian Music Examination Board, has recently introduced Contemporary Popular Music syllabi and examinations. Furthermore, Hannan reported in the year 2000 that "at least 8 of the 37 universities in Australia are offering degrees servicing aspects of the popular music industry in Australia" and that "all the state Technical and Further Education (TAFE) providers offer programs at certificate, diploma and advanced level."[61]

With respect to the incorporation of popular music content in Australian secondary schools since the 1970s, the most obvious changes have occurred in the modification of curriculum content and may be illustrated by syllabi prescribing particular types of repertoire and skills to be developed. These modifications have been overt and instigated by policy. Change, however, has also occurred at a deeper level, as teachers have responded to the method-

ological challenges of dealing with such content. Inherent popular music approaches to integration, creativity, aurality, vocabulary, learning structures, and larger underlying philosophical questions have challenged teachers. Changes seem to have sprung from the actions and philosophies of the teachers themselves as they implement the specified content, rather than being driven by policy or executive personnel. Popular music, as was the case with Dylan's antiwar songs and the anthems of the sit-ins of the Civil Rights movement, seems once again able to mobilize change, albeit in another context. Most interestingly, many of the modifications made as a result of popular music being included in Australian secondary school music curricula have started to influence the ways other musics are taught. These new methodologies and ideas are being fed back into traditional Western art music and educational approaches and provide a greater variety of ways of understanding, experiencing, and knowing music.

Notes

1. See, for instance, R. Serge Denisoff, *Sing a Song of Social Significance,* 2nd ed. (Bowling Green, OH: Bowling Green State University Popular Press, 1983); R. Serge Denisoff and Richard A. Peterson, eds., *The Sounds of Social Change: Studies in Popular Culture* (Chicago: Rand McNally, 1972); Simon Frith, *Performing Rites: On the Value of Popular Music* (Cambridge: Harvard University Press, 1996); Philip Hayward, ed., *Widening the Horizon: Exoticism in Post-War Popular Music* (London: John Libbey, 1999); Greil Marcus, *Lipstick Traces: A Secret History of the Twentieth Century* (Cambridge: Harvard University Press, 1989); Greil Marcus, *Mystery Train,* 4th ed. (New York: Plume, 1991); Greil Marcus, *The Dustbin of History* (Cambridge:

Harvard University Press, 1995); and Greil Marcus, *Invisible Republic: Bob Dylan's Basement Tapes* (New York: Holt,1997).

2. Ron Eyerman and Andrew Jamison, *Music and Social Movements: Mobilizing Traditions in the Twentieth Century* (Cambridge: Cambridge University Press, 1998), 7.

3. See, for instance, Patricia Shehan Campbell, "Of Garage Bands and Song-Getting: The Musical Development of Young Rock Musicians," *Research Studies in Music Education,* no. 4 (1995): 12–20; Lucy Green, *How Popular Musicians Learn: A Way Ahead for Music Education* (Aldershot, England: Ashgate, 2001); David G. Hebert and Patricia Shehan Campbell, "Rock Music in American Schools: Positions and Practices Since the 1960s," *International Journal of Music Education,* no. 36 (2000): 14–22; and Kathryn Wemyss, "From T. I. to Tasmania: Australian Indigenous Popular Music in the Classroom," *Research Studies in Music Education,* no. 13 (1999): 28–39.

4. See Peter Dunbar-Hall and Kathryn Wemyss, "The Effects of the Study of Popular Music on Music Education," *International Journal of Music Education,* no. 36, (2000): 23–34.

5. Martin Comte, "The Arts in Australian Schools: The Past Fifty Years," *Australian Journal of Music Education,* no. 1 (1988): 112.

6. See, for instance, Curriculum Corporation, *A Statement on the Arts for Australian Schools* (Victoria, Australia: Curriculum Corporation, 1994); and Curriculum Corporation, *The Arts: A Curriculum Profile for Australian Schools* (Victoria, Australia: Curriculum Corporation, 1994).

7. Doreen Bridges, "Music in Australian Education: Origins and Backgrounds," *Australian Journal of Music Education,* no. 15 (1974): 11–13.

8. Laurence Lepherd, *Music Education in International Perspective: Australia* (Queensland, Australia: University of Southern Queensland Press, n.d.), 9.

9. Comte, "The Arts in Australian Schools," 111–12.

10. Gillian Weiss, "Fundamental or Frill? Music Education in Australian Schools since the 1880s," *Research Studies in Music Education,* no. 5 (1995): 58.

11. Ibid.

12. Comte, "The Arts in Australian Schools," 117.

13. Graham Bartle, *Music in Australian Schools* (Victoria, Australia: Australian Council for Educational Research, 1998), 238.

14. Ibid.

15. Comte, "The Arts in Australian Schools," 117.

16. Bartle, *Music in Australian Schools,* 125.

17. Ibid., 189.

18. Ibid., 193.

19. Ibid., 189.

20. Ibid., 4.

21. Ibid., 3.

22. Lepherd, *Music Education in International Perspective: Australia,* 79.

23. Secondary Schools Board, *School Certificate Syllabus in Non Elective Music* (New South Wales, Australia: Secondary Schools Board, n.d.), 5.

24. Ibid., 11.

25. Comte, "The Arts in Australian Schools," 116.

26. Secondary Schools Board, *Syllabus in Music Elective: Years 7–10* (New South Wales, Australia: Secondary Schools Board, 1986), iii.

27. Ibid., 11.

28. Gary McPherson and Peter Dunbar-Hall, "Chapter 2: Australia," in *Musical Development and Learning: The International Perspective,* ed. David J. Hargreaves and Adrian C. North (London: Continuum, 2001), 14–26.

29. Ibid., 15.

30. Lepherd, *Music Education in International Perspective: Australia.*

31. Victorian Curriculum and Assessment Authority, *Curriculum and Standards Framework II* [online document] (East Melbourne, Australia: Victorian Curriculum and Assessment Authority, 2001 [cited 22 January 2003]); available at www.vcaa.vic.edu.au/csfcd/home.htm.

32. Curriculum Council, *Curriculum Framework for Kindergarten to Year 12 Education in Western Australia* (Western Australia: Curriculum Council, 1998).

33. Curriculum Corporation, *A Statement on the Arts for Australian Schools* (Victoria Australia: Curriculum Corporation, 1994), 22.

34. Ibid., 12.

35. Victorian Curriculum and Assessment Authority, *Curriculum and Standards Framework II.*

36. Board of Studies, *Music Syllabus, Years 7–10: Mandatory Course and Additional Study Course* (New South Wales, Australia: Board of Studies, 1994), 4–5.

37. Ibid., 7.

38. Graham Vulliamy, "Definitions of Serious Music," in *Pop Music in School,* ed. Graham Vulliamy and Ed Lee (Cambridge: Cambridge University Press, 1976), 33.

39. Office for Curriculum, Leadership, and Learning, *The Arts: Music* [online document] (Tasmania, Australia: Government of Tasmania, n.d. [cited 22 January 2003]); available at www.discover.tased.edu.au/arts/music.htm.

40. Board of Studies, *Music Syllabus, Years 7–10: Mandatory Course and Additional Study Course.*

41. Board of Studies, *Music Years 7–10: Draft Syllabus* (New South Wales, Australia: Board of Studies, 2002), 37.

42. Board of Senior School Studies, *Music Syllabus Years 11 and 12: New 2 Unit A Course. Draft Document* (New South Wales, Australia: Board of Senior School Studies, 1977), 1.

43. Board of Studies, *Stage 6 Syllabus: Music 1* (New South Wales, Australia: Board of Studies, 1999), 1.

44. Ibid., 6.

45. Tasmanian Secondary Assessment Board, *All Current Syllabus Documents: Arts: Music* [online document] (Tasmania, Australia: Tasmanian Secondary Assessment Board, n.d. [cited 22 January, 2003]); available at www.tassab.tased.edu.au/0770/RND01.

46. Queensland Board of Senior Secondary School Studies, *Arts in Practice: Study Area Specification* (Brisbane, Australia: Queensland Board of Senior Secondary School Studies 2001), 9.

47. Ibid., 48–51.

48. Ibid., 2.

49. Board of Senior Secondary School Studies, *Appendix for the Senior Syllabus in Music Extension (Performance): Prescribed List of Notated Solo Works for Prepared Performance* (Queensland, Australia: Board of Senior Secondary School Studies, 1997), 1.

50. Ibid., 60–63.

51. Peter Dunbar-Hall, "An Etic and Emic Model for Teaching Popular Music," in *Association of Music Education Lecturers Proceedings of XIVth Annual Conference,* ed. Vanda Weidenbach and Jean Callaghan (Sydney, Australia: University of Western Sydney, 1993), 79.

52. Piers Spencer, "The Creative Possibilities of Pop" in *Pop Music in School,* ed. Graham Vulliamy and Ed Lee (Cambridge: Cambridge University Press, 1976), 98.

53. Board of Studies, *Music Years 7–10: Draft Syllabus.*

54. Board of Studies, *Music Syllabus, Years 7–10: Mandatory Course and Additional Study Course.*

55. Board of Studies, *Music Years 7–10: Draft Syllabus,* 25.

56. Spencer, "The Creative Possibilities of Pop," 98.

57. New South Wales Department of Education, *Syllabus in Music* (New South Wales, Australia: New South Wales Department of Education, 1956), 5.

58. Board of Studies, *Music Syllabus, Years 7–10: Mandatory Course and Additional Study Course,* 18.

59. See Board of Studies, *Stage 6 Syllabus: Music 1;* and Board of Studies, *Stage 6 Syllabus: Music 2 and Music Extension* (New South Wales, Australia: Board of Studies, 1999).

60. Christopher Small, *Music, Society, Education* (Hanover: Wesleyan University Press, 1996), 211.

61. Michael Hannan, "The Training of Contemporary Popular Musicians," *Music Forum, Journal of the Music Council of Australia* 7, no. 1 (2000): 18

Kathryn L. Wemyss is currently a lecturer in music education at the Sydney Conservatorium of Music and has previously held teaching positions in several Sydney schools. She has performed as a session trumpet player with some of Australia's premier performing artists, such as Midnight

Oil. She was cofounder of the Jackson
Code, who released five CDs and were twice
nominated for Australian Recording
Industry Awards. Her current band, Wemo,
released their eponymously titled debut CD
in March 2003. She presents at national and
international music education conferences
and holds graduate and postgraduate
degrees in music education, trumpet, and
voice, her major research areas being
Australian Indigenous education (music
and literature) and popular music.

Teacher Education Perspectives

9

Preparing Teachers for Popular Music Processes and Practices

Scott E. Emmons

When comparing the music teacher training I received twenty years ago with the training given to students today, I find many changes. Many music education curricula now include courses in American popular music, world music, and musical creativity (improvisation and composition). These subjects did not exist in my training. Unfortunately, I still find many similarities in curricula that make the knowledge of music teachers entering the profession today largely irrelevant. Even with the curricular changes of recent years, music teacher preparation courses address a very narrow range of literature from a small cultural perspective. Beginning teachers are well prepared to provide experiences in choir, band, orchestra, and general music from a Western European art tradition. This training alone, however, will not be enough to motivate the vast majority of students in today's schools. Many students in today's schools did not grow up listening with this cultural perspective. Music teacher training programs must identify the needs and interests of students and prepare teachers to overcome students' unique problems.

Only by doing this will we prepare teachers to experience the unique rewards found in music education.

School music must begin to reach a much broader range of students by representing music from many different styles. Bennett Reimer says:

> The key to our continuing relevance to the musical interests of those who choose to learn to be performers is not to abandon the excellent opportunities we have made available in bands, orchestras, and choruses, but to encourage and hasten the already existent movement toward adding a greater diversity of performance opportunities reflecting a more accurate representation of the musics thriving in contemporary American culture. This means much more than the (healthy) use of more small-group literature as related to the repertoires of bands, orchestras, and choruses. It means, also, an expansion of musical literatures far beyond those school-sanctioned styles to the diverse domains of popular styles and styles related to cultures from around the world.[1]

Children love to participate in music, both in and out of school. The music they most fully experience, however, is the music that they enjoy the most. Patricia Shehan Campbell says that children "choose music for which they have a special affinity and which suits their own particular personality and mood. They sing songs by modeling their favorite singers, and they play keyboard, guitars, and drums by listening, watching, and exploring their possibilities."[2] Music teachers must provide broader musical experiences for students, especially those who do not play a band or orchestra instrument or sing in a chorus. Many of these students would benefit from an alternative way of making music, such as performing on a guitar, keyboard, or bass or even experimenting with electronic composition.

Along with reaching a broader range of students, offering music ensembles and classes that use instruments commonly found in popular music will allow us to focus our attention on National Standards 3 and 4, the "creativity standards" of improvisation and composition. We commonly use creativity to justify music's place in schools. Frequently, however, in our traditional performance-based band, orchestra, and choir rehearsals, the only person allowed to make creative musical decisions is the teacher directing the ensemble. To meet the needs of current students as well as future generations, music teachers must rethink their roles. They must begin to meet the needs of students, not merely ensembles. Since music education is tied historically to ensemble performance, augmenting traditional offerings in order to serve different kinds of musical needs is a formidable challenge.

What is possible with popular music in our schools today? While it is easy for students to be interested in popular music, this music may not be easily institutionalized. How can popular music be included in our schools and still maintain its "popular" qualities, performance practices, and creative possibilities? The answer, I believe, lies in allowing students to make as many musical decisions as possible. Our role as music teachers in this environment becomes that of a facilitator or coach. Let us take a glimpse at a pilot program that focused on popular music in one suburban Milwaukee school.

Popular Music in the Schools—A Pilot Program

During the summer of 2000, one of my graduate students, a middle school band director, came to me with an idea for an independent study project. Her idea was to provide a location for rehearsals and instruction for students who wanted to start a rock band. This idea for an "institutionalized garage band" led to a four-month program, team-taught by the two of us, culminating in a performance at a February "pops" concert.

The first step in planning the curriculum for this project was to brainstorm what skills students needed to perform and create music in popular styles. We thought about the informal learning process many professional rock musicians follow as they master the skills they need to succeed. It seemed to us that most rock musicians begin by learning and performing "cover" tunes originally performed by their favorite artists. After learning songs by others, many pop musicians begin creating their own music, usually trying to emulate, at least at first, the music of their favorite performers or groups. Musicians need to develop many skills in this process. We determined that basic skills needed for students to succeed in performing and creating music in popular music styles include the following:

- playing instruments used in rock music (enough to allow for success with the literature performed)
- singing with good technique (both lead singing and harmony singing by ear)
- independently selecting, analyzing, interpreting, and developing the performance of music for personal use
- learning vocal and instrument parts from recordings without the aid of notation (record copy, discussed in more detail on page 170)
- improvising in popular music styles
- writing songs, including melodies, lyrics, and chord progressions (composition)
- developing instrumental accompaniments in the desired styles
- forming vocal/instrumental groups
- evaluating personal performances
- using sound-reinforcement equipment to enhance performance
- using recording technology to preserve songs and evaluate performances

We began in October by asking seventh- and eighth-grade band members, "Who plays a rock instrument and is interested in being in a band?" We then announced that we were going to open the band room for interested students two mornings a week before school for rehearsals and rock music coaching. This schedule was designed to complement the existing before-school jazz band program. During the next few weeks, two groups

emerged, one from the eighth-grade band and one from the seventh-grade band.

The students in the eighth-grade band—two guitarists, one keyboard player, one bass guitarist, and one drummer—approached us as a preexisting band. All of the students had taken, or were currently taking, private lessons on their instruments. They shared with us that they had "jammed" a few times at the drummer's house. We asked what they had been playing, and they listed several songs by some of their favorite groups. They also mentioned that they really wanted to learn enough songs so that they could perform for their friends. They also expressed a desire to begin working on their own original tunes.

The three students in seventh grade were all taking guitar lessons outside school. One guitar player said he was interested in learning bass guitar but did not have an instrument. We assured him that he could use the school-owned bass guitar as part of this program. The students also expressed concern that they did not yet have a drummer. At first, we solved this problem by using Band-in-a-Box computer software as a drum machine (with all the instruments except the drum turned off). Four weeks into the program, a percussionist in the seventh-grade band became excited about the band's progress and became the group's drummer.

In November, we began meeting with each group to discuss cover tunes they wanted to learn. We purchased the recordings for the students and helped them "record copy" the selections they chose. Patricia Shehan Campbell says:

As in the case of choosing exemplary works to represent lullabies or singing games, the same careful choices must be made to represent swing, rock and roll, 60s rock, soul, heavy metal, grunge, rap, doo-wop, and techno. Not just any piece will do, though, and those that do not offer a hearty taste of the best of the batch (or genre) are probably not worthy of children's time and attention.[3]

As much as possible, we attempted to follow the students' lead in selecting tunes. Occasionally students selected songs that demanded more technical achievement than what was possible in the time allotted. While students were not always interested or able to perform popular music of the highest quality, they did try to make choices based upon group discussions about quality. "Quality" for the students did not always match my views. Fortunately, the students chose material that would stretch their abilities yet seemed within their reach.

Lots of individual effort by the students, coaching from us, and help from the students' outside private teachers combined to produce success. Each band quickly transferred several cover tunes to their instruments and began working on the vocal parts. The eighth-grade band had a natural leader in one of the guitarists. The drummer and keyboard player quickly imitated harmony vocals found on the original recordings. Because of the group's interest and skill, the eighth-grade group quickly learned to perform "Say It Isn't So" by Bon Jovi and "Everything You Want" by Vertical Horizon.

Members of the seventh-grade band began performing songs by doubling lead vocals and leaving out the harmony parts. As they became more comfortable with

singing, two of the guitar players traded lead vocals and shared harmony vocals with the bass player. The seventh-grade students quickly learned to perform "All the Small Things" by Blink 182 and "Kryptonite" by 3 Doors Down.

As the students continued learning cover tunes, I presented several improvisation and songwriting clinics during the last part of their before-school sessions. The improvisation approach I used with students began with call-and-response exercises using a gradually expanding minor pentatonic scale over a twelve-bar blues background. The composition exercises, derived from my research, began with instructional strategies requiring students to compose their own songs based on the cover tunes we were learning. Our goal was to encourage students to perform their own compositions as soon as possible, so we used lessons and instructional strategies that allowed students to feel confident about their early efforts. These included limited-note, limited-function, and limited-form compositions. Giving the students a small number of choices provided success and motivation for students. As Stephen Nachmanovitch says, "structure ignites spontaneity."[4] As students gained confidence with their skills, we encouraged them to incorporate additional musical tools, such as harmonic functions or forms, into their work.

In my previous research, I found that students used nonlinear and nonsequential processes to complete their composition assignments.[5] The student behaviors I observed could be grouped into three categories: formation, preservation, and revision (see Figure 1).[6] The first category, "formation," includes exploration, improvisation, thematic selection, and rehearsal. Formation accounts for harmonic and melodic exploration that eventually leads to a selection of harmonic and melodic ideas. During the formation phase, I observed nonlinear and nonsequential behaviors that occurred throughout the creative process; they were not limited to the beginning of the process.

The second category of behaviors I observed was "preservation." In preservation, students actually notate or record their work. The third category of behaviors, "revision," is where students correct or refine their ideas. I observed behaviors in this category throughout the composition process. Students continually revised or corrected their work while notating or sequencing.

The work of the students in the Milwaukee project as they composed their original songs reinforced this model. The interplay between each category of behaviors was clear as they formed, revised, and preserved their work. Some students related better to harmonic approaches, while others related better to melodic approaches; thus, individual differences in student creative processes were permissible and highlighted. Students used cover tunes that they were learning as models for their compositions. Studying these models, especially the chord progressions used and the relationship between melody and harmony, increased the sophistication of the students' work.

Our teaching goal was to encourage student decision making. This created well-defined roles for the band director and myself. My role, because of my experience performing popular music, was that of guitar, drum, and bass coach; record-copy helper;

and improvisation and composition clinic presenter. The band director's role was that of equipment and room facilitator, ensemble coach, vocal arrangement assistant, and computer software instructor. As much as possible, we tried to get the students started with their work and then get out of the way. We then tried to answer questions and help students through difficult times when they could not determine chord progressions while record copying or in composing.

While working on creating their own originals, students used a collaborative approach common to rock musicians. One student typically came to rehearsal with a chord progression or riff that, through experimentation, quickly became expanded into a song. Occasionally, one of the eighth-grade students (the lead singer) came to rehearsal with a song nearly completed. The other band members then negotiated with him about the style or "feel" of the song. The collaborative approach the students in our project used closely resembles the approaches demonstrated by the rock bands Lucy Green examined in *How Popular Musicians Learn:*

> Amongst my sample, group composition occurred, usually by having one or two main songwriters who would come to the rehearsal with ideas which were then embellished to varying degrees by the other band members, such that everyone to some extent, provides an original contribution to the finished product.[7]

The collaborative approach Stephen Nachmanovitch describes is successful because "it's much easier to learn from someone else than from yourself. And

Figure 1

Model of the creative process of students composing music

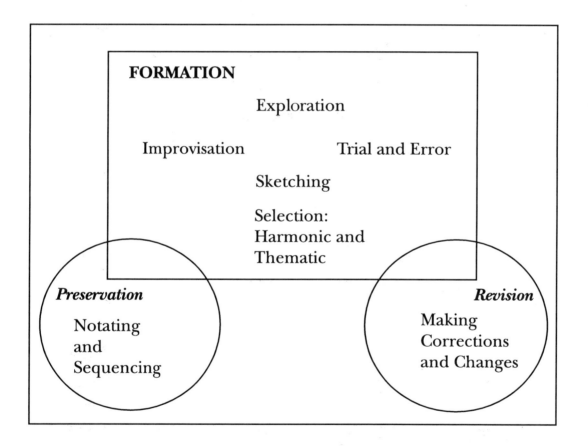

inertia, which is often a major block in solitary work, hardly exists."[8]

At the conclusion of our program, both groups were featured in the school's February "pops" concert. They were clearly the highlight of the evening for student and parent audience members. This performance was followed by several appearances by both bands at school dances and local YMCA band nights. At the time of this writing (two years after the program ended), two members of our eighth-grade band are still performing together at coffee houses and teen nights. The seventh-grade students, now a trio (guitar, bass, drums), have also continued to perform and have completed their first recording session of original works at a professional studio.

Understanding and Teaching Popular Music Styles

Music teachers must face many institutional challenges if they are, as Reimer says, to feature "an expansion of musical literatures far beyond those school-sanctioned styles."[9] One major problem is that many music teachers do not come from a musical environment that encourages popular music performance, experience, or informal listening. A woodwind player being prepared as a band director, for example, rarely has an opportunity to participate in popular music idioms. It is also common for public school and university music instructors to discourage participation, or even interest, in popular music. If music educators are to succeed in reaching the next generations of students by making connections with popular music, college music education curricula must feature

methods class experiences that provide students with popular music skills on par with their skills in "art" music.

Learning the Instruments of Popular Music

Music teacher preparation programs must broaden the list of instruments that students learn in their techniques classes to include guitar, bass guitar, drum set, and electric keyboard. Although many institutions provide some experience with these instruments, the techniques frequently taught do not provide the experience or knowledge needed for success with popular music. Guitar classes, for example, currently educate students in folk music accompaniment and simple melodic performance. This knowledge should be supplemented with skills in improvisation (especially minor pentatonic and blues scale), bar chords used in rock, and accompaniment styles used in today's popular music. Bass guitar experience, when offered in university methods classes, is typically limited to learning the instrument's first-position notes. This experience needs to be augmented with instruction on how to perform bass accompaniments while reading chord symbols. All music education majors would benefit from learning a few basic rock beats (e.g., the shuffle) on drum set. Keyboard experience should include functional experience in reading and playing from chord symbols. Reading standard notation from sheet music has minimal value in popular music.

Learning Improvisation for Popular Music

Most styles of popular music require more improvisation skill than is generally taught to music education majors. A few years ago, while presenting a workshop on implementing the National Standards, I asked the teachers to identify the Standards that they felt least prepared to teach. They overwhelmingly chose Standards 3 and 4—improvisation and composition. Stephen Nachmanovitch reminds us that "improvisation is the most natural and widespread form of music making."[10] The ability to improvise demonstrates an understanding of the workings of music. Until the past century, improvisation was believed to be an integral part of our literate Western musical tradition. Music history books are filled with accounts of musicians—including Leonardo da Vinci, Bach, Mozart, and Beethoven—impressing audiences with their abilities to improvise. During the late nineteenth and early twentieth centuries, however, Western art musicians were taught to trust the composer and the conductor. Many pianists were even told *not* to play by ear.

Today, skills in improvisation are again being viewed as important. Music education majors must be given strategies throughout their preparation that provide them the ability to give future students experiences creating music through improvisation. Unfortunately, we tend to provide only those students interested in performing jazz with a broad background in improvisation. This leads to the continuing myth that improvisation is mystical, something that only special or gifted individuals can do, or worse, that it is something stylistically connected to jazz alone.

Fortunately, students of any instrument or voice can learn improvisation. Several strategies exist to help music educators teach improvisation in their classrooms. The most basic of these, and one of the most important for teaching popular music styles, is to have students sing a harmony line to a given melody. This activity is similar to the informal activity that many of us have experienced in our cars while singing along with the radio. Another nonthreatening way of introducing methods students to improvisation is to perform a body-drum improvisation. Begin by having half of the class provide a steady beat (stomp, stomp, clap, rest—the famous "We Will Rock You" rhythm). Other students in the classroom can improvise rhythmic patterns to this beat by clapping hands and tapping thighs.

Limited-note pitch activities can be a good way to introduce improvisation to students. See Figure 2 for a sample lesson I have used successfully. Along with being important as a tool for teaching the theoretical nature of music, experience in improvisation is an essential component for providing students with the understanding needed for teaching popular music.

Learning to Compose Music

Most music education majors today have little experience composing in popular music styles. However, elementary and secondary general music methods classes provide fertile ground for such experiences. Beginning strategies for teaching composition should only use rhythm or a limited collection of tones. One activity that uses temporal elements alone is the rhythmic round. To begin, break students into small groups and have them complete these steps:

• Individually compose four measures of

Figure 2
Improvisation Lesson Plan

Objective
- Students will improvise variations to "C Jam Blues" by Duke Ellington.

Materials
- Printed handout with the melody for "C Jam Blues" in the key of E
- E Blues rhythm background using Band-in-a-Box (See handout for chord changes.)

Prior Knowledge and Experiences
- Students have sung and played on their instruments (soprano recorders or resonator bells) the notes of the E-minor pentatonic scale (E–G–A–B–D).
- Students have been taught the melody to "C Jam Blues." The melody uses two notes found in the minor pentatonic scale.

Procedures
1. Perform the melody of "C Jam Blues" as a group along with the computer's Band-in-a-Box rhythm background.
2. Start the background track. With good swing feel, model short "blues licks" for students (two to four notes maximum length) using the notes E and G. Have students echo them back immediately as a group in correct time to background music.
3. Do the above with a gradually expanding collection of notes. Add notes in this order: E–G–lower D–A–B.
4. Ask the students to improvise full choruses softly as a group to the background track using licks they learned in the above procedures.
5. Give students chances to improvise solos to entire choruses when they feel comfortable.

Indicators of Success
- Students will improvise short melodic "licks" and solos.

Follow-up
- Transfer the information learned above to other blues songs.
- Repeat the lesson with various background styles (both swing and "straight").

music in common time (use quarter, eighth, half, and dotted-half notes and their corresponding rests) appropriate for clapping.
• Combine these compositions into one longer work.
• Rehearse the composite rhythmic composition.
• Perform the rhythm composition as a round with each entrance beginning four measures apart.

An exercise for introducing composition using a limited number of notes is to assign students to complete a sixteen-measure piece using only the notes found in a pentatonic scale (for example, C–D–E–G–A). Another easy-to-master strategy may involve giving students beginnings of short melodies to complete. An instructor may give students the first phrase of a simple folk melody and ask them to create ending phrases.

Students in the Milwaukee project composed melodies using chord tones over chord progressions from songs they were analyzing. This activity led to discussions of how chord tones may be connected with nonharmonic material. Figure 3, another sample lesson, illustrates this approach.

An eighth-grade student completing the lesson in Figure 3 composed the song shown in Figure 4. It is noteworthy that the student attempted to use nonchord tones in his work, although they do not always occur on the weak beats as assigned.

Another valuable composition technique for university methods students to experience is the collaborative approach commonly used in popular music creation. Patricia Shehan Campbell has observed successes in elementary students composing collaboratively:

Figure 3
Composition Lesson Plan

Objective
• The learner will compose melodies over simple chord progressions.

Materials
• MIDI setup
• Musical examples
• Staff paper or notation software

Prior Knowledge and Experiences
• Students have listened to teacher-selected single-line melodies and discussed the harmonic function (using I–IV–V chords) implied by the melodies.

Procedures
1. Discuss single-line melodies with simple chordal (I–IV–V^7) accompaniment. Give special attention to use of nonchord tones, phrase structure, and form.
2. Compose melodies using chord tones to a teacher-provided I–IV–V chord progression.
3. Use connecting nonchord tones on weak beats.
4. Record, discuss, and revise compositions using MIDI equipment.

Indicators of Success
• Evaluation will be based upon class discussion and performance of the compositions.

Figure 4
Song One

Collaborative and cooperative learning works quite well in the music class, as children guide, stimulate, teach, and check each other on assignments in which they are engaged. The more expert musicians can lead the novices, as the less musically enriched children provide the more musically experienced with challenges for articulating and demonstrating what they know.[11]

Music education majors can benefit from using collaborative strategies. Activities might include group experimentation with a chord progression or riff until it expands into a song or experiences in rearranging a song by altering its "feel" or style.

Learning to "Record Copy"

The traditional way of learning someone else's song, in the popular music model, is to transcribe the song from the recording. At times, the transcriber actually writes down the music. Usually, however, the musicians simply memorize the music as it is repeatedly sung or performed on an instrument. They memorize the music by listening and repeatedly performing it along with a recording. This skill of "record copying" is valuable in the university for providing opportunities for student musicians to apply their skills in ear training and analysis and in instrumental and vocal technique. In the Western art-music tradition in which most music education majors are trained, students learn songs from notation. Although reading from notation is important for a developing music teacher, music education students will benefit from learning to transcribe music in the same manner as popular musicians because it helps them bridge the gap between music theory and

the aural aspect of music. Students may find that they do not have the technique necessary for performing the song. This process of methodically transcribing a line on one's instrument helps students internalize the sound of difficult sections. This can be a valuable aid in gaining the technique necessary for performing difficult passages of a musical work.

Learning the Technology of Popular Music

Young teachers are expected to be proficient in the use of technical equipment when they begin their careers. Unfortunately, instruction in the use of sound-reinforcement equipment, electronic keyboards, and digital recording software is limited in traditional teacher preparation programs. If music educators are going to use this equipment in the field, they need preservice experiences using these tools. The best way to give this experience is to require students to utilize technology to complete assignments in methods classes as well as in other music subject areas.

The Best Way—Doing Popular Music

The most effective education in popular music is achieved by actually creating and performing popular music. Music teachers, as Lucy Green says, must "put themselves into the position of young popular musicians, and try out some informal learning practices for themselves."[12] A popular music lab could link popular music skills together in the same way a senior recital ties together the skills of a music performance major. Students in the lab could participate in activities like these:

- forming their own popular music chamber groups (combo)
- selecting songs for the group to perform
- record copying songs on a popular music instrument that they play
- assigning vocal parts within the group
- experimenting with riffs, lyrics, and chord progressions as they create their own songs individually and collaboratively
- improvising solos within their songs
- learning to use and rehearse with live sound-reinforcement equipment
- performing for other lab ensembles
- recording their covers and original music using computers, mixers, and digital-audio equipment
- studying their recordings and evaluating their performances

Creating and performing popular music helps students acquire the skills necessary for teaching popular music and encourages them to respect the skills of popular musicians. Musicians trained to perform music in the Western art tradition have much to learn from those who have learned music aurally.

How Shall We Prepare Future Teachers in Popular Music?

Providing our students with the skills needed for teaching popular music will take additional time in university methods classes. Some may argue that this time does not exist. Many of these skills, however, can be taught in music core areas such as music theory, music history, and performance. If the music community really believes in the breadth of the National Standards, it will

become natural to teach improvisation, for example, as a part of music theory instruction. Popular music can be a greater part of our music history curriculum. Popular music performance labs can be used to fulfill part of university performance requirements. One of the greater challenges for the music education community will be convincing non-education university music colleagues schooled in the Western art tradition that making curricular connections to popular styles is important. This challenge cannot be solved quickly or easily. It may take many generations of university music professors to change established traditions. But in order to remain a viable subject area in our changing world, we must broaden our range of "sanctioned styles" used for musical instruction.

Popular Music as Chamber Music

Will Schmid, past president of MENC: The National Association for Music Education, challenges music educators to expand their idea of the traditional band, orchestra, and choir approach to performance ensembles by encouraging more chamber music opportunities:

Chamber music, in the most liberal interpretation of the word, can provide a good deal of the change needed within instrumental programs. If we really aspire to the goal of having students become independent musicians who can find their own music, form their own ensembles, interpret music on their own, find venues for playing (and singing), and present music well, then we will value chamber music. We must, however, see chamber music as style neutral. This interpretation allows a five piece rock band to be considered a chamber group. It also makes room for the myriad hybrid groups so interesting to students today. It allows for the use of instruments (such as guitars, keyboards, synthesizers, electric basses, and world music instruments) that are not normally part of either band or orchestra programs."[13]

The sort of chamber music Schmid endorses allows for active involvement in the kind of creative music making that we commonly use to justify our position in the schools. These chamber music ensembles, especially those that favor popular music, will truly allow students to make creative decisions and be active in every aspect of the musical world, from conception to performance.

If music educators are to teach students to be independent musicians, a new view of the role of music teacher is needed. Music educators must consider themselves "music educators," not simply band, orchestra, or choral directors. Music educators, especially in high schools, must provide additional offerings during the school day to allow for chamber music opportunities in a wide variety of musical styles—pop, jazz, or Western art music.

Scheduling and Administering a Popular Music Performance Program

When music educators rally around slogans such as "Music for All," we can take comfort in knowing that we do reach most of America's children, especially in the elementary grades. However, our success at reaching children as they pass through middle and high school greatly diminishes.

Music educators seem to think that if students do not perform in a band, choir, or orchestra, they must not be interested or able to succeed in music. Unfortunately, many general music offerings for middle and high school students are completely divorced from making music. Instead of actively engaging in concrete musical experiences, students and teachers merely talk about music in these classes.

Imagine the interest and excitement that could be generated by offering popular music ensembles and singer/songwriter classes that allow students to create, perform, and record their work. The difficulty is fitting these possibilities into the day of already busy teachers. Music educators will need to work with university music methods teachers, state education officials, community members, and administrators to examine educational priorities in order to include alternative ensembles or popular music courses in the school day.

In recent years, I have had many conversations with teachers who have had pull-out lesson programs cancelled. Although I view individual and small-group lessons as vital to a successful performance program, this scenario may inspire the use of creative music offerings. Many teachers in this situation face traveling from school to school when lessons are no longer part of their teaching load. One way to retain a full-time position in one building is to offer a popular music option during the time that was previously devoted to lessons. Most administrators are willing to try new courses that they see as meeting educational needs. The key in convincing an administrator to add a popular music course is demonstrating that students will be actively engaged in making music through composing, improvising, performing, and preserving their work—all activities that are part of the "real" world of music making.

Along with opportunities for students to play popular music in chamber ensembles, other classes can augment the program. Keyboard, guitar, world-music drumming, and recording courses can attract students who may not be motivated by traditional school ensembles. The curricula in these classes need not be limited to building performance skills. Just as in a complete and balanced traditional performance class, good teaching involves educating students for the broad range of understanding expected in the National Standards.

Conclusion

Our society continues to value music. As we go through each day, we are constantly surrounded by music. We hear music on our radios, televisions, movies, and computers. We have the opportunity to hear many styles of music performed live in concert halls, parks, churches, and clubs. We can also purchase an endless amount of recorded music through vendors or Internet downloads. We will still enjoy listening to the cherished music of the past, and we will continue to look forward to hearing new styles, performers, and creators of music. As we train our students to actively create and perform music and allow them to make musical decisions, the possibilities are great. Popular music offerings can help us achieve many of our goals, including the following:

• greater participation in school music activities

• more meaningful experiences in improvisation and composition for music students

• real-life music-making experiences similar to those of professional musicians

• greater understanding of music for those interested in a wide variety of styles

• high-level understanding of music from a greater number of consumers

We will not achieve these goals without overcoming a number of challenges. Areas of greatest need include the following:

• embracing of a broader spectrum of musical styles and traditions

• preservice training in popular music traditions

• flexibility in public school scheduling

When examining our current music education programs and assessing our abilities to meet the needs of a quickly changing population, it becomes clear that we must adapt our programs for our future students. Our students possess very different cultural interests from the narrow focus we currently serve. They are no longer likely to adapt to us. Music opportunities will continue to be all around future students. In broadening our appeal, we will maintain our ability to offer high-quality music education to a much larger percentage of these students.

Notes

1. Bennett Reimer, "An Agenda for Teaching Performing with Understanding" in *Performing with Understanding*, ed. Bennett Reimer (Reston, VA: MENC, 2000), 193.

2. Patricia Shehan Campbell, *Songs in Their Heads: Music and Its Meaning in Children's Lives*

(Oxford: Oxford University Press, 1998), 182.

3. Ibid., 214.

4. Stephen Nachmonovich, *Free Play: Improvisation in Life and Art* (New York: Tarcher, 1990), 83.

5. Scott Emmons, "Analysis of Musical Creativity in Middle School Students through Composition Using Computer-Assisted Instruction: A Multiple Case Study" (Ph.D. diss., Eastman School of Music, 1998), 177.

6. Ibid, 166.

7. Lucy Green, *How Popular Musicians Learn: A Way Ahead for Music Education* (Aldershot, UK: Ashgate, 2001), 80.

8. *Nachmanovitch, Free Play,* 96.

9. Reimer, "An Agenda," 193.

10. Nachmanovitch, *Free Play,* 6–7.

11. Campbell, *Songs in Their Heads,* 220.

12. Green, *How Popular Musicians Learn,* 214.

13. Will Schmid, "Challenging the Status Quo in School Performance Classes," in *Performing with Understanding,* 54.

Scott Emmons is music education professor and music chair at the University of Wisconsin–Milwaukee. Emmons is a widely sought clinician in the fields of music technology and creativity. Along with many book and journal publications, he is a program author for Silver Burdett Ginn's *Making Music* series.

10

K–12 Music Education at the Rock and Roll Hall of Fame and Museum

Craig Woodson

Two current trends in popular music are changing the scope of resources music educators use. First, rock and roll education is entering the mainstream of public education, growing beyond its oral/aural tradition to be included in the general music curriculum and in musical performance ensembles. There are popular music programs for preschool children and elementary through high school students, and there are postsecondary teacher training courses. Second, during the second half of the twentieth century, rock musicians have drawn on cultures outside their own. Rock music has increasingly become a global expression and is now found in most countries of the world, where it is mixed in with local music and customs, including clothing, language, instruments, and dance. This chapter will review the traditional ways performers learn rock music and explore educational programs at the Rock and Roll Hall of Fame and Museum, with specific references to a class that emphasizes multicultural awareness. Music educators can take advantage of these and other programs as school systems strive to satisfy emerging

academic standards in all subjects through music education.[1]

Why Rock and Roll?

While the stereotypical lure connected rock music has been "sex, drugs, and rock and roll," listeners have more often experienced it as the "teen CNN." Songs expressing the passion, confusion, exasperation, and yearning of youth come from songwriters who might be saying, "I know what you are going through" or simply, "Let's party." When assisted by advances in recording and transmission technology, these artistic expressions can be financially profitable.

Teen talent has been an important part of the music business for decades with such artists as LaVern Baker, Stevie Wonder, and Elvis Presley. But superstar status is now coming to preteen performers—Lil' Bow Wow and Lil' Romeo, for example. These changes are making pop music more attractive for the "tween" market (ages eight to twelve) as the marketable age of pop listeners continues to drop. The toy market reveals this trend with rock star dolls that include a full complement of associated equipment. Parents can now buy afford-able, small-sized, playable rock instruments at toy stores, while high-end children's ver-sions are available at music stores. Manufacturers have increased the number of guitars, keyboards, and drum sets for five- to eight-year-olds, and Asian manufac-turers continue to inundate this market with even less expensive instruments.[2] Additionally, while the market for rock music continues to expand to younger ages, the rock "oldies" market also continues to increase as baby boomers age.

How Rock Music Is Learned

Since it is not typically included at the teacher-training level, music educators who want to include rock music for general study or performance need to start with an understanding of how rock and roll listen-ers and performers learn rock music. Rock musicians may learn the craft by emulating someone they admire, learning by rote, singing in church choir, visiting clubs and talking with artists, going to concerts, play-ing records over and over to learn the lyrics or get the "lick," or, if possible, finding a performer who is willing to teach. For students wanting to learn to play popular music, the radio is often only the begin-ning. In the past, a would-be performer simply had to have access to the chosen record, and with a record player, repeat the part until mastering it. Cassette players enhanced this technique by including a counter that helped learners find the exact position of a musical excerpt. This simple technology allowed musicians to listen to musical segments over and over, repeating brief sections for mastery. Compact discs,

along with the now enormous video and DVD libraries available, make traditional oral/aural learning a more complete sensory experience.[3]

For performers, a major source of infor-mation comes from either the "grapevine" or other musicians who can recommend types of music, specific tracks on a record, or even special places on a track. Meeting and taking phone numbers of new musi-cians while on "gigs" has become a resource for finding backup personnel when book-ing casual or steady club work. Going to jam sessions at clubs is tremendously inspir-ing and gives the live experience an up-close-and-personal reality that is not possi-ble anywhere else. During the breaks, musi-cians can mingle to get ideas.

In the absence of private lessons, young people today can learn from downloads of MP3 files or tablature and then form bands in which they start to learn melodies and rhythms through listening and imitation. Semiprofessional gigs such as socials, wed-dings, and bar mitzvahs are important venues for playing rock music. "Fake books" provide lead sheets for standards and har-monic structures for improvisation. The church has provided a musical education for many artists. For example, Aretha Franklin learned to sing from her father, who was legendary as a singing minister. The influence of gospel music is evident in the music of Mahalia Jackson, LaVern Baker, and Dinah Washington. The general influence of the church as a musical source of education continues today. All of these oral/aural traditions remain to this day and will no doubt continue.

It is probably safe to say that most rock

musicians have learned by listening and imitating. Stories from the early days of the Beatles, the Rolling Stones, Bob Dylan, and many others are prime examples of this. In short, the way to learn rock music has been to do it on your own without formal instruction and certainly not in an elementary or secondary educational setting. Today, students who want to learn about rock music, especially as a performance art in an academic setting, quickly find that there is little instruction available. While the oral/aural method has worked and continues to work, private lessons, both formal and informal, have increasingly become a major source of instruction.

Private teachers have traditionally not specialized in rock but have often added it as needed to a general course of study.[4] Today, formalized rock instruction is taking the route of jazz and world music instruction by becoming institutionalized in teacher training courses. Specialized postsecondary institutions such as the Musicians Institute (Hollywood), Berklee College of Music (Boston), and many others have introduced rock instruction as part of a general course of study.

Organizations for private teachers have traditionally focused on classical music.[5] The first official national private drum teachers' meeting was held through the Vic Firth drumstick company in November 2002 at the Percussive Arts Society International Convention in Columbus, Ohio, where nationally recognized drum teachers discussed issues of their business. Taking drum lessons in the 1950s meant playing on a rubber drum pad in a music-store studio. Drum instruction today is video-assisted, distance-learning-capable, and replete with sound proofed, air-conditioned studios. Electric guitar, bass, keyboards and vocal instruction have developed in a similar way. Students now expect to receive rock music instruction through the full range of available technologies, including play-along videos and DVDs.

Notation

The least-used method for learning how to play rock music has been through musical notation. Recently, however, notated songs and solos of rock musicians have become available and are a serious option for rock instruction. Arrangers such as Ed Lojeski have long used popular music to reach band and choir students. Publishers such as Mel Bay, Hal Leonard, and Warner Brothers have devoted large portions of their catalogues to rock music instruction. Books teaching the systematic techniques of hip-hop scratching or "turntablism" are also now available. Another notation system that is commonly used today is tablature, or the graphic representation of finger positions and strokes for guitar, bass, and drum parts. Tablature provides instant access to a wide variety of contemporary rock and other styles and helps those who do not read traditional notation.

The TUBS, or Time Unit Box System, designed in the early 1960s by Phil Harland is useful in teaching the music of other cultures, especially Africa and Asia. This system makes use of what Harland called "rhythmic density," which was the fastest pulse of a rhythm. For example, in a 12/8 beat slow blues the performer might bring in references to a 24/16 density. Today this system has become popular as an introduction to traditional Western notation and, in some cases, is used in its place.

The Use of Pop Music in Schools

Performing groups in elementary, middle, and high school increasingly include arrangements of rock music. On occasion, these ensembles require improvisation in a variety of rock styles. Under the best circumstances, students can demonstrate their skills at school events and competitions. Currently, many schools incorporate rock music through a variety of disciplines such as English, social studies, history, and political science. However, music teachers have yet to fully embrace rock and roll, especially in its typical form as a small ensemble, including singers, electric guitars, bass, and drums. The following reasons for resisting the use of rock music have dominated for many decades:

• Students are exposed to rock music outside of school, so why teach it in school?
• The stereotypical message of "sex, drugs, and rock and roll" is inappropriate.
• There is a presumed lack of intrinsic musical value in rock music.
• There is insufficient time in the curriculum for additional repertoire and skill development.
• There are limited resources and teacher training courses.
• There are insufficient curricular guidelines.

As baby boomers have matured, one would expect that such questions might have abated. Rock and roll, however, has continued to evolve with its cutting commentary and disrespect of authority, so parents today might find themselves asking the same questions that their parents asked.

One answer might be that we need to use rock music to teach across the curriculum and as a performance art because (1) students are familiar with it, (2) it is a source of artistic information for today's youth, (3) it addresses difficult issues that concern young people today, and (4) it has evolved into an international art form with a distinct history that has received academic attention for decades.

Rock music continues to be learned in the oral/aural tradition, through private lessons and tablature, and in schools; but there are large institutions solely devoted to rock and roll education, one of the most notable being the Rock and Roll Hall of Fame and Museum in Cleveland, Ohio.

Teacher Training at the Rock Hall

Henceforth referred to as the "Rock Hall," the Rock and Roll Hall of Fame and Museum is the only institution of its kind dedicated to rock and roll education. Providing educational resources even prior to its opening in 1995, its mission statement is as follows:

> The Rock and Roll Hall of Fame and Museum exists to educate the world about the history and significance of rock and roll music. The Museum carries out this mission through its efforts to collect, preserve, exhibit and interpret this art form.[6]

A vice president leads the Education

Department, while the senior director of education, education staff, and outside consultants implement programs with assistance from volunteers, docents, and interns. By placing education at the top of its priorities, the museum is in a unique position to assist teachers and students who want to learn more about rock music. Currently, there are four ways that music and general classroom teachers from around the country can receive formal training in rock education from the Rock Hall:

- **Graduate teacher training courses:**
  . *Summer Teacher Institute at the Rock Hall.* A weeklong, two-graduate-unit course for general K–12 classroom teachers on the history of rock, with specialized workshops for various disciplines, including music, English, social studies, history, political science, art, and technology.
  . *Teacher training course at Cleveland State University.* An annual collaboration between CSU and the Rock Hall that focuses on a special topic each year. The topic in 2003 was "Rock and Roll for the Multicultural Classroom—Grades 4–12."
- **Online lesson plans:** The Rock Hall's Web site offers over seventy lessons on a variety of subjects, including English, social studies, history, and music.
- **Resource guides for teachers:** Materials, such as the *Hip-Hop Educator's Guide,* can be found at the Rock Hall Web site and are available through the mail.
- **Distance learning:** Videoconferencing, to begin in 2004, will include K–12 classes that support state academic content standards.

Additionally, the Rock Hall provides a performance venue for local and national student groups. It has been presenting annual collaborative programs with the Cleveland Contemporary Youth Orchestra (CCYO) for several years. The program, called "Works for Orchestra by Rock Artists," features original compositions and arrangements of rock classics for high school orchestra, giving students the opportunity to explore ways of applying classical training to the performance of popular music.[7]

In 2003, the Rock Hall provided a venue for the first electric rock and roll high school orchestra as a special feature of the Ohio Music Education Association's Winter Conference. Under the instruction of and with a performance by Mark Wood, electric violinist with the Trans-Siberian Orchestra, and under the leadership of Beth Hankins, director of the Lakewood High School orchestra, this rock orchestra performed arrangements of rock songs and classics from Led Zeppelin to Mozart. Some string players performed on electric instruments (designed and manufactured by Mark Wood) while others played on acoustic instruments. The fact that students in these programs learned to improvise in, for example, a blues form, was a vital exercise in exposure to rock music. Their previous training had been traditional, and helping students overcome their reliance on notation was a critical obstacle. Beth Hankins comments about the Lakewood Project in the program notes:

> A happy discovery was uncovering the wealth of talent that existed outside the traditional music classroom. Embracing and welcoming the "garage band" popu-

lation allowed us to combine the unique talents these musicians can offer the classically trained students. We managed to create a fresh and more exciting musical education for all.[8]

At the national level in 2002, the Rock Hall worked with the International Association for the Study of Popular Music, United States Branch. This organization provides for the academic study of popular music around the world and is an excellent resource for music educators.

Rockin' the Schools

The primary mission of the Rock Hall's K–12 educational program is to serve local students in classes that are collectively known as *Rockin' the Schools*. Since these programs form the basis of the education department's current K–12 curriculum and the upcoming 2004 distance learning programs, it is important to understand the program mission and implementation. Public schools in the greater Cleveland area and many from Northeast Ohio can choose from ten fifty-minute classes (listed below) for elementary and secondary students. These courses are presented without cost, twice a day, five days a week in the museum's fourth-floor theater. These classes cover age-appropriate subjects that address state academic content standards. Approximately eighteen thousand K–12 students attended these classes between September 2002 and June 2003.

Each event includes lecture, demonstration, audience participation, videos, stage visuals, musical performance, dance, and educational materials for teachers. All *Rockin' the Schools* programs use visual aids

to guide the audience through the story line; they act as the script, or storyboard, of the class. The story is presented with words, drawings, and pictures on colorful poster-board-sized panels that are placed on stands. If it is necessary to change the script, it is easy to take one posterboard out and replace it with another. This system works better than a PowerPoint presentation because the story remains onstage throughout the class. The content and variety of these programs might change based on internal and external evaluations, but as of June 2003, they were as follows:

"Kids Can Rock," for grades K–8, focuses on four early Rock Hall inductees who began music at an early age and in some cases even educated themselves.[9] For example, Bo Diddley made his own guitar as a teenager, Bill Haley started on a box guitar at the age of seven, LaVern Baker brought her early gospel training into her work as a singer in nightclubs, and Elvis Presley performed as a teenager, having been exposed to many types of music at a very early age. Audience members participate by playing a simple three-in-one musical instrument—a bell-drum-shaker with a metal lid at one end for a cowbell sound, a plastic lid at the other end for a lower-pitched drum sound, and mung beans inside for the shaker sound. Students drum and shake a 3:2 clave rhythm with Bo; shake, rattle, and roll with Bill; and play a mambo bell rhythm with LaVern's Latin-flavored "Tweedlee Dee." There are opportunities for students to dance throughout the class, either at their seats or on the stage.

"Fifty Years of Rock and Roll: Sock Hops to Hip Hop," for grades K–12, takes the audi-

ence through five decades of the music and dance of selected Rock Hall inductees with a live four-piece band and dancer. Beginning with songs dated from the time of the 1952 Moondog Coronation Ball, the band plays two selections from each decade while the dancer performs appropriate dance movements, including the twist, the swim, disco, and break dancing. Students depart with an overview of selected inductees and an enhanced understanding of the sounds that make up rock music.

"Ohio Rocks," for grades K–12, explains how rock music has been connected to Ohio for over fifty years, beginning with Alan Freed's Moondog Coronation Ball at the Cleveland Arena in 1952, through legendary radio announcers such as Casey Kasem, TV shows like *Upbeat,* and rock groups such as the James Gang, Devo, Bootsy Collins, Phil Ochs, the O'Jays, and the Raspberries. The story of the Rock and Roll Hall of Fame, beginning in 1983 and continuing through the opening of the museum in 1995, brings the story of rock in Ohio up to the present. The program concludes with a description of how the building itself was designed to reflect the story of rock and roll.

"The Roots of Rock and Roll," for grades 4–12, is about the seven roots of rock: blues, jazz, rhythm and blues, gospel, country, folk, and pop. The museum's definition of rock and roll is multicultural in its scope: rock and roll is the confluence of African-American and European American popular musical cultures. Each of the seven roots is traceable back to either an African or European influence, sometimes both. The African roots include syncopation, domi-

nance of percussion, call and response, singing and dancing, five-tone scale, and use of small ensembles. The European influences are 4/4 rhythm, use of strings and horns, four-part harmony, auditorium venues, seven-tone scales, and the use of large orchestras. The class contrasts seven roots artists with those they have influenced. For example, Robert Johnson's "Cross Road Blues" was continued in the Cream version, the danceable music of showman Louis Jordan's "Caldonia" was carried on by Chuck Berry in "Johnny B. Goode," and the folk style of Woody Guthrie's "Hard Travelin'" was continued in Bob Dylan's "The Times They Are a-Changin.'"

"Multicultural Rock," for grades 4–12, presents how rock and roll represents the musical cultures of Africa, Europe, Asia, and the Americas. (This program is discussed later in more detail.)

"Rock-It Science," for grades 4–12, explores the connections among four scientific arenas—Earth, life, time, and space—and rock and roll. Part of this class traces the four families of musical instruments: winds, drums, strings, and idiophones. Four major scientists representing each scientific discipline—Buckminster Fuller for Earth, Donald Johanson for life, Stephen Hawking for time, and Edwin Hubble for space—connect to rock in surprising ways. The course features rock musicians such as Afrika Bambaataa; Earth, Wind, and Fire; the Who; the Beatles; Parliament Funkadelic; the Beach Boys; David Bowie; and Elton John.

"Hip-Hop: A Cultural Expression," for grades 6–12, includes the four elements of hip-hop—DJs, MCs, B-boys/B-girls, and

graffiti artists[10]—presented by local hip-hop artists. The history lesson begins with reference to the griots (storytellers) of West Africa who used poetry juxtaposed with drum rhythms to transmit history. The modern story continued when young people heard Louis Jordan, Bo Diddley, James Brown, and the Last Poets in the 1960s and the Sugar Hill Gang in the 1970s, and turntables eventually become beat generators on the streets. Hip-hop gained greater commercial success in the 1980s when it drew on inspiration from Kool Herc, Grandmaster Flash, and Afrika Bambaataa—and especially when Run DMC recorded a cover of Aerosmith's "Walk This Way" with Steven Tyler and Joe Perry. The MC's microphone, the DJ's turntables, the gymnastic dance moves of B-boying and B-girling, and graffiti art have remained part of the hip-hop experience. These elements have merged with local traditions in many countries around the world.

"Women in Rock," for grades 6–12, presents women's issues such as feminism, sexism, racism, careers, marriage, and drug abuse. The history begins with women who contributed to the roots of rock music—such as Bessie Smith and Ma Rainey—and continues through five decades of artists who have significantly addressed women's issues, including LaVern Baker and Ruth Brown in the 1950s, Aretha Franklin and Diana Ross in the 1960s, Janis Joplin and Patti Smith in the 1970s, Tina Turner and Madonna in the 1980s, Melissa Etheridge and Janet Jackson in the 1990s, and Sheryl Crow and Lauryn Hill in the twenty-first century.

"Songs of Social Protest: Vietnam Era," for grades 6–12, shows how songs have brought about change in social consciousness, especially in reaction to the Vietnam War. The class is organized into four ten-minute sections. First, students learn how songs can explore a variety of human themes, such as love, unity, pain, and protest, using John Lennon's "Imagine" as one example. Second, students learn a brief history of protest songs from 1955–1975, including Jimi Hendrix's version of "The Star-Spangled Banner." Third, they learn about affirmation in music, with examples including the self (Aretha Franklin's "Respect"), family (John Lennon's "Mother"), neighborhood (Marvin Gaye's "What's Going On"), and school (The Raiders' "Indian Reservation"). In the final segment, they hear about songs of war protest in the 1960s—Tom Paxton's "Lyndon Johnson Told the Nation," Edwin Starr's "War," and Phil Ochs's "I Ain't Marching Anymore."

"Difficult Issues in Rock and Roll," for grades 8–12, addresses hearing conservation, First-Amendment and free-speech concerns, and how drug abuse has affected rock stars. Students see and discuss a fifteen-minute video segment called "Listen Smart" about the dangers of listening to loud music that features testimonials from prominent rock stars like Ozzy Osborne, Russell Simmons, Blondie, and Wyclef Jean. In the second part of the class, students learn how rock lyrics have challenged First-Amendment rights to free speech with songs by Frank Zappa and others. Finally, students learn how drugs and alcohol have taken the lives of stars like Elvis Presley, Janis Joplin, Jimi Hendrix, and others, and also how survivors of substance abuse like Joe Walsh of the Eagles and Steven Tyler of

Aerosmith have a message about the need to face addiction and take action.

World Music

While all the *Rockin' the Schools* programs deal with cultural issues, "Multicultural Rock" has a strong ethnomusicological component. Ethnomusicology is the study of music in cultural context. One ideal of this discipline is to achieve bimusicality, that is, to become sufficiently proficient in music of another culture that members of that culture recognize you as a competent musician in their tradition. This entails exposure to multiple aspects of the tradition, including language, food, clothing, and stories, ideally experienced through immersion in the culture. Those who teach rock music can view its culture on VH1 or MTV, learn the language and the stories, listen to the music and to artists speaking, and attend concerts.

Throughout the history of rock music, there have been cultural artifacts that are appropriate for all ages. At the Rock Hall, one exhibit allows visitors a chance to hear five hundred songs that experts selected as the most influential in rock history. Many of these are appropriate for K–8 students. For example, LaVern Baker sings the song "Tweedlee Dee" about her dog, her hit "Jim Dandy" is about rescuing, and "Shake a Hand" is a gospel-style song about friendship. She dresses in high fashion with abundant jewelry and comes from a church background. Such elements are relevant to K–8 students.

Hip-hop is actually a world culture, since it embraces an entire lifestyle and appears around the globe. The museum's hip-hop class presents a positive message by invoking students' understanding of metaphor, phrase, and rhyme as they compose rap poetry and "free style," or improvise, on a subject. Academic references support this instruction.[11]

Designing a Multicultural Rock Lesson for Grades 4–12

As the metaphor of the "global village" becomes more of a reality, rock music provides music teachers with an opportunity to discuss the familiar and the unfamiliar. Students need to connect with cultures other than their own, as indicated in academic content standards in many states. Learning rock involves learning about other cultures, including other languages, styles, costumes, and customs. Musicians in the United States have directly and indirectly imported elements of the cultures of Africa, Europe, Asia, and the Americas. The multicultural origins of rock and roll are varied, difficult to isolate, and often can only be inferred; but there is an attempt to develop understanding of the multicultural aspects of rock and roll in all of the museum's K–12 classes.

For purposes of the fifty-minute classes at the Rock Hall, it is necessary to generalize. For the "Multicultural Rock" class, it means that world musical cultures and their characteristics are approximated. What follows is a brief synopsis of the class, consisting of world regions and their characteristics, followed by examples of performers who incorporate these characteristics in their music.

Africa
• *Rhythm:* Based on speech (e.g., the *dondo*, the talking drum of West Africa).

- *Melody:* Commonly uses pentatonic scales; intervals are not based on European scales.
- *Harmony:* Uses thirds, polyphony, and hocket (i.e., melody is arranged among several voices).
- *Instruments:* Percussion is dominant but also includes strings and winds. In a set of two drums, the low-pitched drum represents the male and the high-pitched drum represents the female voice.
- *Size:* The organization of an African ensemble is described in Ghana as being like a family. A repeated bell pattern would represent a crying baby, other rhythmic drum parts would stand for other children who interact with the baby and parents, and the most complicated rhythms, usually played on low- and high-pitched instruments, represent the parents. The musical organization of a rock band is probably based on this family model from Africa.
- *Place:* Performances are often outside, environmentally friendly.
- *Dance:* Dancers are possessed by their ancestors' spirits. They experience a religious connection to ancestors.
- *Purpose:* Used in ceremonies related to chieftaincy, religious events, rites of passage, ancestors.

Earth, Wind and Fire's leader Maurice White saw an African "thumb piano," or *kalimba,* in a store window; it "spoke" to him and became the inspiration for songs. This plucked lamellophone is commonly in the pentatonic scale, with the lowest notes in the middle and ascending notes on either side. The notes of this instrument represent the members of a family, with the parents being the longest two notes and the

children being the other shorter notes, making a connection to the family model mentioned above.

Mick Fleetwood's 1981 album *The Visitor* contains a selection titled "The Visitor" sung in the *Ga* language and consisting of Fleetwood playing drums with the Ghanaian National Folk ensemble from Accra in 1980.[12] Fleetwood wanted to fuse the two cultures, having admired African drumming for many years; he had been using the Nigerian pressure drum, the *dundun,* as a solo instrument in his Fleetwood Mac performances.

Paul Simon used music to make a political statement against apartheid in South Africa. In the 1986 album *Graceland,* he performs with Ladysmith Black Mombazo and over fifty musicians, including many from Africa. The filmed concert of Simon's 1987 event in Zimbabwe shows a packed audience in a soccer stadium and features the highly poetic "Diamonds on the Soles of Her Shoes," performed with a large ensemble of white and black African and American musicians.

Europe

- *Rhythm:* 4/4 meter and measure are based on notation and form; first and third beat are stressed.
- *Melody:* Uses seven tones, based on the keyboard system of tetrachords; notated music is important.
- *Harmony:* In four parts, SATB, a choral orientation from early European religious music.
- *Instruments:* Strings and winds are used in string quartets, orchestras, and wind ensembles.
- *Size:* Full orchestra evolved over five

hundred years, based on violins for soprano voice.

- *Place:* Performed in auditoriums, evolved from church performances.
- *Dance:* Used in ballet and has choreography and structure.
- Purpose: Presented for public viewing and listening, with minimal audience participation.

The Beatles' "Eleanor Rigby," from the 1966 album *Revolver,* contains a string quartet arrangement that students hear while watching a segment of the animated film *Yellow Submarine.* The repeated notes in the music complement the theme of a lonely woman who died disenchanted by the routines of life. The cartoon shows the animated yellow submarine passing through frames that are a humorous, tragic, and stark commentary on the potential for meaninglessness in our everyday lives.

Kraftwerk, a German group of classically trained musicians who favor electronic music, provide a source of inspiration to hip-hop artist Afrika Bambaataa and his Soul Sonic Force in "Planet Rock," which samples a cut from Kraftwerk's 1977 "Trans-Europe Express." Using twin drum machines and a synthesizer, Ralf Hutter and Florian Schneider of Kraftwerk created a legendary minimalist pop album. Finding the right beat for rapping takes an artist to many sound sources and countries, in this case to sampling and synthesizing sounds of trains in Europe.

The Doors' "Riders on the Storm" from the 1971 album *L.A. Woman* has been arranged for full orchestra by Jaz Coleman and performed by the Cleveland Contem-

porary Youth Orchestra. Students pass around John Densmore's autobiography, *Riders on the Storm,*[13] as a preview of suggested follow-up reading. The orchestral arrangement combines European and Asian music, making this song a cross-cultural resource for music educators. The link to Asian culture becomes a natural segue into the discussion of rock's connection to that culture.

Asia

- *Rhythm:* 3+2+2, often in combinations of three and two.
- *Melody:* Embellishments are part of melodic style and even of scale.
- *Harmony:* Drone is common; melody rhythm dominates.
- *Instruments:* Strings and percussion used. Includes single stringed instruments and board zither, pitched percussion (e.g., *tabla*).
- *Size:* Trios or ensembles common, may perform with soloists.
- *Dance:* Uses storytelling motions, sometimes of epic stories.
- *Place:* Played in temple, place of worship.
- *Purpose:* Used for religion, with connections that date back several thousand years.

Jimi Hendrix's album *Axis: Bold As Love,* features cover art portraying Jimi Hendrix, drummer Mitch Mitchell, and bassist Noel Redding in a Buddhist setting with repeated religious figures on either side of them. In this case, repetition is a statement of devotion to the Buddhist and Hindu deities. During this segment of the class, students see a video about album covers created between 1967 and 1983 that feature multicultural art. The video, produced by the art department at Lansing Community College (Michigan), documents the use of world cultures on album covers, beginning with the Beatles' *Sgt. Pepper's Lonely Hearts Club Band.*

Junoon is a group composed of members from mixed cultures in the United States and Pakistan that is dedicated to peace. Its music is rock and roll with a decidedly Eastern rhythm and feeling. From the 2000 album *Parwaz,* the selection "Mitti" means "ashes to ashes." The Urdu lyrics say that no matter who we are or what we do, we all go back to dust. This group has toured the United States and performed at the United Nations promoting peace in the world.

Madonna appropriates images of Japan in her video of "Nothing Really Matters" from her 1998 album *Ray of Light.* Wearing a kimono, she cradles a clear plastic pillow filled with clear fluid, then uses rapid editing to bring viewers images of Asian men and women in white jump suits with fencing masks on, performing a dance. Students have to opportunity to evaluate her approach in this video.

Americas
- *Rhythm:* Used for dance, drumming for pow wow.
- *Melody:* Nature is source of scales (e.g., animal sounds).
- *Harmony:* Includes fifths, open harmonies; but melody dominates.
- *Instruments:* Winds and percussion reflect sounds of nature and animals, (e.g., flutes=birds); *cuica,* a friction drum, is a common percussion instrument.
- *Size:* Performed by soloist and chorus, as in Africa; also played by groups at pow wow.

- *Dance:* Celebrates spirits of ancestors and has some connections to African dance.
- *Place:* Played in sacred places, for communing with the ancestors.
- *Purpose:* Honors related ancestors, less to facilitate possession by ancestors.

Bob Marley performs "Is This Love?" from his 1978 album *Babylon Bus.* In the music video "Legend," Marley attends a child's birthday party, singing and dancing in celebration of youth and fun. Children of many cultural backgrounds appear with him as he demonstrates his appreciation for youth and diversity. This video might be considered a child-friendly example of the Rastafarian movement in reggae music.

Paul Revere and The Raiders' 1971 album *Indian Reservation (Lament of the Cherokee Reservation Indian)* reveals that lead singer Mark Lindsey is one-sixteenth Cherokee. The lyrics of the title track express the plight of Native Americans through references specific to the Cherokee nation. Written by John D. Loudermilk, the song was a number-one hit on the Billboard charts in 1971.

Gloria Estefan's song "Tradición" from her live HBO show *Que Siga La Tradición* pays tribute to her Cuban heritage through the *rumba guaguanco* rhythm that is used in a large stage production. Recalling the 3:2 rhythm from West Africa at the beginning of this class, the drums begin with a clave beat as Estefan sings about her desire for a continuation of her heritage and traditions. Soon traditional Cuban dancers join, the stage band begins, and the stage shakes with a long conga line.

In all of these segments, students can participate by moving in their seats and drumming on tambourines. Teachers receive a summary of the program with suggestions for follow-up activities, as well as an evaluation form to give feedback about the class.

Conclusion

Music educators are facing the new challenge of bringing rock and roll into the curriculum. The first task is to understand the past and present ways that young people learn about rock music and how to perform it. Many cultures have directly and indirectly influenced rock music, and during the second half of the twentieth century rock music has become an artistic force in most countries. These facts present many possibilities for music teachers. When educators make use of rock, it will help them meet academic content standards in a cross-disciplinary way, enabling discussions in music, politics, social studies, psychology, science, English, history, and art. The study and implementation of rock education will be a valuable resource for the next generation of teachers, and providing this resource will continue to be the priority of the Rock and Roll Hall of Fame and Museum.

Notes

1. This paper represents my views and not necessarily those of the Rock and Roll Hall of Fame and Museum. Other notable museums with rock-related music education programs include the Experience Music Project in Seattle, Washington, and the Country Music Hall of Fame in Nashville, Tennessee.

2. Based on my experience at the National Association of Music Merchants Convention, Los Angeles, in 2003.

3. There are educational robotic musical instruments at the Experience Music Project in Seattle.

4. I have acquired this view from my personal experience as a private drum teacher since 1959.

5. The Music Teachers National Association, founded in 1876, is primarily for private teachers who cater to teaching classical music.

6. This statement appears in the 2002 Annual Report of the museum.

7. The inaugural concert, conducted by Liza Grossman, was held on June 8, 2001, at the museum and featured a guest appearance by Ray Manzarek, keyboard player with the Doors. It presented the world premiere of *Riders on the Storm: The Doors Concerto* by Jaz Coleman, a nine-movement violin concerto with each movement based on the Doors' best-known tunes. The second concert in 2002 presented *Kashmir: Symphonic Led Zeppelin* by Jaz Coleman. The third concert, called *Classical Nash,* took place in May 2003 and featured Graham Nash performing "Teach your Children" with the orchestra.

8. Beth Hankins, program notes for performance of the Lakewood Project, 24 January 2003.

9. Artists become eligible for induction twenty-five years after release of their first record. Categories include Performer, Nonperformer, Early Influences, and Side Men.

10. *B-boys* and *B-girls*, also known as breakboys and break girls or break-dancers, dance during drum breaks in a song when the singer or lead instrument stops for a few measures. *Graffiti art* is brightly colored art that is usually displayed in public places, often created with aerosol spray paint and incorporating a type of secret or encrypted language.

11. Alonzo Westbrook, *HipHoptionary: The Dictionary of Hip Hop Terminology* (New York: Harlem Moon, 2002).

12. I assisted Fleetwood in this project.

13. John Densmore, *Riders on the Storm: My Life with Jim Morrison and The Doors* (New York: Delta Trade, 1991).

Craig Woodson is a music educator, ethnomusicologist, and performing musician with a Ph.D. in music from the University of California at Los Angeles. He specialized in the making of music instruments for young people, which led to a small business, twelve patents on instrument technology, and a three-year research project in West Africa. His forty-year career in the music business, including credits as a rock and roll drummer and kindergarten through college-age music teacher, brought him to the Rock and Roll Hall of Fame and Museum, where he is senior director of education.

Performance and Composition Perspectives

11
The Pop Music Ensemble in Music Education

George Boespflug

Since the middle of the twentieth century, pop music has played an increasingly prominent role and served a variety of purposes in the music classroom. Whether examined from a historical or sociological perspective, analyzed for musical content, or used in traditional ensemble arrangements, pop music has become more commonplace and accepted within music education. *However, we have been unable to find a way to approach the making of pop music in an ensemble that would ensure its status as a standard school ensemble similar to the choir, band, orchestra, or jazz band.* In this chapter, I will examine why we have not been able to find a place for the pop music ensemble and what must take place to make it a viable ensemble option in schools.

We must first define "pop music ensemble." The pop music ensemble is as much about creating music as it is about performance. Composition in the pop music ensemble is collaborative, improvisatory, and aurally conceived—without music notation. Pop ensemble music, style, and membership can vary greatly. Musical styles may include rock, heavy metal, rhythm and blues, techno, soul, hip-hop, alternative, reggae, and so on. For the most part, it is youth-oriented music with or without words. The ensemble can consist of a singer and a guitarist accompanied by a variety of sequenced or prerecorded tracks, or perhaps a quartet of singers accompanied by a full rhythm section, assorted keyboards, and brass section. There are no limitations or prerequisites to membership; the musical material determines the nature of the ensemble. The emphasis is on creating and performing music in an improvisatory, collaborative environment.

For decades, music educators have sought ways to incorporate popular music in music curricula. The Tanglewood Symposium, a gathering of U.S. music education leaders sponsored by MENC, took place during the summer of 1967. Symposium participants drew up a declaration summarizing their discussions and providing guidance for the future of American music education. The Tanglewood Declaration consisted of eight major points. The second point read:

> Music of all periods, styles, forms and cultures belong in the curriculum. The

musical repertory should be expanded to involve music of our time in its rich variety, including currently *popular teenage music* and avant-garde music, American folk music and the music of other cultures. [1]

The declaration was written thirty-five years ago and the "popular teenage music" referred to in the Tanglewood Declaration is now "classic rock," the music of choice for many young and middle-aged Americans.

It is clear that popular music has had, and will continue to have, enormous influence on our culture and economy. In 2001, the recording industry netted $33.7 billion worldwide,[2] the majority from pop music sales. The music product industry, which produces recording software, sound-reinforcement equipment, amplifiers, electric guitars, keyboards, and other equipment used in popular music, grossed $6.88 billion in the United States in 2001.[3] Although not all of those sales were for pop music, pop-related spending did make up a substantial portion of industry receipts. Pop music culture has influenced politics, art, literature, film, fashion, and practically every aspect of society. It has become a worldwide cultural force, yet the making of pop music is not typically addressed in music education.

The influence of popular music upon our culture is significant and has not gone unnoticed by some in music education. The examination of the global, social, and cultural impact of popular music has become increasingly prevalent in university music courses and public school general music curricula. It is not uncommon for a university to offer courses that examine the social roots and cultural evolution of pop music.

These courses are often enormously popular and at some institutions have taken the place of more traditional music appreciation courses based upon Western art music. K–12 music materials use pop songs to teach elements of music and fundamental music skills that in the past were taught using folk songs and classical music. Using pop music examples that are often more recognizable, memorable, and meaningful to students has proven effective. Arrangements based upon pop songs have become more prominent in choral and instrumental literature. It is now unusual to attend a junior or senior high school ensemble performance without hearing at least one arrangement of a Top 40 hit.

We have learned to use pop music for traditional educational purposes. Just as we once studied the development of the classical era and the effects of the French Revolution on Beethoven, young students now study the Vietnam War and the effects of the peace movement on John Lennon; as students examined Mozart's "Twinkle, Twinkle, Little Star" piano variations in order to study theme and variation form, they now also examine mixed meter by studying the songs of Radiohead; and as school choirs sing Alice Parker's arrangements of traditional gospel songs, they also present arrangements of Elton John songs in concert.

The methods of examining pop music from a historical or sociological perspective, analyzing its musical content, or using it for traditional ensemble arrangements have become increasingly popular and accepted. Yet we have been unable to find a generally accepted way of making pop music in the schools. The reasons we have been unable to incorporate the making of pop music include aesthetics, pedagogy, logistics, and the most common educational obstacle, funding. These impediments are surmountable and must be overcome if we are to bring the making of pop music on a large scale into the schools.

Obstacles to Teaching Popular Music

Perhaps the most fundamental obstacle is that music educators have generally not been taught how to make pop music. Traditionally, music students have learned that creating music involves a composer, paper, and pencil. Pop music, on the other hand, is typically the product of an improvisatory, "by ear," collaborative process.

The pop ensemble creates an environment rich with improvisation. When faced with improvisation, traditionally trained musicians often find themselves at a loss because their education did not sufficiently address improvisation, either in classroom training or in recognition of it as a useful skill. Many traditionally trained music educators believe that improvisation should certainly lie within the skill-set of the professional music educator, but it typically does not. This deficiency is not the result of a lack of talent but of a paucity of training. Improvisation is therefore often a source of embarrassment for traditionally trained musicians. For music educators, working within the realm of improvisation often requires a willingness to be vulnerable and to accept the fact that they may be less capable than some students in this area.

A second musical skill essential to the pop ensemble is playing by ear, which involves hearing music, remembering it, and replicating it without notation. This demands deft musical memory, as well as pitch- and rhythm-matching skills. The pop musician must be able to hear a musical idea live or on a recording, remember it, and then replicate it. This is essential to building a vocabulary of ideas and for sharing and receiving ideas collaboratively. Working by ear can make the traditionally trained music educator feel vulnerable. Those accustomed to reading music from a page may find it difficult to remember musical ideas or capture the melodic and rhythmic nuance of a musical idea without notation. Again, these are skills and do not necessarily indicate an individual's musical giftedness. Traditional music education, because of the emphasis it places on reading music, does not give adequate attention to "by ear" musicianship. Still, many great composers, including Bach, Mozart, Chopin, Brahms, and Dohnányi, were able to recall music that they heard and then embellish and develop it without notation. In the pop music ensemble setting, the teacher and students should be able to quickly grasp and replicate musical ideas, manipulate and explore the potential of those ideas, and shape and hone them without notation. These skills need to be sharpened with practice. Though they are not developed in traditional music education, these skills are essential to the pop ensemble. We are a very notation-reliant profession, and to become less so will be, to say the least, a challenge.

Popular Music and Instrumentation

Directing a pop music ensemble requires some basic understanding of pop instrumentation. Just as the band teacher needs basic training in woodwinds, brass, and percussion, so the pop ensemble director needs to know something about electric guitar, electric bass, drum set, and keyboard.

Many music education programs now offer music education students the opportunity to study some of the instruments used in popular music. It is not unusual for a music education curriculum to include an acoustic guitar class, percussion class (with perhaps some exposure to drum set), and an electronic music class, which may include an introduction to sequencing and sound synthesis. Pop music, however, involves other instruments and technology that are typically not offered, such as the electric guitar, electric bass guitar, electric keyboard/synthesizer, and more recent additions that include samplers, drum machines, and turntables. These instruments are not commonly taught in university music programs, perhaps in part because most higher education music faculty have little or no experience with these instruments.

Along with the skill required to physically manipulate these instruments, stylistic and aesthetic considerations, which are fundamental to playing these instruments, must be addressed. Pop musicians spend a great deal of time developing a vocabulary of musical ideas and seeking ways to recreate sounds and create new, compelling sounds. They spend much time exploring and experimenting with various brands of instruments, amplifiers, and effects units. Textbooks rarely address these activities, although more publications concerned with these matters are appearing. For the most part, pop musicians learn aurally by experimenting, listening to recordings, observing those successful in the profession, and sharing ideas informally. Teaching these instruments, therefore, requires years of listening and experimenting with the technology involved, as well as actually playing the instruments.

If pop music is to be taught in the schools, then teachers must be familiar with pop music language and style, have some understanding of music technology, and have the technical skills needed to create and perform pop music. Typically, pop musicians have spent more time doing music than accruing academic degrees. Higher education, generally, has been hesitant to hire these kinds of musicians. So when pop music is addressed in music education courses, it is often by faculty who are teaching out of their sphere of experience, for example, a piano teacher with a traditional educational pedigree teaching pop keyboard. The piano instructor will most likely understand what chords pop symbols on a chart represent but may not understand the subtleties of voicing, rhythm, accent, and timbre choices that are essential to pop style. If pop music is to become part of the music education curriculum, it needs to be taught by those who know it intimately.

If music education students intend to guide pop music ensembles when they become teachers, they need to know something about the instruments used in pop recordings, have a basic understanding of pop styles and musical vocabulary, and have had opportunities to interact with teachers who know pop music intimately.

Attitudes toward Popular Music

Many in music higher education have been hostile toward pop music, often considering it inferior, crude, and unsophisticated. These attitudes have created tension in the minds of music students because for virtually all of them, pop music is an important part of their musical lives. Their music teachers often denigrate the music that they most identify with and enjoy. When interviewing prospective music students, I will invariably ask them about the music they listen to and recordings they own. Most, with some prodding, will almost apologetically admit that they listen to some popular music. Perhaps unintentionally, we have created an environment in which serious music students have become closet pop music listeners, embarrassed to talk to music faculty about the music they listen to the most.

During their student years, future music educators may spend hours listening to popular music, music that is rarely relevant to or even mentioned in their musical studies. And when pop music is discussed or examined in classes, it is often accompanied with derogatory comments about the music's content, quality, and sophistication. Music education students are rarely, if ever, given the opportunity to actually perform or record pop music. Composing popular music may be relegated to a single unit of study in a music education methods class, and this experience is seldom the product of group composition.

If the pop ensemble is to become part of the school, then its value must be promulgated at the college level. In addition to the processes of production, performance, analysis, and reflection, there must also be a viable aesthetic component included at all levels of instruction.

Pop Music Pedagogy

The pop ensemble requires new ensemble pedagogy. The traditional method of teaching an ensemble will not work. Although researchers have studied the dynamics of the collaborative pop ensemble, further research and thought need to be invested in exploring how teachers might best guide this process. Relatively little research is being done in this area.

As mentioned previously, creating pop music is usually a collaborative undertaking. Rather than re-creating what others have made, pop musicians typically work together to construct original material. The interaction between those involved in the composition process is multidimensional and dynamic. Ensemble members might create a part for themselves or other members or play parts created by other members. All members are simultaneously creators, teachers, and learners. Ideally, there is a sharing of ideas, with some of the better ideas prevailing through consensus. Of course, due to human nature, factors at work in the collaborative process do not always ensure that the best ideas are ultimately used. The process requires communication, discrimination, and creativity, which is the underpinning of the Manhattanville Music Curriculum Project as described by Ronald Thomas:

> If music is an expressive medium, learning involves expressing. If it is a creative art, learning means creating. If music

has meaning, personal judgments are fundamental to the learning process. If music is a communicative art, the educational process must involve students in communication. Fact may be taught, but meaning is discovered. There is nothing antecedent to discovering meaning.[4]

This process is vastly different from what typically occurs in the music classroom or rehearsal room. Rather than being the authority figure at the front of the room, the teacher becomes more of a facilitator, monitoring musical and lyrical content and group interaction and stepping in as needed to help coordinate the collaborative composition process. The pop ensemble director needs to step in and make suggestions about the music and help the group work through issues that might arise because of the collaborative nature of the process. The pop music ensemble experience is about exploration, so the teacher must observe, encourage, and provide guidance at the appropriate time.

In the traditional ensemble, it is common for a music director to work with fifty students who are all striving together for one goal, the effective performance of a written composition. The students and director have well-defined roles. Students and conductor learn their parts, then come together under the guidance of the director to create a convincing performance that is faithful to the score. The process is orderly and (from a school administrator's point of view) fairly cost-effective. There is a clear outcome to the process, the performance of the score. The audience, faculty, and administration evaluate the school concert, but other methods of appraisal have evolved, including festivals and other forms

of competitive and noncompetitive evaluation. From beginning to end, the process is relatively clear-cut.

Pop music cannot be addressed this way. Pop ensembles do not begin with a completed work. Group members are responsible for creating new compositions, or at least original arrangements of preexisting compositions. Teachers must evaluate and critique work in each phase of the creative process, evaluating the quality of the lyrics, the effectiveness of chord progressions, or the appropriateness of individual parts, such as a bass line or background vocals. There are no standard guidelines for evaluating these elements. Assessing a composition or performance rests on the shoulders of the ensemble director. Thus, the ensemble director must have at least some understanding of vocabulary, style, and taste. In the pop music realm, there is no tradition of evaluation and assessment as there is in other ensembles. At this point, assessment is in large measure subjective, resting on the experience and taste of the ensemble director.

Facilities and Schedules

Pop music ensembles are typically small, usually less than ten members. In order to reach a student-to-faculty ratio acceptable to most school administration, the ensemble director will need to work with a number of groups, perhaps four or five, each working at its own pace in developing compositions, arrangements, and performances. It is perhaps too demanding to expect a single director to meet with four or five ensembles simultaneously, using the traditional ensemble schedule, that is, meeting in one place for three to five hours a week.

In the traditional sound-reinforced pop music environment, two bands cannot rehearse simultaneously in the same room. The director must meet with groups separately to assess their progress and critique their ideas. If the traditional ensemble schedule were used, a number of rehearsal spaces would need to be simultaneously in use with the pop ensemble director rotating from one group to another throughout the period. In most schools, the space issue alone would make this impossible. With technology, however, this problem can be overcome. A solution will be addressed later in this chapter.

All of these issues—a nontraditional approach to class meeting and rehearsal, steering of the collaborative compositional process, and evaluation of the quality of work—are not commonly addressed in higher music education. Sensitivity to group dynamics, proficiency in improvisation, "by ear" skill, familiarity with electronic instruments and digital recording technology, and appreciation and understanding of a wide array of popular music styles are often foreign to the traditionally trained musician. Yet, in order for the pop ensemble to become legitimate, teachers need strategies to address these issues.

Music Technology

In addition to understanding the basics of various electric instruments, the pop ensemble director must also have a functional understanding of recording and sound-reinforcement gear. Understanding current music technology requires time and equipment. In most music education programs, students are briefly exposed to technology and rarely in a creative group environment. The role of technology in pop music is far too great for a cursory survey of elementary functions. Technology now provides creative tools far beyond electric instruments. It is not uncommon for a song to feature a computer-generated sampled loop or synthetically altered drum sounds that provide the texture and timbre that give the composition its unique character, its timbral "hook." Understanding the path of an audio signal through a mixer, the difference between low and high impendence microphones, the effects of compression on a recording, the effect that equalization has on various instruments, and the basic principles of digital editing is as indispensable to the creative process as the electric guitar or drum set.

Using technology, even amateur musicians can remove wrong notes, change tempi, add notes, or even change the pitch and timbre of existing notes. Just as a wall is built brick by brick, now compositions can be digitally constructed, note by note. This technology is no longer the rarified realm of the audio engineer; it has become a creative resource for the modern musician. Technology makes it possible to shade, accent, mute, highlight, expand, and refine musical ideas on a digital "canvas." Some claim that the most prominent performance venue of the twenty-first century is the digital domain of recorded sound, supplanting live performance. It is hard to imagine a music education curriculum that does not provide more than a perfunctory introduction to this important realm of aural creativity.

A number of problems unrelated to education and pedagogy may seem to be insurmountable obstacles to legitimately bringing the pop ensemble into the mainstream of music education. Pop music ensembles are loud, the technology is complex, and the equipment can easily become disorderly and is quite expensive, making security a concern. I believe the solutions to these issues will come from the music products industry. Most of the technology to address these issues already exists, but the music products industry must make an intentional effort to create a rehearsal environment in which pop ensembles can exist in schools.

The current generation of electronic instruments is not designed for junior high or high school pop ensembles (though some in the industry that would probably vehemently disagree with this statement). The music industry seems to have structured technical advancement with the amateur and professional user, not the public school student, in mind. Students need access to technology that will enhance the creative process, not detract from it or impede it. I have seen many talented young musicians retreat from using technology because of its complexity. The thought of wading through the complicated manual that invariably comes with each piece of equipment is often daunting. When one is caught up in the fervor of inspiration, nothing can ruin the moment like a problem with equipment or the need to go to the manual to clarify an involved process— many a brilliant idea has evaporated because of the complexity of the technology. The music product industry continues to find new and exciting musical possibilities that new technologies permit. However,

users typically must find these applications by wading through layers of functions that are accessed through a field of buttons and knobs and a small 3"x 5" LED screen. What is needed is equipment of the highest sonic quality with a limited number of easily accessed functions. For example, a typical keyboard will have not one, but perhaps twenty varieties of reverb with the capability to compound echoes, simulate reflections, and adjust the decay of high and low frequencies. For the experienced musician, this is useful, but it is not necessary for the beginning student interested in using technology to create music.

Another example of needless complexity for a junior high student is the sound resources, or "patches," found on a typical synthesizer. The average synthesizer will have in the neighborhood of one to two hundred basic sounds, with another one to two hundred complex combinations of the basic patches. Sounds include some basics found in much pop music, such as string pads, bass sounds, drums, electric organ, piano, acoustic guitar, and others. These are the primary colors of pop music. However, the manufacturer also usually includes many other sounds that might serve as interesting effects for the introduction of a song or as unusual effects at some point in a composition, but these patches are essentially of little use. These sounds are included because the resources of the synthesizer make them possible, not because they will be widely used. Moreover, the novelty of these sounds is often quickly lost.

Most synthesizers will allow users to manipulate a variety of sound parameters by layering sounds, digitally adding low-frequency oscillators, altering the sound envelope, passing a wave shape through simulated hi- or low-pass filters, and manipulating sounds in other ways. These options are perhaps useful for the synthesizer enthusiast but are not necessary for the keyboardist in a school pop ensemble. It is not uncommon for novice users of this kind of keyboard to inadvertently hit a button, only to be faced with a screen designed to change the envelope of a sound or do some other complex function. The students must then find their way back to the original screen where they began. In the middle of a rehearsal, this kind of occurrence can quickly deflate any creative momentum that might be developing. I advocate equipment that is easily manipulated and furnished with sumptuous, compelling sounds and rich basic effects that are easily accessed and reminiscent of, or similar to, what students hear in popular recordings.

When attending a pop ensemble rehearsal or a live pop concert, one is impressed with the complex tangle of chords; the countless modules with red, green, and yellow blinking lights; the meters; the faders; and bank after bank of knobs and controllers. While visually impressive, the complexity of sound equipment is often enough to thwart the creative impulses of even experienced musicians. Managing sound equipment can prove to be overwhelming for the pop ensemble director. It is time-consuming and complex, demanding an understanding of how each piece of equipment functions and how it is routed within the system.

Networking equipment almost invariably creates a jumble of cables often strewn dangerously across the floor. In a classroom or rehearsal room, this becomes a problem because cables are stepped on and often disconnected or broken. Often students will alter cable configurations without returning them to their original configuration before leaving the studio. The next group may then be unable to reconfigure cables and settings to their original state and therefore may be unable to rehearse. Another problem is that maintaining equipment can be very time-consuming. Troubleshooting difficulties increase exponentially with each additional piece of equipment and its attendant cables. Not only is maintaining equipment time-consuming, but it can also be very expensive. *The point is, technology should not be an obstacle to the creative process, but often it is.*

Security is another concern that could persuade an administrator not to fund a pop ensemble. Electronic music equipment is expensive. A compressor can run from $100 to $3,000. A quality vocal microphone can easily cost $1,500, and even basic microphones can cost more than $100 each. A basic, functional electric guitar can easily cost $500; a good keyboard, $1,500. Ideally, a studio should be equipped with instruments and sound production devices that are made available to students working on popular music projects. Unfortunately, sound modules, microphones, and some instruments are easily removed from an unsecured rehearsal area. Securing school-owned equipment is an important concern schools must address if they are to invest in electronic instruments and equipment.

Volume is an obvious problem for pop ensembles. Individual pop musicians armed with 100-watt amplifiers rehearsing alone can be deafening. This simple yet crucial issue could be the deciding factor in a school administrator's mind when determining whether to allow a pop music ensemble in the school. Technology, however, may provide the solution to this problem. Using digital technology, manufacturers continue to seek ways of replicating wave shapes created by analog equipment driven at extreme voltage, replicating the sound but not the volume required to create it. Often the timbre that a pop musician is seeking is the result of an overdriven amplifier, taxing equipment to the edge of its capacity. This is a recurring timbral feature of pop music, particularly rock. With current technology, the distorted sound of an overdriven tube amplifier can now be realistically reproduced digitally at tolerable decibel levels.

The electronic drum set is another example where technology is addressing the issue of volume. In order to get the stylistic sound they desire, drummers may play with great force and volume. This may not be acceptable in a school rehearsal space while classes are in session nearby. The solution to this problem again exists in developing technology. Electronic drums with touch-sensitive drumheads and cymbals allow drummers to play forcefully but with complete volume control. Therefore, a drummer can play with great force but minimal volume. Drummers often play electronic drums wearing headphones, allowing them to rehearse without disturbing anyone nearby. Headphones, used not only for drums but also for keyboards and guitars, provide rich sonic quality and a wide volume range without disturbing anyone in the same room.

One of the great challenges of amplifying or recording acoustic instruments, particularly drums, is effective miking. It usually takes an experienced engineer and excellent microphones to record or amplify a drum set effectively. The smallest change in microphone placement can affect the entire drum mix. Moreover, in any live, sound-reinforced environment, feedback from microphones is a constant problem, and sound from other instruments tends to bleed into drum microphones. With electronic drums, there is no need for microphones, and mixing bass drum, snare, tom-toms, and cymbals becomes much simpler. When electronic drums are used in a sound-reinforced environment, feedback is not a concern, and controlling the sound and mix of drums becomes simpler and more manageable. Although the current generation of electronic drums produces a sound inferior to acoustic drums, they are becoming more sensitive and realistic-sounding with each passing year. As technology becomes more able to replicate sounds once only available in the analog realm, volume will become more controllable.

Anyone who has been to an amplified band rehearsal knows that balance and volume are chief concerns. It is often difficult to hear what each band member is playing and the role that individual instruments play in creating a larger aural landscape. Instead, it can sound like a piercing confusion of sound. A bass player can easily get lost under a heavy-handed drummer. An electric guitar player with a powerful amplifier can easily overpower a keyboardist whose instrument is only amplified through a PA system. And a PA that amplifies keyboards, drums, and vocals can create an almost indistinguishable wall of sound. Balancing all of these elements in the sound-reinforced environment is very difficult. Also, there are often problems with feedback, particularly in a small rehearsal space where it is difficult to allow for adequate space between microphones and amplified speakers.

Decibel levels tend to increase with each additional amplified instrument added to an ensemble. The result can be deafening and can compromise the teaching environment. I was told of a school pop ensemble rehearsal in which the drummer was playing very loud. The guitarist, armed with a large amplifier, rose to the occasion, matching the drummer's sound, while the keyboardist and singer, amplified by an inadequate sound system driven to the point of distortion, struggled to be heard. Meanwhile, the ensemble director stood in the middle of the group shouting instructions at the top of his lungs trying to direct the rehearsal. The result was a wash of jumbled sound. This is not the kind of learning environment that will bring the pop ensemble into the mainstream of school music.

These issues of complexity, noise, order, and security must be addressed if the pop ensemble is to become viable in schools. The question is how? *I believe the solution to these problems lie in what could be described as a "virtual studio."*

A Virtual Studio

The virtual studio would be a completely digital musical environment that would primarily be experienced through headphones. Instruments would be electric or fitted with digital pickups that could be attached to acoustic instruments, such as violins, saxophones, and French horns, all equipped with wireless technology so cables would be unnecessary. The virtual studio would provide a musical environment in which volume levels would not be harmful to students, sound would not disrupt activities happening in adjacent spaces, and in which a teacher could easily direct rehearsals. In addition to being relatively quiet, the studio would require equipment that is compact, simple to use, easy to maintain and secure, and designed specifically for the school setting. The virtual studio would be a place to record as well as to rehearse, both of which are key pop ensemble activities. In this setting, the group could rehearse without struggling with noise issues that are part of the sound-reinforced environment. Limiters would be placed on headphones so that students could not damage their ears.

The teacher and students would wear wireless headphones equipped with microphones that they would use to communicate with one another, similar to the technology presently used in the keyboard laboratory. With a push of a button, the instructor could interrupt the music to make comments, or perhaps while the ensemble is playing the director could make a comment to an individual ensemble member without distracting others in the ensemble. The instructor would be able to mix the ensemble while the rehearsal is in progress, perhaps adding effects, changing equalization, and recording as needed.

Current technology now offers effective wireless systems for microphones and guitars, but imagine a room without cables—all speakers, instruments, and headphones would be connected by wireless technology: headphones fitted with attached microphones, unrestricted by cables; speakers that could be moved to any place within a room without concern about the length or path of a cable; and wireless pickups for all acoustic instruments, electric guitars, keyboards, and controllers, making it possible to bring violins, cellos, and oboes into the virtual studio.

Rather than a number of modules—such as amplifiers, equalizers, delay devices, compressors, preamplifiers, recorders, and headphone distribution units—one or two master units would serve all of these functions. These units would be designed with the student, not the professional, in mind; simple controls would allow students to easily access various functions. Functions would be sonically rich but simple to use. The master units would also handle all aspects of the recording process. These master units would provide basic functions needed to record or rehearse in the virtual realm, designed with the junior high and high school student in mind. Rather than being plugged into amplifiers, all instruments would be connected directly to the master units. Effects modules for individual instruments would be available within the master units.

Because of the quiet, compact nature of the virtual studio, it would be available to students for rehearsal any time of the day. Students would be able to write to disc anything they create in rehearsal, everything from mix information to track recordings. A student could go to the virtual studio, load a mix of a recent recording session,

mute parts as needed and then practice, improvise, or create a part over other prerecorded parts, and then play the new part later with the rest of the ensemble. Perhaps at the junior high level, the students would only play and record with the help of the teacher, but high school students would be able to manage more sophisticated engineering tasks. At some high schools a second, smaller room might be available for mixing and editing.

Within the virtual studio, two groups could rehearse simultaneously in the same space, each in its own virtual domain, perhaps with a simple portable wall panel between them. As digital technology improves the ability to replicate sound waves created by acoustic and analog electronic instruments, the virtual realm will continue to grow as a colorful, rich, and vital sonic environment.

All equipment and instruments could be tagged with magnetic strips. Entrances to the virtual studio could have detectors that make it impossible for anyone to remove equipment from the studio without setting off an alarm. A security system would stop theft and discourage students from "borrowing" or inadvertently walking off with equipment. Such a security system would save money and ensure that students have easy access to equipment for rehearsals.

Along with allowing work in the rehearsal room, virtual studio technology would provide students new ways to share and store ideas. A student could work on a track at home in the evening, download the track to the school's system via high-speed cable, and have that track available for a recording session or rehearsal the following day;

or the student could send that same track to ensemble members on the other side of town so they could learn it before the next ensemble practice.

Music technology has grown by leaps and bounds over the last fifty years, and that process has quickened in recent years. The exponential growth of technology has made possible what was once only imaginable. Most elements of the virtual studio already exist. The music industry has committed vast resources to the continued development of technology, but what is needed is a concerted effort to create a musical environment friendly to the young student pop ensemble member.

Conclusion

If we truly intend to make the pop music ensemble viable in schools, we must begin with teacher training. We must see the intrinsic value of popular music and genuinely encourage music education students to make pop music. We must help future teachers develop the tools to join in the pop music creative process and assessments. Furthermore, we need to work with the music products industry to develop a creative environment that is conducive to the making of pop music in schools, while at the same time is unobtrusive and able to function and even flourish.

Music educators long to influence our culture, yet we remain disconnected from contemporary culture. I often wonder what popular music would sound like today had the music education community embraced the Beatles and Beach Boys. What would the connection between music education and popular music be if music educators had embraced the creative potential of the collaborative process and espoused the value of "by ear" skills or perceived the expressive potential of new instruments like the electric guitar? What would pop music be like today if fifty years ago music teachers had begun exploring alongside junior high and senior high students the potential of electronic instruments and music technology? What songs would have been written by young energetic creative minds drawn to pop music had they had the input of teachers who could have expanded their musical and poetic sensibilities? What would be the aesthetic values of the current generation of pop musicians if during their formative years they had explored form, color, harmony, rhythm, and melody with their school music teachers? Would young people be listening to Public Enemy, Kid Rock, or Marilyn Manson? What price have we paid as a musical community and as a society? I believe it's not too late, and indeed it is the perfect time, to consider these changes.

Notes

1. Michael L. Mark and Charles L. Gary, *A History of American Music Education,* 2nd ed. (Reston: MENC, 1999), 312, emphasis mine.

2. IFPI, "Global Music Sales Down 5% in 2001" [online press release] (London: IFPI, 2002 [cited 17 January 2003); available at www.ifpi.org/site-content/press/20020415.html

3. NAMM, "MusicUSA: Uniting the World Through Music" [online document] (Carlsbad, CA: NAMM, 2003 [cited 12 March 2003]); available at www.namm.com/musicusa.

4. Ronald B. Thomas, "Rethinking the Curriculum" *Music Educators Journal* 56, no. 6 (1970): 70.

George Boespflug is the director of the Biola University Conservatory of Music in La Mirada, California. He has served in higher education for the past seventeen years, both in the classroom and as an administrator. He is a graduate of the Eastman School of Music, holding a doctorate of musical arts in piano performance and literature. He has appeared as a soloist with the Rochester Philharmonic Orchestra, Colorado Symphony Orchestra, Boulder Chamber Players, Alfred University Orchestra, and Houghton College Philharmonia. He has collaborated with members of various major orchestras, including the Boston Symphony Orchestra, St. Louis Orchestra, Rochester Philharmonic, and Chinese National Orchestra. He has appeared on public radio as a soloist and recorded a compact disc of solo piano works, *From Wesley Chapel.*

12

Of Concert Bands and Garage Bands: Creating Democracy through Popular Music

Randall Everett Allsup

This chapter will examine the structure of middle and high school band programs with an eye toward introducing the informal processes associated with making popular music. Band, in this context, does not refer to Bon Jovi or the local garage band, but to school-sponsored activities like wind ensembles, pep bands, marching bands, jazz bands, and pit bands, as well as small-group ensembles, sectionals, and lessons. As band directors and music educators, we will look for ways to appropriate the best of popular music making, borrowing what works to create shared understandings, hybrids, and links to our own programs. I will affirm and critique the values of both cultures—school music and popular music–so that together students and teachers might consider school-based instrumental music from a broader, more potentially rich perspective. In my conclusion, I will avoid prescribed guidelines or recommended practices (as we shall see, the processes of popular music making thrive within the local, the inimitable) in favor of *more* questions—thinking that reconceptualizes the role of school-based instrumental music.

High School Band and Popular Music

Before I begin my investigation, allow me to establish my credentials. In high school—and grade school, for that matter—I was a bona fide "band geek" (although I now prefer the more generic label "music geek"). Not only did I participate in every musical activity my high school offered, I ate lunch in the band room, did homework after school in the band room, and spent most of my time outside school with the friends I met in music classes. Band was a community, a place of evolving identity—it was what philosophers call "a way of being."

In an article in the *Music Educators Journal* titled "The School Ensemble: A Culture of Our Own," Steven Morrison postulates that band programs represent an indigenous North American culture, which, like all musical subcultures, lays claim to specific "customs, conventions, and conversational manner[s]."[1] These include traditional practices, social contracts, group identifiers, and organizational hierarchies.[2] Because bands serve functions that their members value, they produce a kind of "right result" for those involved.[3] These values are far ranging, and some may have less to do with music making than with identity and community making.

As teachers in the twenty-first century, we are more aware than ever of the role culture plays in learning. My investigation of band culture and popular music is framed by the proposition that *culture*—understood in its broadest sense—*shapes minds,* situates our thinking and understanding, and contextualizes learning.[4] Cultures are not benign, but ideological, and cultural membership is designed as much to constrain as to enable. Even a band program as diverse as the one I enjoyed produced results that were often at odds with a larger shared community—and even antithetical to later musical pursuits. The music I played in the car and at home seemed far away from the music I was playing in high school band. I was listening to one kind of music, but performing another.

This dichotomy seems built into band culture. Even from the very beginning, when our students choose their first instruments, our programs require them to leave their musical world behind and enter one that is new and has little to do with the music they may already know and like. Who will deny that beginning band music is so tepid and bland that young musicians may wait years before they play something that is recognizable, age appropriate, or even likable? Band arrangements of popular songs, moreover, have a shelf life so brief that the music becomes passé by the time the work is finally ready for performance.

Outside the band room, our students' lives are filled with diverse musical activities, from impromptu dances in homes and hallways to garage band rehearsals in windowless basements. Researchers who have looked at informal music making (the processes associated with the creation of popular music by popular musicians) have noted that these self-selected communities place a premium on spontaneous and creative activity.[5] In schools, by contrast, structured creative experiences (occurring primarily in general music classes) are likely to end around the sixth grade.[6] This is especially true for students who wish to take up a wind instrument or sing in the choir, as the institutional structure of large ensembles de-emphasizes experimentation and creativity in favor of a standard or canonical repertory.

Large musical ensembles, from post–Civil War to the present, have tended to exist under the exclusive province of educational or professional organizations.[7] Instrumentalists who create groups outside these systems tend to be hidden from institutional view. In Ruth Finnegan's 1989 ethnography of music making in a small town, she observed that the purposes of private music making—especially in the idioms of rock and jazz—differ greatly from those of public school bands and choirs.[8] Rather than performing already written works, these independent groups compose their own self-reflective and intrinsically meaningful music.[9] Consequently, the popularity of so-called garage bands reveals an intriguing discrepancy between the practices of a local, or hidden, musical world and the broad pedagogical objectives of institutionalized music. We might ask ourselves whether our traditional musical outlets sufficiently satisfy an aesthetic need—specifically, the desire to create and share.

Band programs need spaces where students can carve out an identity that is linked intrinsically with music that reflects—as much as possible—the convergence of multiple cultures, the more total self. Small groups may seem a logical way to attain this outcome. However, band students have few approved opportunities to interact in small groups with their peers. The chamber music that does occur during the school year is frequently linked to musical organizations, as in state-run solo and ensemble contests or all-district and all-state competitions. These networks unequivocally emphasize performance outcomes and their assessment. Moreover, they are typically reserved for the school's most proficient (though not necessarily most talented or musical) students—players who can afford private lessons, young musicians who have dedicated themselves to one instrument and style of playing, and students who are unafraid of competition.

I know of very few band programs in which students are asked to explore, experiment, and create their own music. The format of a large concert band necessarily precludes such experiences, and unless a studio instructor is particularly inventive, students are given little opportunity to compose or improvise in private lessons.

Often the responsibility to teach improvisation (to say nothing of composition) falls largely to the jazz band instructor. Although the study of jazz necessarily emphasizes creativity, jazz music itself has an inherent, idiomatic structure—it is a musical world or culture in which basic

instruction is as teacher-centered as the traditional band experience.[10] Even more problematic is the fact that instruction is likely to be limited to the instruments that comprise a big band: five saxophones, four trumpets, four trombones, a piano, bass, guitar, and drums.

The good news is that what is sometimes missing in school band programs is often occurring on the outside. I am referring not simply to the informal practices of popular musicians but also to associative methods of thinking and being, what psychologists call "frames of mind."[11] Band directors (or anyone) can learn a great deal from popular music—how it is created, how it is organized, and what it means to take part in it.

Big Cultures and Little Cultures

Let's continue to examine the term "culture," as it will provide us with a starting point from which to explore. Culture—represented here as all encompassing—is the very backdrop of every human activity, artistic or otherwise. In the societal sense, culture depends upon learning for the reproduction of values, while its manifestations—laws, languages, art forms, and so forth—provide the medium through which we understand our world.[12] Jerome Bruner considers culture a kind of "toolkit" by which we "construct not only our worlds but our very conceptions of ourselves and our powers."[13] We learn through context—through interactions with the world around us, "around the dinner table when family members try to make joint sense of what happened that day, or when kids try to help each other make sense of the adult world, or when a master and apprentice interact on the job."[14] Learning depends upon being with others in the world.

From this view, it would be a fiction to conceive of formal education as somehow fixed, neutral, or objective. Too often, Bruner writes, learning in school is viewed as detached from so-called real life; rather, school, like band, "is a culture itself, not a 'preparation' for it, a warming up."[15] For John Dewey, school should respect the "social basis of living," integrating "the concrete, the human side of things" rather than the abstract, "the academic—unsocial."[16] Physician-educator Maria Montessori decried the compartmentalization that occurs when academic institutions act apart from practical life experiences. She wrote, "Often the education of children consists in pouring into their intelligence the intellectual contents of school programmes. And often these programmes have been compiled in the official department of education, and their use is imposed by law upon the teacher and child."[17]

These authors are suggesting that when teachers, schools, or colleges "educationalize" experience, they may be entertaining only a partial sense of life's possibilities. Equally, when music educators "educationalize" music, we place limits on what is musically possible. When we remain fixed within the confines of a content area or specialization, we further exacerbate the dichotomy between what students see as school music (or band music) and "real" music.

I readily admit that investigating social theories of music learning is problematic. Cultures cannot be easily classified—they resist stasis, they blur at the edges. Edward

Said reminds us that relationships within larger cultures are often fluid, with members participating in a variety of groups— even those ostensibly opposed to each other.[18] Patricia Shehan Campbell observed that even very young children splinter from the larger culture, or "big culture," into subcultures, or "little cultures," very early in their lives.[19]

An examination of big and little cultures is important in many ways. *While all students belong to a range of musical subcultures, schools sanction (and finance) only a few such groups.* Because a larger school- and industry-based infrastructure, or superculture, supports authorized activities like wind ensembles, saxophone quartets, and marching bands, the actual participants rarely determine the rules for membership. A big culture—say, publishers of curriculum guides, how-to books, and periodicals like the *Instrumentalist;* professional organizations like MENC: The National Association for Music Education and NYSSMA (New York State School Music Association); sponsors of national and statewide competitions and festivals; or teacher training programs at universities and colleges—often predetermines the character of school music groups. Because so much musical activity is prescribed and codified, school music programs serve as good examples of what Paulo Freire calls the "banking concept of education."[20] Music teachers begin to resemble a kind of banking guarantor with musical activities existing primarily on fixed terms or according to regulations and standards; our students, meanwhile, act as the beneficiaries of our largesse.[21]

In spite of the educational superstructure

that supports it, the irony of high school band is that it is isolated within the world of music. Band music, after all, is rarely heard on the radio (even classical stations), and its recordings are next to impossible to buy at the local mall. At the same time, its structure—its ideology—is hierarchical, dogmatic, even undemocratic. This creates a kind of lose-lose scenario. Here is an organization that is not supported within the larger or popular culture but is unable to capitalize on the freedom and diversity typically associated with outsider cultures.

Learning in and out of School

One of the advantages of popular music is that learning is transmitted through enculturation rather than formal instruction. Music anthropologist Allan Merriam characterized enculturation as a lifelong procedure whereby behaviors and concepts are learned through socialization. While Merriam has a behaviorist's point of view, his definition resonates with the reciprocal nature of informal music making. Music learned through enculturation "is judged in terms of its acceptability to [a particular] society as a whole. Thus music sound feeds back upon the concepts held about music, which in turn alters or reinforces behavior and eventually changes or strengthens music practice."[22]

I sense that for Merriam, enculturation is a dynamic process, one in which a particular society or subculture negotiates to some degree the terms of its engagement. A notable difference between enculturation and schooling is that, in the case of enculturation, the less knowledgeable participate more closely with the knowledgeable in the construction of meaning. Schooling, on the other hand, is an authority-directed process of framing young minds. School is set apart from the real world and is where students learn information that is essential to a group or society's survival.[23]

School, unfortunately, can be a place of confusion and irrelevance, and learning is often conceived as being done *to* children, not in dialogue *with* them. John Holt writes:

> Almost every child, on the first day he sets foot in a school building, is smarter, more curious, less afraid of what he doesn't know, better at finding and figuring things out, more confident, resourceful, persistent, and independent, than he will ever again be in his schooling or, unless he is very unusual and lucky, for the rest of his life.[24]

Holt is referring to the unnaturalness of formal education. After all, he contends, a six-year-old preschooler has already mastered at least one language and learned to negotiate his or her world through trial and error.[25] Holt takes a dismal view of formal education, implying that the operations of school deaden curiosity; his assertion that schools actually *interfere* with self-esteem and creative thinking is particularly worrisome.

I wish to return to Paulo Freire's notion of schooling as the "banking concept of education." In this scenario, students are seen as empty minds, "passively open to the reception of deposits of reality from the world outside."[26] The following attitudes and practices within this banking concept will almost certainly be familiar to any school of music or conservatory graduate:

1. the teacher teaches and the students are taught;

2. the teacher knows everything and the students know nothing;

3. the teacher thinks and the students are thought about;

4. the teacher talks and the students listen—meekly;

5. the teacher chooses and enforces his choice, and the students comply;

6. the teacher acts and the students have the illusion of acting through the action of the teacher;

7. the teacher chooses the program content, and the students (who were not consulted) adapt to it.[27]

Ideally, teachers in school should not separate the world into one that is known, approved of, and then taught and one that students are expected to leave behind as they enter the classroom. Who will argue, however, that almost all music course work, from studio lessons to band rehearsals and theory classes, is structured around the banking approach to learning?

By contrast, the informal learning that occurs outside school is socially shared and democratic by nature. In an article titled "Of Garage Bands and Song-Getting: The Musical Development of Young Rock Musicians," Patricia Shehan Campbell observed teenagers working collectively outside school in a kind of mutual learning community.[28] Membership centered around pedagogy, with participants teaching and learning the rules of rock music in a spontaneous and self-directed manner.

The experience of performing changes when it is brought into the schools. While the musical purpose of concert bands and garage bands is basically "song-getting," the means or pedagogy of these groups noticeably diverge. Jeffery, one of the fourteen-year-olds in Campbell's study, describes the discrepancy between music making in school and out:

> Well, [general] music at school is boring because we just sit and listen to stuff. And band goes too slow, 'cause the bulk of the kids don't practice. And I quit my piano lessons 'cause I wasn't getting anywhere—just playing "Feelings" and "Scarborough Fair" over and over again. But I got a guitar at home, and a couple of guys from school and I formed a band this summer. It's working out.[29]

School music did not work for Jeffrey because it conflicted with his own understanding of what real music is. It is not, for example, talking *about* music or playing the popular music of an older generation. Nor, with reference to the school band, did Jeffrey wish to be with players who did not share his commitment or enthusiasm. Jeffery dropped out of school music because only one view or methodology was offered—but importantly, he did not drop out of *home* music, choosing instead to create a learning environment that better suited his needs.

Introducing democratic processes into a formal music setting is a complex task, more nuanced than letting a choir select the color of its robes or allowing a pep band to vote on music. Democracy requires cooperation and collaboration, and it must involve more than just adults—it should incorporate the rights of *both* teachers and students. James Beane and Michael Apple identified the following seven conditions upon which democratic learning depends:

1. the open flow of ideas, regardless of

their popularity, that enables people to be as fully informed as possible

2. faith in the individual and collective capacity of people to create possibilities for resolving problems

3. the use of critical reflection and analysis to evaluate ideas, problems, and policies

4. concern for the welfare of others and "the common good;"

5. concern for the dignity and rights of individuals and minorities;

6. an understanding that democracy is not so much an "ideal" to be pursued as an "idealized" set of values that we must live and that must guide our life as a people;

7. the organization of social institutions to promote and extend the democratic way of life.[30]

Beane and Apple's view of democracy is action oriented; a group does not wait for democracy to happen, nor does one person implement it for the sake of others. Rather, democracy must permeate an organization's structure to the extent that it includes the processes of cognition, behavior, and emotional well-being, as well as the arrangement of structural relationships. We need only compare Beane and Apple's seven characteristics of democratic learning with the seven characteristics of the banking approach to see that one is the antithesis of the other.

If we compare popular culture with band culture, we can see that the former provides more possibilities for democratic relationships than the latter. At the same time, popular culture exists at the nexus of adolescence, identity making, and community, creating (in contrast to band culture) a win-win situation for its participants: support from the larger society with myriad spaces for self-expression and self understanding. This is not to say that all associations with popular music are flawless. However, some criticisms of popular music are contradictory, overly generalized, and perhaps a bit superficial.

Popular Music and Identity

We know, of course, that teenagers create identity largely through friends and groups of friends, participating in many little cultures. These subcultures, according to Jonathon Epstein in *Adolescents and Their Music: If It's Too Loud, You're Too Old,* are characterized "by the distinct values, beliefs, symbols, and actions which certain youth employ to attend to, and cope with, their shared cultural experience."[31] Concerning music, he states the important, but somewhat obvious, fact that "what you listen to, or do not listen to, partially defines who you are within youth culture."[32] Certainly the same can be said about subcultures within a retirement community or a music conservatory (and, with regard to Epstein's title, I do know a certain professor emeritus who likes his Mahler rather loud).

It is common wisdom that young people join performing and nonperforming musical subgroups in order to define themselves against authority—that is, against adults. According to researchers Zillman and Gan, once participants join a musical subgroup, the following privileges accrue:

- They are defined in their own eyes as elite.
- They enjoy the attendant gratification of belonging.
- They take pleasure, even feel superior, in distinguishing themselves from others.[33]

These researchers contend that shared beliefs and rivalry both define involvement in a subculture: "the stronger the involvement in a particular music genre, the more likely the disparagement of competing ones."[34]

Many studies about youth culture and popular music garner unsurprising results.[35] Popular music plays a key role in mediating one's way in the world.[36] It helps to satisfy emotional needs and relieve boredom.[37] For Simon Frith, popular music is so powerful an influence, it is responsible in large measure for the manufacture of self.[38] "The question we should be asking," he writes, "is not what does popular music *reveal* about 'the people' but how does it *construct* them."[39]

According to Frith, the experience of popular music is communal; it forms around its listeners a collection of shared experiences. Thus, popular music has four social functions:

● *Popular music answers questions of identity.* Popular music helps to create who we are; and just as importantly, it helps us to say who we are *not.* Categories of taste automatically separate us into groups; these can be based on race, gender, class, ideology, age, nationality, and so on.

● *Popular music gives us a means to manage public and private emotions.* The most obvious example of this is the popularity of love songs, which help to illuminate all manner of confusion, satisfaction, or dilemma.

● *Popular music shapes popular memory.* Our experiences with popular music, personal or shared, facilitate recall of significant events later in our lives. Moreover, our greatest investment in popular music usually occurred during adolescence, a time defined by significant developmental concerns.

● *Popular music is something possessed.* This philosophical notion of ownership implies that self-identity and lifestyle are tangled within issues of taste.[40]

For many readers, the aforementioned conclusions will seem rather commonsensical. We should keep in mind, of course, that sociological development need not be limited to popular music. Certainly *all* manner of music—or dance, art, and theater, for that matter—helps us make sense of our world, provided that we seek out, or are exposed to, new forms and experiences. Because of the work my high school band did with *Appalachian Spring,* each time I hear Copland's finale I return, almost viscerally, to the vast cornfields of central Illinois and a tiny farming town called Herscher.

As stated earlier, *cultures shape mind.* Thus, getting to the crux of what makes popular music so important to so many, we can safely say that certain art forms are better at *shaping* particular ways of thinking than others. Dance, for example, addresses the body and movement in a way that poetry does not and cannot. Especially apparent to me is the manner in which popular music facilitates real-life experiences. The structure of the high school band, I contend, often—although not always—neglects to capitalize on shared meanings, constructed identities, and evolving communities. School-based musical learning does a poor job of helping students understand their world, which to my mind, is a reasonable expectation a teenager may bring to a music class.

When, for example, *I* consider questions

of love, I don't look for help from Jim Curnow or Alfred Reed. I am likely to go straight to popular music. Lately I've been listening quite a lot to a song by Sade called "By Your Side." When I hear its simple chords and her smooth-sounding voice, I am transported:

> Oh when you're cold
> I'll be there,
> Hold you tight to me.
> Oh when you're low
> I'll be there
> By your side, baby.[41]

The bass pedal kicks a soft hip-hop beat, and Sade's quiet straight tones feel physically near to me; the sound is intimate, warm, and full of care. Although the lyrics say nothing I haven't heard before—and are indeed exceedingly banal—for a moment I think I understand love just a little bit better.

I would like to emphasize that it is in popular culture that the so-called "real world" (everyday problems and concerns) is privileged. Concerns that philosophers call "material reality" are found in abundance in songs and stories about heartaches, breakups, deceptions, and love.[42] I wonder, furthermore, if there are many instrumentalists like myself for whom the immediacy, the intimacy, of their horn provides only an abstract understanding of everyday emotions, of self or place. My high school band program did many wonderful things, but it did not try very hard to address my lived world, which included the cruel hierarchies of high school life, the vagaries of friendship, and the confusions of love. In retrospect, I wish that there were places for me to connect across cultures so that the music

I played in the car and at home were relevant to my formal instruction.

Making Connections

The astute reader may at this point wish for a little clarification. How can band be a unique culture full of far-ranging values—a place to eat lunch and do homework, to socialize and make friends—and yet be somehow dislocated from the real world? Indeed, the introduction of this chapter emphasized the special relationship between band, community, and self-identity. To answer this question (and it is a good one), we might wish to examine the kind of music we teach. If *music* is the root of said activities and experiences, what exactly is taking place in the music classroom?

To help us answer this question, I'd like to refer to Christopher Small's book *Musicking*. Small's thesis emphasizes that "music is not a thing at all, but an activity, something that people do," so that the term "music" might be better understood as the old English verb, *to musick*.[43] Musical meaning, for Small, does not reside in the musical object, nor is music autonomous, containing universal values, as some used to believe.[44] Rather, Small contends that musical meaning resides in its relationships—*in its connections between participants*, between performer and audience, in history, interpretation, ideology, ritual, tradition, family, religion, politics, work, play, and ceremony.[45] Such a sociological understanding of music is not a distinct or discrete function of music making. Instead, social relationships are fundamental to understanding music; social relationships (or culture) are music's very essence. This suggests that musical meaning is largely located in both sound and action.

While band programs certainly provide unique opportunities for understanding the beauty of Copland and others, and while such music making is at the nexus of important developmental experiences, I find myself very much afraid for the future of the high school band paradigm. What kind of relationships do we offer that will survive the rapid change occurring in the world around us? I don't wish to devalue activities like eating lunch in the band room and the friendships that spring from performing together, but I wonder if what we are doing *musically* will remain sufficiently compelling to future generations.

I strongly believe that we need to think of high school band—or any formal learning scenario—as a partnership. This means looking at musical relationships as intensely as our students practice their parts and we study our scores. Perhaps the experience of making music will become more important than genre, and process more important than product. In such a learning scenario, interested students will bring unsanctioned genres, like the many that fall under the aegis of popular music, into the curriculum.

One of the main questions of this chapter (indeed, this entire book) is *at what expense do educators ignore the real world as represented by popular culture?* Does band culture have an obligation to be anything other than it is, any more than a ballet company has an obligation to introduce the works of Pina Bausch or MTV? One might argue that the band tradition is actually authentic; our practices imitate real-world practice. After all, on a fundamental level, the high

school band rehearses no differently from the Chicago Symphony Orchestra or the Dallas Wind Ensemble. Proponents of a progressive core curriculum, whose teachers have only recently begun asking math students to think like mathematicians and biology students to think like biologists, might well view bands and choirs with some degree of envy. Our high school musicians are doing, in effect, what professional musicians do.

Well, sort of. They are doing what *classical* musicians do, and that is not a bad thing! However, many classical musicians also collaborate with filmmakers and puppeteers, start improvisation ensembles, and play secondary instruments in ska bands, operating outside the hierarchical structure of classical music culture. This is what I would like to see occurring in schools, in addition to spectacular spring concerts and all-state auditions.

I suggest that we consider two aspects of popular music making that might broaden the typical band experience. First is acknowledging the appeal of popular culture to everyday experience. As we have noted, band is a place and time in which all kinds of personal and artistic growth occurs. Yet this musical development is negotiated through a canonic repertoire— solo works by Paul Creston, marches by Sousa, études, scales, and so on. Students may have few opportunities to create music using their own voice. Can we craft opportunities for young musicians to make sense of their immediate world through sound so that they enjoy the kind of aesthetic understanding that music provides as it relates to friends, love, good times, and bad?

If we create such an opening, *we will democratize band,* which is my second suggestion. Relationships, both musical and social, will be undemocratic if musical activities are not negotiated among all participants. The aesthetic experience is transformed when music making is shared. (By sharing, I refer to the processes of inventing, arranging, voting upon, experimenting with, analyzing, and talking about music.) These processes will materialize differently from school to school. How could they not? If our goal is to introduce the informal practices of popular musicians and the unique thinking associated with popular genres, our methods will produce divergent, rather than convergent, results. To make this point, I would like to share with you two studies that link non-hierarchical music making with the very personal, human need to express one's self and share one's world.

Rethinking Curriculum

In an article titled "'To Say Something That Was Me': Developing a Personal Voice through Improvisation," Ros McMillan describes a course in which music majors at the Victorian College of the Arts in Melbourne, Australia, constructed personally meaningful works of music through composition or improvisation.[46] McMillan asked his students to develop their own "musical voice," a term that is meant to signify "the revelation of self through an expressive act."[47]

Everyday concerns and relationships were common themes among the participants, whose compositions resembled a kind of instrumental autobiography. One student named Belinda wrote her piece at a time in her life when she was "broken-hearted," and her music represented "all my anxieties and all my hurt and all my frustrations." Belinda's work, "Dreaming of the Sea," was "inspired by aspects of the sea as seen from her home town of Sydney, and … consisted entirely of her own words."[48] Students wrote pieces that related to their own lives and values:

> Hugh described *Tip to Toe* as a piece about people "from top to bottom" adding: "We all have disparate elements to our personality … and I tried to represent what's going on in me." Damien noted that his piece *Reconciliation* represented his feelings towards relationships with people and the importance of being reconciled after "disagreements and stuff." Fran summed up her peers' feelings when she stated that it was important "to say something that was just me."[49]

Student compositions were highly diverse, applying "unusual instrumental and vocal sound including distortion, non-Western percussion, a choir and electronics."[50] McMillan's study suggests that where identity and music making intersect, the measures and means of creativity are limitless and unforeseeable. His conservatory-trained musicians—students heavily invested in authorized genres like jazz or classical music—took musical information from a number of subgroups to create personal amalgams that were meaningful and self-reflective.

This is a new consideration for the twenty-first-century music educator. How do we teach in scenarios where the structure of musical learning is more important than the genre of music being investigated—where genre serves expression, rather than vice versa? In our new global world, a limitless and unforeseeable place, no single culture will shape minds, but many. And if this is true, can we in good conscience authorize one tradition of music making at the exclusion of others—as we do now in band and choir?

In my own study, I worked with nine high school band members on a project like McMillan's.[51] To get to know my participants, I asked them several questions about musical experience and taste: "What instruments do you play or have played (in and out of school)? What groups do you play in or have played in (in and out of school)? What kind of music do you listen to?" Their e-mail responses included reference to the following genres: techno, acid, punk, emo, hard rock, contemporary Christian, Christian rock, ska, classical, jazz, "older jazz," Broadway songs, soundtracks, blues, heavy metal, classic rock, funk, folk, reggae, jam band, acoustic rock, bebop, fusion, rag time, swing, and progressive rock. Artists mentioned included Black Sabbath, Steppenwolf, Jackson 5, Linkin Park, Metallica, Supertones, DC Talk, Benny Goodman, Steven Curtis Chapman, Bob Dylan, Styx, Third Day, Newsboys, Phish, Steve Vai, Moe, Allman Brothers, Bach, Skynard, and Sousa. They also referenced influential works, such as "Epinicion for Winds and Percussion" by John Paulson, Suite in E-Flat and *The Planets* by Gustav Holst, "One Note Samba" by Jobim, "Cortez the Killer" by Neil Young, "In the Mood" by Glenn Miller, "Sing, Sing, Sing" by Benny Goodman, and "The Sound of Music" by Rodgers and Hammerstein.

One student confessed to downloading over six hundred works onto her MP3 list (an amount I recently discovered is quite modest). My participants performed in a variety of ensembles such as concert band, orchestra, church praise band, community band, senior band, stage band, jazz band, jazz combo, festival band, choir, garage band, and jam band. Experience on the following instruments was cited: French horn, voice, auxiliary percussion, mallet percussion, saxophone, baritone horn, trumpet, piano, timpani, snare drum, electric guitar, acoustic guitar, kazoo, clarinet, drum set, vibes, cello, acoustic bass, and electric bass. I suspect that nine band students anywhere would supply an equally impressive amount of information.[52]

These students represent a new era, I think. We live in a time of global information where easy access to popular media shapes musical tastes and exposure. In our Internet world of soft boundaries and instant discoveries, we might wish to rethink our assumptions surrounding teens, identity, and music teaching. As I glance over the previous paragraph, I wonder how important any single genre is to today's teens. In my high school, we defined ourselves by the specific type of music we liked; there were groups that liked heavy metal and others that liked new wave. But does one particular musical style suffice as a personal identifier anymore? Does a musical subculture like techno define or represent a person less, I wonder, than the amalgam of music listeners now have easy access to? Is diversity, rather than exclusivity, a new paradigm among young music lovers? Such a contention would challenge the research of Frith, Epstein, and Zillman and Gan.

Let's assume that this notion is even partially true—that our students' personal relationships to popular and canonic genres are today more pliable than rigid—*then here is an opening for band directors and music teachers!* If we create opportunities for students to find their own voice, then maybe, just maybe, the distinctions and dichotomies between school music and popular music will begin to blur. Such an experiment might affect all aspects of musical learning: thinking and feeling, community and identity, creativity and development, action and theory.[53]

I wanted to test this theory, and as part of my doctoral dissertation I worked with the aforementioned nine high school students in rural upstate New York. I was curious to find out what would happen if band students were given institutional space and support to create music that *they* found meaningful. The study (published in the *Journal of Research in Music Education*) produced outcomes that are of interest to our investigation.[54]

Thinking Like Popular Musicians

My nine study participants elected to split into two randomly selected ensembles. Group One chose not to compose on their traditional band instruments, opting for electric guitars, keyboards, electric bass, and drums. This group came to resemble a garage band and adopted an informal, collaborative method for composing. Their time together was productive and full of laughs. Here are some of my notes:

There is unobtrusive sound everywhere.

While Luke and Colin talk, they emphasize and explain their opinions through improvisations on their instruments. The sound of guitars and drums mingle with voices as if they are the natural components of an everyday discussion.[55]

A typical scenario might include four instrumentalists quietly improvising. The players appear lost in thought, impervious to their surroundings. What seems like jumbled sound to me—no unifying theme heard, no single melody explored, no musical or rehearsal objective stated—is a compositional method favored by popular musicians. When, for example, someone's experimentations take shape or a chord progression suddenly begins to speak, a head will lift from a fingerboard, eye contact is made, and disconnected sound begins to meld. The information becomes communal property, with or without talking. This intuitive and democratic process is one of the strongest aspects of popular music making.

Lucy Green recorded similar observations in her book *How Popular Musicians Learn.* One of Green's interviewees, a musician named Andy, describes the communal aspect of composing popular music:

The main writer is the singer—he does come up with all the lyrics—and more often than not he comes up with the basic tune. But as soon as we get into rehearsal it's no longer what he came up with. We pull it apart, we reform it, we re-structure it, add the harmonies, the bass line, the beat, the rhythm, everything to it. And it comes out as a different product. You can still hear the basic thing, but it is more refined, it's more definite in structure.[56]

217

Psychologists might label this process "gestalt," but to me it speaks to the strength of democracy and music education. In a democratic music setting, there is an expectation that each group member brings special qualities that enhance a work so that it is greater for having been shared. Says Josh, one of my study participants, "one person would come up with an idea, and we'd just kinda like work off the idea. Pretty much everybody was receptive. Like if I came in with an idea, pretty much everybody accepted it. If someone didn't like it, they'd say so right away. It works pretty well."[57]

Things didn't work out as well with my second group. Composing for their primary band instruments, these students chose to write what they referred to as "a classical piece." The compositional process had a splintering effect on their community.

The students viewed classical music as having a predetermined structure, so the first stages of music making were more conceptual than exploratory. Before playing a single note, Group Two debated form (aria, slow song, multiple movements, contrasting sections, AABA), tonality (major, minor, modal), historical style (baroque, classical, romantic, modern, mixture), orchestration (brass ensemble, voice, piano, acoustic bass and acoustic guitar), tempo, and even language (Italian, English).

There were several disadvantages. "In the beginning, we moved along pretty slow," said Ryan. "We had a lot of trouble putting our ideas together," another member told me. As an observer of the process, I noticed that Group Two would fix upon an idea, write it down, and rush to rehearse it. The process seemed to leave little room for dis-

covery or surprises. Because musical ideas were not generated collectively, they were more difficult to integrate. Ryan reflected upon this, "When four people have these ideas, it can be kinda overwhelming." He continued, "We did a lot of composing at home instead of as a group." I asked Ryan how this process was different from composing in a garage band. In a garage band, "someone will come up with a riff or something, and we'll just kinda jam. More like the other group did for their thing."[58]

Midway through the process, Group Two began to make adjustments, as Jesse's comments confirm:

> It took us a while to be able to figure out how to do this with more than one person putting their input into it. At the beginning, we thought since we're never going to get along [musically], we'll each do our own thing and then try to improve it. But we never ended up getting something based on that because it was just too hard to put such different ideas together. Eventually, I guess we just started thinking together, trying to work things out.[59]

What Jesse fails to mention is that his group "started thinking together" and "working things out" when they created a jazz piece. "We had a lot less problems with jazz," said Steve.[60] The main difference was individual versus collective, he explains:

> The classical piece, it was more like everyone's individual ideas, and we just lumped them together, except for the very end—that one or two of us did together, and then the jazz piece is sort of like, "What about this here? Oh yeah! That sounds good, we'll put that in."[61]

It was interesting to watch this group evolve. As the compositional process became more participatory, I observed not only musical and individual growth, but also communal growth—echoing John Dewey's notion of democracy as community in the making.[62] Such an experience led to significant insights on community, learning, and responsibility, as noted by Ryan:

> With democracy, the weaker members–everybody–gets a chance to say something, and so the more things go on, maybe, like if I were the quiet one, I would start to say things more and more as it went on 'cause I'd feel more comfortable, I'd feel like they care about what I have to say.[63]

Breaking out of Traditional Instruction

Perhaps it is time to relinquish some traditions within band culture. Can we move away from teacher-focused instruction—away from the notion of training and toward musical learning that is multifaceted and culturally relevant? Don't words like facilitator, instructor, mentor, or coach sound better than Director (with a capital D)? Indeed, this kind of Directorship has a long history in North America. In 1939, a leader in our profession named Theodore Normann created ten basic principles of instrumental music instruction. These included "a generous amount of rote teaching and imitative drill, keeping every child busy, and remembering that the attention span of the average child is rather small."[64]

Unfortunately, the notion that students cannot be trusted to think for themselves is still prevalent today. In an interview published in 1999 by the *Instrumentalist,* a celebrated California band director boasts:

> I follow the 10-second rule, meaning I rarely stop for more than 10 seconds. I have had colleagues time me to be sure I quickly diagnose a problem, give instruction, and start the ensemble playing again. I don't dwell on anything for long because students grow restless. If you lose their mental concentration, the rehearsal is over.[65]

Without opportunities for dialogue, or even reflection, this kind of teaching creates and reinforces the dichotomy between school music (vis-à-vis one person's choice) and music that meets the expectations of a majority.

Compare this traditional style of musical training with the learning I observed in my dissertation study. The following is from field notes taken shortly after Group Two started its jazz piece:

> Work is focused, noisy, productive, and kinetic; there are always jokes, musical or otherwise. For example, while Steve and Priscilla are sketching out a piano riff, Ryan is playing a lick from Miles Davis's *So What,* which Jesse imitates. Steve is a self-taught pianist and it takes longer for him to catch up. Eventually all four players regroup and rehearse a section or two before the process breaks down and starts again.[66]

In this scenario, the primary learning objectives are creative, social, and above all *self-determined.* Learning is not educationalized, existing as some far-off finished product in the mind of an adult. Rather, the students have taken ownership of the process:

the context from which they create musical ideas, the manner in they acquire technical skills, as well as the pace of learning. I can picture Jay-Z, Missy Elliot, or Stephen Sondheim working in a similar manner. If this is a natural method—learning through creating, learning through laughing—why is it so infrequently encountered in schools? These comments are from my December 6, 2001, field notes:

> Tonight, perhaps, I have witnessed more laughing *and learning* than I have ever encountered in a school setting. It makes me wonder why we do not smile and laugh more often in school. Are assignments that boring? Are teachers afraid of losing control? Are schools so unnatural a place that that there is no room for laughter?[67]

I asked Ryan's opinion about the benefits of this kind of group work—how might it help a band program? Is there a place for this kind of learning within our tradition? He answered:

> It kinda makes it [the band experience] more creative, you know, 'cause they [small group participants] realize that they can be creative and have fun with music, and put in what they want to put in. And it might change their attitude in like regular concert band. It might like boost their musicianship.[68]

Looking over Ryan's words, I begin to wonder, Has the band room become a colonized site—a place taken over and changed by more powerful outside forces? How much fun are students having with music? Are they putting in as much as they are getting out? Can we re-imagine the band room

as a site of greater possibility—as a garage perhaps, a basement, a musical study hall, a recording studio? Answering these questions is difficult. It requires reconceptualizing institutional roles, and above all, embracing the complexity of our students. How prepared am I to teach in this undefined world, in a diversity of cultures and subcultures?

I would like to share the following statement from Colin, one of my dissertation participants:

> Well, I really like the [electric] guitar a lot. It's more fun to me than the trumpet. The trumpet is a good instrument—I'm not dissing the trumpet, or anything. I love the trumpet. If it were possible for me to play guitar in band, I'd do it. You can't do that obviously. So I play trumpet as a secondary thing, so I can be involved in band. I like it a lot, it's fun and everything, but I like the guitar a lot more. I practice trumpet because I have to for my grade. I practice guitar because I really want to—you know, to get better. The music is very similar, but to me there's more possibilities with guitar.[69]

I find this statement honest, uncomfortable, but somewhat reassuring. Colin is suggesting that he need not choose between one tradition and another, nor is he abandoning Holst for Hendrix. He is demonstrating a flexibility of taste that is, I think, far more complex and nuanced than that of the average conservatory graduate.

I suspect that Colin is a better guitar player for having studied trumpet and a better trumpet player for knowing guitar. Looking back to when I was Colin's age, I wish *I* had learned to sing in a rock band, write my own music, or play the drums—but I didn't. I knew early on that if I wanted to be a music major, playing anything other than classical saxophone would not get me into the best music schools. While my classical training has made me a better musician, it has always been up to me to transfer what I learned in college to the music of other genres and cultures. I find this kind of education too roundabout, too convoluted, even a bit dishonest. Yet, I have faith that as band directors in the twenty-first century, we can create learning scenarios that exist without tacit barriers or guilty pleasures. Perhaps we need to graduate more music students like Colin, and fewer like me.

Conclusion

Before ending this chapter, I would like to ask readers to revisit Freire's seven conditions of the banking concept of education. We should ask ourselves, Do we want to be part of a system like this? Let's create a democratic alternative. It might look like this:

• The teacher teaches the students, the students teach the teacher, and the students teach each other.
• The teacher knows a lot, the students know a lot, and everyone knows something.
• The teacher and students think together.
• The teacher and students take turns talking, performing, sharing, and listening.
• The teacher and students make choices together.
• The teacher performs what she does best, the student performs what he does best, they share what they know, and they create community by working together.
• The teacher consults students when designing programs, and the students consult the teacher when designing programs.

Every band program has a unique culture. Some schools emphasize jazz band more than marching band. Some tour the country. Yet no matter how proud we may be of what we offer, our programs are incomplete without student-teacher partnerships. If we create spaces for the informal practices of popular music making, we will open the door to democratic music education, to the real world and real feelings. Our students are inventive enough to make this work. We need simply to work with our students—to listen to them, learn from them, and encourage them.

Notes

1. Steven Morrison, "The School Ensemble: A Culture of Our Own," *Music Educators Journal* 88, no. 2, (2001): 24.
2. Ibid., 25–28.
3. Thomas Regelski, "Musical Values and the Value of Music Education," *Philosophy of Music Education Review* 10, no. 1 (2002): 49–55.
4. Jerome Bruner, *The Culture of Education* (Cambridge: Harvard University Press, 1996).
5. Randall Allsup, "Crossing Over: Mutual Learning and Democratic Action in Instrumental Music Education" (Ed.D. diss., Teachers College, Columbia University, 2002); Patricia Shehan Campbell, "Of Garage Bands and Song-Getting: The Musical Development of Young Rock Musicians," *Research Studies in Music Education*, no. 4 (1995): 12–20; Patricia Shehan Campbell, *Songs in Their Heads: Music and Its Meaning in Children's Lives* (New York: Oxford University Press, 1998); Ruth H. Finnegan, *The Hidden Musicians: Music-Making in an English Town* (Cambridge: Cambridge University Press, 1989); and Lucy Green, *How Popular Musicians Learn: A Way Ahead for Music Education* (Aldershot, UK: Ashgate, 2002).
6. Patirica Shehan Campbell, *Lessons from the World: A Cross Cultural Guide to Music Teaching and Learning* (New York: Schirmer Books,1991), 245.
7. Harold F. Abeles, Charles C. Hoffer, and

Robert H. Klotman, *Foundations of Music Education* (New York: Schirmer, 1995), 15–17; John Tasker Howard and George Kent Bellows, *A Short History of Music in America* (New York: Thomas Y. Crowell, 1967); and Michael Mark and Charles L. Gary, *A History of American Education* (New York: Schirmer, 1992), 264.

8. Finnegan, *The Hidden Musicians.*

9. Ibid., 166–67.

10. Having lived and taught music for over a decade in New York City's Harlem neighborhood (a cultural center of jazz music), I have found that for most young people, jazz and the blues are as alien a musical subculture as classical art music.

11. Howard Gardner, *Frames of Mind: The Theory of Multiple Intelligences* (New York: Basic Books, 1983).

12. Formerly, culture was often depicted as the development and refinement of mind or taste. In each view, culture is linked symbiotically to education.

13. Bruner, *The Culture of Education,* x.

14. Ibid., xi.

15. Ibid., 89.

16. John Dewey and Evelyn Dewey, *Schools of Tomorrow* (New York: Dutton, 1915), 121.

17. Maria Montessori, *The Montessori Method,* trans. A. E. George, (1909: reprint, New York: Schocken, 1964), 62.

18. Edward W. Said, *Culture and Imperialism* (New York: Knopf, 1993); and Edward W. Said, *Reflections on Exile, and Other Essays* (Cambridge: Harvard University Press, 2000).

19. Patricia Shehan Campbell, *Songs in Their Heads,* 184–91.

20. Paulo Freire, *Pedagogy of the Oppressed,* trans. Myra Bergman Ramos (New York: Continuum, 1970), 52–67.

21. Paulo Freire, *Pedagogy of Hope: Reliving Pedagogy of the Oppressed,* trans. Robert R. Barr (New York: Continuum, 1997).

22. Alan Merriam, *The Anthropology of Music* (Evanston, IL: Northwestern University Press, 1964), 145.

23. Estelle Jorgensen, *In Search of Music Education* (Urbana, IL: University of Illinois Press, 1997), 4–6.

24. John Holt, *The Underachieving School* (New York: Dell, 1969), 24.

25. Ibid., 24–25.

26. Freire, *Pedagogy of the Oppressed,* 56.

27. Ibid., 54.

28. Campbell, "Of Garage Bands and Song-Getting."

29. Ibid., 12.

30. James A. Beane and Michael W. Apple, "The Case for Democratic Schools," in *Democratic Schools,* ed. Michael W. Apple and James A. Beane (Alexandria, VA: Association for Supervision and Curriculum Development, 1995), 6–7.

31. Jonathon S. Epstein, "Introduction: Misplaced Childhood: An Introduction to the Sociology of Youth and Their Music," in *Adolescents and Their Music: If It's Too Loud, You're Too Old,* ed. Jonathon S. Epstein (New York: Garland, 1994), xiii.

32. Ibid., xviii.

33. Dolf Zillman and Su-lin Gan, "Musical Taste in Adolescence," in *The Social Psychology of Music,* ed. David J. Hargreaves and Adrian C. North (Oxford: Oxford University Press, 1997), 172, 175–79.

34. Simon Frith, *Sound Effects: Youth Leisure, and the Politics of Rock 'n' Roll* (New York: Pantheon, 1981), cited in Zillman and Gan, "Musical Taste in Adolescence," 172.

35. David G. Hebert and Patricia Shehan Campbell, "Rock Music in American Schools: Positions and Practices since the 1960s," *International Journal of Music Education,* no. 36 (2000): 14–22; Peter G. Christenson and Donald F. Roberts, *It's Not Only Rock and Roll: Popular Music in the Lives of Adolescents* (Cresskill, NJ: Hampton Press, 1998); and Denna Weinstein, "Rock: Youth and Its Music," Popular Music Society 9, no. 3 (1983): 2–16.

36. Robert L. Thompson and Reed Larson, "Social Context and the Subjective Experience of Different Types of Rock Music," *Journal of Youth and Adolescence* 24, no. 6 (1995): 731–44.

37. Mark Tarrant, Adrian C. North, and David J. Hargreaves, "English and American Adolescents' Reasons for Listening to Music," *Psychology of Music,* no. 28 (2000): 166–73; and

Walter Gantz et al., "Gratifications and Expectations Associated with Pop Music among Adolescents," *Popular Music in Society* 6, no. 1 (1978): 81–89.

38. Simon Frith, "Towards an Aesthetic of Popular Music," in *Music and Society: The Politics of Composition, Performance and Reception,* ed. Richard Leppert and Susan McClary (Cambridge: Cambridge University Press, 1987).

39. Ibid., 137.

40. Ibid., 140–44.

41. Sade, "By Your Side" on *Lovers Rock,* Epic 085185.

42. Popular music (like all music) is also the repository of a culture's particular ideology so that although these texts deal largely with material concerns, they are in no way neutral, or necessarily harmless.

43. Christopler Small, *Musicking: The Meaning of Performing and Listening* (Hanover, NH: Wesleyan University Press, 1998), 2.

44. Immanuel Kant, *The Critique of Judgement,* trans. J. H. Bernard (Amherst, New York: Prometheus Books, 2000).

45. Merriam, *The Anthropology of Music,* 209–27; and Andrew Gregory, "The Roles of Music in Society: The Ethnomusicological Perspective," in *The Social Psychology of Music,* 123-40.

46. Ros McMillan, "'To Say Something That Was Me': Developing a Personal Voice through Improvisation," *British Journal of Music Education* 16, no. 3 (1999): 263–73.

47. Ibid., 267.

48. Ibid., 271.

49. Ibid., 269.

50. Ibid., 267.

51. Allsup, "Crossing Over."

52. Ibid., 336–37.

53. Asking students to create music that is meaningful to them may also lead to self-actualization, what I have referred to as "liberatory action." See Randall E. Allsup, "Music Education As Liberatory Practice: Exploring the Ideas of Milan Kundera," *Philosophy of Music Education Review* 9, no. 2 (2001): 3–10.

54. Randall Allsup, "Mutual Learning and Democratic Action in Instrumental Music Education," *Journal of Research in Music Education* 51, no. 1 (2003): 24–37.

55. Allsup, "Crossing Over," 331.

56. Green, *How Popular Musicians Learn,* 80.

57. Allsup, "Crossing Over," 269–94.

58. Ibid., 284.

59. Ibid., 259.

60. Ibid., 295.

61. Ibid., 297.

62. See John Dewey, *Democracy and Education* (New York: MacMillan, 1916); or John Dewey, *Freedom and Culture* (New York: Putnam, 1939).

63. Allsup, "Crossing Over," 293.

64. Theodore F. Normann, *Instrumental Music in Public Schools* (Philadelphia: Oliver Ditson, 1939; dist. by Theodore Presser), 149–52.

65. Catherine Lenzini, "With Energy and Discipline: An Interview with Michael Stone," *The Instrumentalist* 53, no. 6 (1999): 12–14, 87.

66. Allsup, "Crossing Over," 188–89.

67. Ibid., 159.

68. Ibid., 287.

69. Ibid., 242.

Randall Everett Allsup is assistant professor of music and music education at Teachers College, Columbia University. He is the author of a number of articles that address the role of philosophy and social justice in arts educations. He can be reached at ALLSUP@tc.columbia.edu.

13

What Can Music Educators Learn from Popular Musicians?

Lucy Green

Formal Music Education and Informal Music-Learning Practices

Most formal music education contains one or more of the following: written curricula, syllabi, or explicit traditions of teaching and learning; paid teachers, lecturers, or "master musicians" who usually possess some relevant qualifications; systematic assessment mechanisms such as graded exams, national school exams, diplomas, or degrees; musical notation, which is sometimes regarded as peripheral, but more usually, central; and finally, a body of literature, including texts on music, pedagogical texts, and teaching materials. Alongside formal music education there have always been other methods of passing on and acquiring musical skills and knowledge. These involve informal music-learning practices, which, in direct contrast to formal education, include no teaching institutions; no written curricula, syllabi, or explicit teaching traditions; no qualified teachers and lecturers; no assessment mechanisms; no certificates or qualifica-

tions; and little emphasis on notation and literature. Formal music education and informal music learning are not, of course, totally separate spheres. The distinction between them is sometimes blurred, and many people experience aspects of both. But there are some significant differences between them, and for some people the two spheres rarely, or never, coincide.

It is unfortunate that formal music education has only had lasting benefits for a minority of the students who come into contact with it, while in many societies without any formal music education, musical participation is part of daily life for everyone. Further, the vast majority of traditional, folk, jazz, and popular musics of the world originated and developed through informal learning, which in many countries existed alongside formal music education while remaining quite distinct from it.

During the last thirty years of the twentieth century, many of these musics made inroads into formal education, and in some countries they now have a presence in schooling, higher education, private instrumental programs, and even conservatories.

Initially, this represented something like an invasion of new *curriculum content,* with very little attention being paid to the implications it carried for *teaching strategy.* The nature of the informal learning practices of the musicians creating these styles was almost completely overlooked. However, there is currently a surge of interest and a new respect among music educators for these musics and their informal learning practices.

Why Is Popular Music Important for Music Educators?

Over 94 percent of world record sales are in the realm of popular music, while a mere 3.5 percent are in classical music, and 1.5 percent are in jazz.[1] It hardly needs adding that children and young people overwhelmingly favor and identify with popular musics above all others. This is, of course, no reason why popular music should be important for music educators. If the students are already fully imbued with this music, there seems little point in including it in their schooling, where the aim is to introduce them to knowledge and skills that they do *not* already possess. But there is a reason for music teachers to come to a better understanding of not only the music that moves their students but also the learning practices, attitudes, and values of the musicians who produce that music. We must ask ourselves why, despite their evident commitment to music and music learning, so many popular musicians turned away from the formal music education they were offered during their school years. How do they manage to produce music that attracts the interest and enjoy-

ment of the vast majority of the world's population? If we continue to ignore such questions, we will deprive the vast majority of students of that spark that attracts so many musicians and listeners to popular music. A greater understanding of and respect for the informal learning practices of popular music could help educators attract larger numbers of young people and ultimately reinvigorate musical participation in the community at large.

This chapter offers a general overview of the informal learning practices of popular musicians and the attitudes and values associated with these practices. Toward the end, I outline some popular musicians' responses to music in school and to instrumental tuition, and I conclude with a very brief discussion of the possibilities that I believe a serious consideration of popular musicians' informal learning practices, attitudes, and values might offer to formal music education.[2]

Research Methods

I interviewed fourteen English popular musicians living in and around London who were involved in what can broadly be termed Anglo-American guitar-based pop and rock music, as well as other styles cutting across jazz and theater music. I excluded rappers, DJs, and musicians who produce highly electronic, synthesized, and sampled musics, because the learning practices involved in such musics contain significant differences from those of guitar-based rock. I wished to enable a deep treatment of the issues within one substyle, leading to findings that could be compared to learning practices, attitudes, and values in other substyles. In checking the validity of my findings by reviewing existing literature on popular musicians' practices, I found a high degree of commensurability between the responses of the musicians in my sample and those of musicians other researchers have studied.[3]

The musicians were divided into two age-groups so that I could ascertain how much, if at all, informal learning practices and experiences of formal music education had changed over the last forty years of the twentieth century. Those in the older group were aged twenty-three to fifty and had started secondary school between 1960 and 1987, before popular music become part of schooling in England. Those in the younger group were aged from fifteen to twenty-one and had started secondary school after 1988, when popular music

became a normal, established part of the curriculum. The youngest four interviewees were still in school at the time of the research. Apart from age, the only other selection criteria were that none of the interviewees could be personally acquainted with me (there were two minor exceptions), the older ones should be professional or semiprofessional popular musicians, and the younger ones should either play in a popular band (professional or not) or be just about to start one. I interviewed the first fourteen musicians I came across who fit these criteria, accessing them in various ways, from purely coincidental meetings to networking.

I did not seek to interview any famous stars; I was interested in the acquisition of

Table 1
Musician Profiles

Name	Age	Main Instrument(s)	Main Musical Activities
Bernie Holland	50	**Guitar**, Bass, Drums, Keyboards, Perc.	Session, Composer/arranger
Terry Ollis	46	**Drums**	Originals band, Covers bands
Rob Burns	45	**Bass**, Guitar	Session, Composer/arranger
Nanette Welmans	38	**Voice**	Covers/originals bands
Brent Keefe	34	**Drums**	Freelance/session
Peter Williams	27	**Bass**	Covers band, Originals band
Will Cragg	23	**Guitar**, Drums, Bass, Voice	Covers band, Covers duo
Steve Popplewell	21	**Bass**, Guitar	Originals band
Simon Bourke	19	**Drums**, Guitar, Bass	Originals band
Andy Brooks	19	**Guitar**, Sax	Originals band
Michael Whiteman	17	**Drums**, Guitar, Keyboard	Covers/originals band
Emily Dicks	16	**Guitar**	Rehearsal band
Richard Dowdall	15	**Guitar**, Drums, Keyboard	Rehearsal band
Leo Hardt	15	**Sax**, Voice, Keyboard, Guitar, Bass	Planning a band

Note: The main instrument for each person is shown on bold. Many of them had also played other instruments that they had given up.

musicianship, rather than stardom, and of course, the two do not always coincide. However, the oldest five musicians had worked with several well-known artists and bands, including Joan Armatrading, Long John Baldry, Jeff Beck, Eric Burdon of the Animals, Ian Carr, Georgie Fame, Isaac Hayes, Hawkwind, Van Morrison, Leo Sayer, the Stylistics, Danny Thompson, Pete Townshend of the Who, and more. The next six in age were in semiprofessional originals, covers, and function bands; two of the youngest were in their first rehearsal bands with school friends; and the very youngest was planning to form a band soon. Table 1 gives a summary profile of the interviewees.

Popular Musicians Acquiring Skills and Knowledge
Enculturation

By "enculturation," I mean immersion in the music and musical practices of one's environment. This is a fundamental aspect of all music learning, whether formal or informal. However, it is more prominent in some learning practices and styles of music than others. Imagine a baby banging a spoon or some other object on the kitchen table of a white English family in London. The adults are liable to take the spoon away or somehow get the baby to stop "making noise." By contrast, in his observations of the Venda people of South Africa, John Blacking observed that in such a situation the adults or other children would be likely to join in, adding a polyrhythm to the baby's banging in such a way as to turn it into music.[4] In both cases, the baby is being encultured into the music and the music-making practices of (or their absence from)

its surrounding environment.

As soon as banging a spoon becomes a *musical* activity, it involves all of the three main ways by which we engage in music making: performing (whether playing or singing), creating (whether composing or improvising), and listening (to ourselves and to others). All the musicians in my study, regardless of age, had acquired musical skills and knowledge through being encultured in these three activities. This involved the equivalent of banging spoons: they had an instrument, experimented with it, and discovered what sounds it could make through trial and error. However, there are some crucial differences between how these young people learned and how the Venda baby learned. Most folk and traditional musics of the world are learned by enculturation and extended immersion in listening to, watching, and imitating music-making practices of the surrounding community. In some folk and traditional musics, as well as in many art musics and jazz, there are systems of what might be called "apprenticeship training" whereby adult experts explicitly train or help young musicians. In relation to Western popular music, I wish to highlight two main departures from these tendencies.

First, most young popular musicians in the West are not surrounded by an adult community of practicing popular musicians who they can listen to live, watch, and imitate, or who initiate them into the relevant skills and knowledge. Hence, young musicians tend to engage in a significant amount of *solitary* learning. Secondly, insofar as a community of practice *is* available to young popular musicians, it tends to be a community of *peers* rather than "master musicians" or adults with greater skills.

The Main Learning Practice: Listening and Copying Recordings

By far the overriding learning practice for popular musicians, which is already well-known from the few existing studies (see endnote 3), is to copy recordings by ear. It seems extraordinary that this practice has developed in only the eighty years or so since the invention of recording technologies and is now found across many countries of the world. Children and young people can and do learn basically in isolation from each other, outside any networking or formal structures, and largely without adult guidance. I wish to distinguish two extreme ways of conceiving of this practice, each situated at the opposite ends of a continuum. At one end is what I call *purposive* listening, that is, listening with the conscious purpose of adopting and adapting what is heard into one's own practices. At the opposite end, *distracted* listening (or even hearing) occurs when music is heard in the background and enters the mind almost entirely through unconscious enculturation.

Here are some examples of the musicians in my study, from the oldest to the youngest, talking about how they had approached copying recordings, in relation to the first category, *purposive listening*. It is worth noticing that although they all did this, each interpretation and use of the method was idiosyncratic.

> *Rob:* I'd listen to the line over and over again till I could sing it, the bass line. And then I'd work it out from singing it.

Andy: Without even knowing at the time, I'd get a phrase, just one single phrase, and I'd do that, and I'd copy it, get it perfect, and move on to the next bit, and then once I'd got it all, I'd play along with it, and I'd keep on playing along with it.

> *Will:* At that age [c. ten to twelve] I was really, really into the Beatles, and a lot of Ringo's stuff is very easy to follow, and I was just learning about where you put the bass drum, where you put the snare, where you put the hi-hat, and just, and I was just trying to coordinate the three— to be able to do that.[5]

In contrast to purposive listening, some practices involve a very *distracted* approach to listening or even just rely on inattentively hearing a large variety of music. For example, as youngsters the musicians would play, from a mixture of memory and imagination, the kinds of sounds they heard around and about them.

> *Terry:* Well, I mean I'd be listening to the record anyway, so it would probably be on the radio, or I'd be playing it. It was obviously one that I liked, and so I'd know it.

> *Richard:* You just listen to it and—at that time I just kind of played the—moved the chords around til it sounded right ... Usually when I'm at home on my own, I play along to it just like that, and if there's nothing on I'll just think, "I feel like playing that song," so I just play a bit of it.

Both purposive and distracted listening carry on beyond the early learning stages and into professional realms. For example, Terry was a founding member of the British psychedelic band Hawkwind, which had a large cult following during the early 1970s. He left the band just before it achieved some mainstream chart success, when he was about nineteen. During his lifetime there followed many periods when he was not making music at all. Once, after one such gap of seven years, he had an unexpected phone call asking him to play in a covers band. Playing in a covers band obviously requires memory of a large number of songs, which can range from fifty to several hundred, depending on the individual and the band. Further, it requires the ability to reproduce songs at short notice, in ways that sound as exactly like the original recordings as possible, in conditions far removed from the rather more ideal setting of a recording studio.

Terry had never played in a covers band. So I asked him if before the first gig he had to refresh his memory by listening to and playing along with a lot of recordings. He responded:

> *Terry:* No, because it's like, you know, the bass player or someone would say, "Oh, it's 'High Heeled Sneakers,'" and there's loads of songs that are the same as "High Heeled Sneakers" for the drums to play; or it's a shuffle, you know, and I'd just do it from that.
> *Lucy:* And you do the fills and stuff from feel?
> *Terry:* Just feel, yeah.

At the time of the interviews, he was playing in a Hendrix tribute band:

> *Terry:* It's a bit like the Hendrix stuff, I was saying, because I'd know the stuff so well I could remember how it goes, do you know what I mean?
> *Lucy:* Right. Well that's slightly different

though isn't it, if you're doing it by memory without ever having sat down and played along, or listened over and over to the recording, you're not attempting to get exactly what Mitch Mitchell [Hendrix's drummer] did, or whoever it happened to be, are you?
> *Terry:* Well I was, well I am you know, we try to play it almost exactly how it's played.
> *Lucy:* Yeah, right.
> *Terry:* As opposed to a band playing Hendrix stuff, in *their* style, we play it in Hendrix's style, you know.
> *Lucy:* And you don't have to go back and check your memory very often then now?
> *Terry:* Well, yeah, I mean you listen to the tape and think, "S— I'm not doing that!" things like that, you know what I mean.

However, a comparison of his band's performances with some of the original Hendrix recordings not only revealed a high level of accuracy but also reproduced the "feel" of the original (a view that has been confirmed by a number of musicians to whom I have played the music).

Playing with Peers

Copying recordings is almost always a solitary activity, but solitude is not a distinguishing mark of the popular music learner. On the contrary, group activity is of great importance and occurs in the absence of adult supervision or coordination. It is characterized by two aspects. One is peer-directed learning, which involves the conscious sharing of knowledge and skills, through, for example, demonstration. The other is group learning, where there is no *conscious* demonstration or teaching as such. Learning takes place through watching and imitation during music making, as well as talking endlessly about music in and out of rehearsals.

Players form bands at very early stages, even if they have little control over their instruments and virtually no knowledge of any chord progressions, licks, or songs—or even if they have no instruments to play! All but two of the musicians in this study had started up a band within a few months of beginning to play their instrument. The youngest age was six, but most were between ten and fifteen. Although early bands are nearly always formed with peers, age is less important than musical ability— the band members all need to be at a roughly similar standard.

The bands jammed, played covers they knew and liked, and made up their own music. In all cases, different band members would demonstrate learned or original musical ideas, and usually each member of the band would put in his or her own touch.

> *Andy:* The main writer is the singer—he does come up with all the lyrics—and more often than not he comes up with the basic tune. But as soon as we get into rehearsal, it's no longer what he came up with—we pull it apart, we reform it, we re-structure it—add the harmonies, the bass line, the beat, the rhythm, everything to it. And it comes out as a different product.

So musicians acquire performance, composition, and improvisation abilities not only as individuals but, crucially, as members of a group, through informal peer-directed and group learning, both conscious and unconscious, that occur in the absence of an adult or other person who can provide leadership or greater musical experience.

Notation

Scores are very rarely used in popular music, apart from a few cases, such as highly professional function or theatre bands, or in an occasional manner, such as when a musician in a rehearsal scribbles something down on a piece of paper (usually to be thrown away as soon as the instruction is internalized). Session musicians are more likely to have constant work if they can read music. But the main means of learning and passing on music is through recordings, either commercial ones or "demos" passed between musicians. Even when it *is* used, notation is always heavily mixed with purposive listening and copying, using recordings as the central resource.

Six of the fourteen musicians in this study used notation, mostly having been introduced to it through some fairly minimal amount of formal music education. However, even given this adult guidance, they all nonetheless adapted the relevant skills to their own use through highly idiosyncratic means. Here is the oldest musician, Bernie Holland, talking about his use of notation when he was first learning. He explains how, having had a year of guitar lessons from a musician in his father's factory dance band, he extended the skills:

> *Bernie:* [By] listening to records … I'd buy the LP and it would run at thirty-three revs per minute. I had a record player luckily that had a sixteen-and-a-half rpm speed, and what I'd do is, 'd get their guitar solos, and I'd play them at sixteen-and-a-half revs, and write them down, because at that speed I could write it down onto paper, and then I'd learn them …

Another very experienced session musician, Rob Burns, had a grounding in the treble clef through classical trumpet lessons as a boy. But he was entirely self-taught on the bass guitar, and in his own words, never connected what he was learning on the trumpet with what he was teaching himself on guitar. Then, early on in his professional career, the following occurred:

> *Rob:* As far as reading bass goes, it was an ordeal by fire, because I'd just got a gig in this band that backed soul artists, the Stylistics, and it was the first tour I ever did, and they had an MD [musical director] who took no prisoners, and he just gave us all the charts [notation], counted us in, and I learnt to read bass clef in an hour!
> *Lucy:* You understood the principle of it before?
> *Rob:* Oh yes, I knew treble clef pitch, it was only a question of reading everything a third down, but it was nerve-wracking. But I was determined not to fail.
> *Lucy:* Was it a completely notated part, or sort of just partially—
> *Rob:* The majority of it was completely notated. I was just flying on adrenaline.

Aural copying pays attention to a number of factors that notation does not readily communicate. These include idiosyncratic and nonstandardized timbres, rhythmic flexibility, pitch inflection, and many other aspects, including qualities such as groove, "feel," and swing. Here again, not only conscious, focused, purposive listening and copying but also loose imitation related to continuous, unconscious enculturation and distracted listening are essential parts of the early learning process and continue to be the principal means through which musicians transmit and reproduce music.

Acquiring Technique

The concept of technique as a *conscious*

aspect of controlling the instrument came late to most of the musicians and was, in many cases, incorporated into their playing either immediately before, or some time after, having become professional. For example, Rob was a highly proficient, virtuosic bass player who, at the time of the interviews, was head of bass guitar at one of the first popular music colleges in Britain. Here, he responds to my question about how he went about learning bass guitar technique:

> *Rob:* I didn't. I did it all by ear until at the age of—I'd just turned nineteen, it must have been around March or April when a guitar playing friend of mine said, "Your hand technique's dreadful," and I said, "Well I'm fast, I can do this, that and the other," and he said, "No, no, no, it's dreadful." And he showed me correct classical guitar technique.
> *Lucy:* Right. And you were nineteen?
> *Rob:* I was nineteen. And I turned professional in the September … By this time I'd become obsessed with technique, and I used to watch every bass player that I regarded as being an icon at the time, and I noticed that the majority of them did use the technique that [my friend] had shown me.

Acquiring Knowledge of Technicalities

By "technicalities," I do not mean the executive psychomotor *technique* involved in playing or singing, but rather knowledge and understanding of music "theory." This came haphazardly, according to whatever the musicians were playing and enjoying at the time. To begin with, the musicians could *use* musical elements in stylistically appropriate ways, but usually without being able to apply names to them or to discuss them in any but vague or metaphorical terms:

Will: I mean when I first started playing I didn't know the names of things, like modes, but it was more about the feel of it.

I asked Steve, "So how did you acquire your understanding of harmony?"

Steve: Um. Trial and error. [Laughs] What sounds right. Just get the bass note, the first note that they're playing, then work around that.

As a rule, all the responses to such questions referred to listening as the prime source of the learning, with working out the relationships between sounds following on from that. Thus learning about theory was led by the excitement of the music.

Michael: My dad said, "Well, put in this F in the C chord here and then make it go down to the E," and I thought, "Ooh, that sounds nice." I started doing it all the time after that.

Later he referred to this as a "sus4," or the rock term "suspended 4th." Another commentator, on reading a draft of this research, responded (again using rock terms):

You discover A-augmented-6th because you want to play a Stevie Wonder song; you discover A-augmented-9th because you want to play a Jimi Hendrix song; you discover A-major triad over a B bass note because you want to play a Carole King song.

As time goes by, the pieces of the jigsaw puzzle fall into place to differing degrees, depending on the individual, and can lead to highly sophisticated levels of theoretical knowledge and understanding.

The Development of the Ear

Not surprisingly, all this emphasis on listening also leads to the development of quite sophisticated aural capacities. Here are three examples of how some of the musicians surprised even themselves in this respect:

Andy: Through [listening and copying], you don't just pick up what they're doing, you pick up techniques, you pick up common sorts of progressions and so forth. And nowadays I can hear a record, and I just know what's coming next. I know exactly what the notes are as well. This is a recent thing. I can listen, and I can pick out the pitch. I know that's a C major or whatever. And I never thought I'd be able to do that, the way I've learned music, you know, it's really strange.

Richard: You just listen to it and—at that time I just kind of moved the chords around til it sounded right, but now I can usually tell, like if it's in A it's going to be that chord next because it's got, you know what I mean? It's … I can't explain it.

Michael surprised his schoolteacher:

Michael: I can often pick out chord sequences just from … if I know a song I can play it … I do remember once a teacher playing us two pieces of music and asking us what the connection was between the two. And she was quite surprised when I said they were both in the same key. She didn't think anyone was going to spot that.

Practicing

Some of the musicians practiced their instruments for five or six hours a day in the early stages of learning, others practiced for considerably less time, and one (Terry) hardly ever practiced at all. They all approached practice according to their mood, other commitments in life, or motivation by external factors such as joining a new band or composing a new song. Their development was marked by some periods of relatively intensive practice, interspersed with other periods without any practice. Most importantly, practice was something they did as long as they enjoyed it. If they were not enjoying it, they did not do it.

Popular Musicians' Attitudes and Values toward Music and Musicianship

"Feel"

I asked every interviewee, "What do you value most highly in another musician?" Unsurprisingly, nearly all of them gave one type of answer, which I would expect of any musician the world over. They valued "feel," "sensitivity," "spirit," or similar attributes over and above technical ability. For example, Bernie described attending a concert of virtuoso guitarists:

> *Bernie:* And for the first half an hour my tongue was hanging out, my jaw dropped, but after that I thought, "Well was that it? Well, come on what else?" And it was rather like a circus act … You've got this chord sequence, and you've got these bars, and you've got to make sense of it, and be musical as well. It's not enough to be clever and technical. You've got to be musical, you've got to sing, you've got to be lyrical, you've got to make your instrument sing.

All the others echoed these sentiments, as in these examples:

> *Terry:* I think with all music, it's the feel that makes the music, you know you could be technically brilliant and as boring as anything. I think it's what people put into it really.

> *Rob:* Passion I think, I've got to be moved by music.

> *Brent:* Spirit, I would say. Spirit or feel or whatever, however you want to describe it, the sort of, the way in which they play. The way they attack things for want of a better word. You know you can get people who don't have much technique but really have a great feel about what they do, and you can get people who've got phenomenal technique who are just totally soulless. So you know when it comes down to it, I think it's feel or spirit.

> *Leo:* Um, really, I'm not quite sure I think … especially if it's improvisation, then, the melody, or how they're playing it, how they've interpreted it, is more important than their actual quality of playing.
> *Lucy:* Right, so, what do you mean by "how they interpret it"?
> *Leo:* Um, well, whether they play it, say, just if they put their own life into it like, I mean like, interpret it their own way … they've added something extra.

Friendship and Cooperation

More unexpectedly, in answer to the same question on what qualities they value most highly in another musician, many of them said they valued friendship, tolerance, and shared taste: "being a nice person," "being able to fit in with the band," "people that can sit in a tour bus or on an aeroplane week after week and not drive everybody else insane or have murderous thoughts," people with whom they had "had a great sense of sort of a bond." Commitment to the music and to the band were also immensely important. As Andy said in an aside, "I value loyalty above all else actually." I am not suggesting that all young popular musicians are exceptionally well-balanced individuals who never have arguments. But what does emerge is that the musicians highly *value* cooperation, sensitivity to others, commitment, and responsibility.

This emphasis on friendship and commitment not only concerns the social relationships that surround the band practice or performance but are necessary conditions of two further aspects. One is that since the music being played is arrived at through choice and group negotiation, all the productive activities of the band rely on a consensus of taste, or the willingness to tolerate others' potentially differing tastes, as well as the ability to cooperate and to arrive at rehearsals and concerts at the correct place and time with the correct equipment, all without any adult guidance. Without such cooperation (especially in the absence of incentives such as fame and money, but even with such incentives), a band will eventually disintegrate. Most fundamentally, friendship, cooperation, and sensitivity to other people also affect the precise nature and feel of the music being produced:

> *Michael:* The most important thing to me in, well in pop music certainly, is empathy with the rest of the band. And in my band I play in we're very empathetic, whatever that word is. Having played with the guitarist for five years of course it helps that, but occasionally from time to time I'll think, "triplet run coming up

here," and I'll play a triplet run and the guitarist will also play a triplet run without having communicated beforehand and that—I think that's absolutely excellent when that happens.

Enjoyment

Enjoyment was very high on the agenda. As I mentioned earlier, musicians did not practice unless they were enjoying it. But more than that, love, even passion, for music were explicit in the words of everyone I interviewed. Rob's sentiments are one example:

> *Rob:* Most of my colleagues now are sort of over forty. I mean we've been working together since we were all in our mid-twenties … I like them to still be as passionate about what they do as I am. I'll never forget my first BBC session where we had a string section playing with us, and all the rhythm section, i.e., the kind of young guys, dashed into the control room at live break to hear what we just put down, and all the string players pulled out their *Guardians* and sat reading the paper. I thought, "I never want to end up with that kind of, 'it's a job' attitude." So I think it's like, if they still have a great enthusiasm. I can still walk into certain music shops and it's still like being fifteen—it's like, "Oh, wow, want one of those, want one of those too." And a lot of people tend to think of it just as a means of earning a living and that's—if somebody has that same view as I have, that they can still be excited, then, you know, I like working with people like that.

Terry shares similar thoughts in his memories of Hawkwind:

> *Terry:* It was almost a spiritual thing, you know what I mean, particularly when we

were playing, because ... I believed, you know I think we all did really, totally in what we were doing, absolutely. I mean I always remember if I had died at the point, at any time when I was playing, I couldn't have died doing anything better, you know, I'd have been completely fulfilled, if you like, doing my utmost for something I believed in you know, it was great.

Self-Esteem

I didn't ask the musicians any direct questions about self-esteem, but nonetheless several of them indicated that playing music raised their self-esteem and their own perceptions of their status amongst peers. This was often, again, a source of pleasure:

Steve: You just want to learn a song, and you just want to learn it so bad so you can play it so when you go to school next day with your guitar you can show your mates—"Oh guess what I can play!"

Andy: Yeah, I mean, first of all it was getting the right chord progressions—you'd walk into school, you'd just learned "Knocking on Heaven's Door" or something, sit in the music centre in front of everybody else, and you'd play it and they'd be like, "yeah, that's right, yeah."

Emily: Well it's really nice when someone says, "Oh that's really cool, did you write that?"

Nanette, a professional singer since she was seventeen, told how at the age of nine her low self-esteem and general maltreatment at the hands of her peers due to a lisp were reversed in the space of two minutes when other girls accidentally heard her singing "Hey Big Spender," the contempo-

rary hit by Shirley Bassey, in the girls' room. The girls at first thought it was the original record playing, and they were so impressed that they took her all over the school and got her to repeat the performance standing on tables, from which time she felt well-liked and accepted by her peers.

"Other" Music

I also asked all the musicians how they felt about music other than their favorite styles, including classical music. The majority were bursting with enthusiasm for a wide range of music, and no one showed the slightest disrespect, least of all for classical music. Many of them had taught themselves to play a variety of classical pieces—especially J. S. Bach in the case of guitarists—to widen their knowledge and skills or just for fun. The youngest interviewee explained:

Leo: I find that when I listen to classical music, I feel very belittled. Because it's so big, there's like, so much in it, and it must be so hard to write a classical piece because it's just so much more than what I, what I do, like when I write a piece I just sit down at my keyboard or computer; but when I think about classical, sort of it, it's mostly in the head, and the parts are massive, the scores are huge, and that just sort of baffles me how people can do it, but it's amazing I guess.

Popular Musicians in Formal Music Education

Many children and young people who fail and drop out of formal music education, far from being either uninterested or unmusical, simply do not respond well to the kind of instruction it offers. Nine of the fourteen musicians in this study had taken classical instrumental lessons at school. Of these nine, seven got little out of the tuition and found the lessons boring, the progress slow, and the music difficult to relate to. None of them made any links between those lessons and their informal popular-music-learning practices. Only Rob Burns and Emily Dicks had positive experiences of instrumental tuition, but as mentioned earlier, Rob did not made any links across the formal and informal spheres, and Emily, age sixteen at the time of the interviews, saw her cello lessons as the "complete opposite" of her popular music practices on the electric guitar.

The nine oldest musicians, who were at secondary school between 1960 and 1987, almost without exception felt alienated and bored during their class lessons. Although the resources and the presence of other young people in their schools made it possible for many of them to set up and even perform in their first bands, the school had in general not recognized, rewarded, or helped them to pursue the popular music skills and knowledge that they were developing outside formal education, nor had their teachers apparently been aware of, or interested in, their high levels of enthusiasm and commitment to music.

Nine of the musicians had taken *popular* music instrumental tuition, and their experiences were in general much more positive than those within classical tuition, not necessarily because the approaches of the teachers appear to have been particularly different so much as because the learners liked and identified with the music and the instrument. Nonetheless, the young players had not necessarily stuck with their lessons.

For various reasons, five of them had quit after a year or considerably less, and only one returned to lessons much later in life.

At school, the younger musicians who had attended secondary school since 1986, when popular music was officially recognized in the English National Curriculum, were far more appreciative of the music course than their older colleagues had been. Teachers' attitudes towards popular music were generally positive by the end of the century and had largely lost the implicit denigration of earlier times. Teaching strategies had also undergone radical changes, emphasizing classroom performance, composition, and links between different musical styles from around the world and across the vernacular/art music divide.[6] Young popular musicians were able to make connections between many of the skills and knowledge they were acquiring formally and informally. In spite of this, their informal learning practices were unaffected and continued unabated.

Toward Formal Music Education

Although popular music has recently entered formal music education in many countries, informal popular-music-learning practices have not done so in any real sense. Even some popular musicians themselves, once they become instrumental teachers, seem to overlook and downgrade the importance of their own informal learning practices. Perhaps teachers from many walks of music education might consider developing a deeper understanding, taking more seriously, and to some extent adopting and adapting some aspects of informal popular music learning for the benefit of all. Below are some suggestions that might take us toward that end. These are only suggestions and need further research to ascertain their value and feasibility.[7]

Teachers could pay more attention to the role of enculturation in music learning and recognize how important it is for learners to *like,* as well as be familiar with, the music they are studying. Teachers could perhaps develop courses of learning based on personal choice, enjoyment, and deep enculturation, rather than mainly introduce learners to new and often unfamiliar music. Most young people—including those taking classical instrumental lessons—are encultured into popular music, not classical music. Yet classical instrumental tuition pays relatively little attention to popular music, or to the importance of enculturation generally. Listening to recordings of the music being studied has not typically been part of tuition during the lesson itself—in fact, some approaches *forbid* recordings, for fear they will destroy students' individual expression, and some regard listening to a piece before reading the notation as a form of cheating! In such an atmosphere, it is quite common for pupils to reach even advanced stages without ever hearing another human being play some of the music that they themselves play. It is not surprising that a common complaint of teachers is that students play without musicality, or the "feel" that enculturation can engender. Similar issues pertain to the extended activities arising from instrumental tuition. How often does the youth orchestra or band sit down and listen together to a recording or two of the pieces

they are learning? Perhaps instead of putting their energies into supervising practice sessions, parents could ensure that their children regularly hear some of the music they are learning to play, or similar music, in the home, not necessarily in focused listening sessions but as aural enculturation and a normal part of everyday life.

More radically, we could try introducing some *purposive* listening alongside close copying, using recordings rather than notation or other written or verbal instructions as the means of transmission. For some activities and some students, there is no reason why purposive listening could not play a useful part in learning to play classical as well as popular music. Instrumental teachers could build it in as a part of the weekly session and homework, providing their own tapes for students to copy where suitable commercial recordings are not available, so that the copying exercises can be tailored to the needs and standards of the individual learner.

Although a far greater variety of musics has entered the curriculum than ever before, this usually means emphasizing musics that are *unfamiliar* to the majority of the students, rather than building on their enculturation, liking, and identification. Ways that classroom teachers can recognize their students' music go far beyond the tired technique of allowing them to bring their own records in at the end of semester for a "treat." Students' recordings could be used as central learning resources, again not only for general listening but for purposive listening and copying exercises. I have piloted such an approach in one school classroom at the time of writing, and it has brought about some fascinating results.

Perhaps we can relax a bit about the necessities of "good" technique or regular daily practice right from the start of a young instrumentalist's life. Maybe these are not necessary, or even constructive, for every child, and some might benefit more from being allowed to play in ways they find comfortable. We should trust children's and young people's instincts and natural inclinations for music learning, sometimes allowing them to go where their interests and passions take them, rather than imposing our definitions of what counts as music on them. We could be less concerned with structuring their learning progressively from simple to complex, allowing them more freedom to follow their inclinations. This might mean that their learning is somewhat haphazard at times, but it would be held together by the music itself and their enjoyment of the music and therefore would be more likely to be meaningful and useful for them. By the same token, we could organize, or simply allow and respect, more peer-directed and group learning and rely less on teacher direction, curricula, syllabi, and exams.

To put suggestions like these into practice, teachers would not need to know how to play popular music or be up-to-date with the latest hits. Indeed, many approaches would require teachers to be confident enough to be *inactive* rather than proactive, a confidence that is likely to arise not only through further research but also through having enough courage to try out new, more informal methods of teaching and learning. For those music educators who are entirely classically trained, the best first

step is perhaps to sit down and learn to play a pop song off a recording themselves. It is likely to be more of an ear-opener than anticipated.

I would like to end by suggesting that popular musicians—including many who have turned away from formal music education in the past—seem to have a number of approaches, attitudes, and values that many formal music educators already share. These include, for example, valuing the integration of composing, improvising, playing, singing, and listening; valuing and developing personal qualities that include cooperation, commitment, and self-esteem through music making; appreciating a wide range of music, including classical music; and perhaps above all, discovering and nurturing a deep enjoyment, love, and even passion for music and music making.

Notes

1. International Federation of Phonographic Industries, *The Recording Industry in Numbers* (London: IFPI, 2000).

2. The issues discussed here are much more fully treated in my book *How Popular Musicians Learn: A Way Ahead for Music Education* (London and New York: Ashgate Publishing, 2001).

3. See for example, H. Stith Bennett, *On Becoming a Rock Musician* (Amherst: University of Massachusetts Press, 1980); Odd Are Berkaak, "Entangled Dreams and Twisted Memories: Order and Disruption in Local Music Making," *Young: Nordic Journal of Youth Research* 7, no. 2 (1999): 25–42; Patricia Shehan Campbell, "Of Garage Bands and Song Getting: The Musical Development of Young Rock Musicians," *Research Studies in Music Education*, no. 4, (1995): 12–20; Mary Ann Clawson, "Masculinity and Skill Acquisition in the Adolescent Rock Band," *Popular Music* 18, no. 1 (1999): 99–115; Sara Cohen, *Rock Culture in Liverpool* (Oxford: Oxford

University Press, 1991); Ruth Finnegan, *The Hidden Musicians: Music-Making in an English Town* (Cambridge: Cambridge University Press, 1989); and Lars Lilliestam, "On Playing by Ear," *Popular Music* 15, no. 2 (1996): 195–216.

4. John Blacking, "Versus Gradus Novos Ad Parnassum Musicum: Exemplum Africanum," in *Becoming Human through Music: The Wesleyan Symposium on the Perspectives of Social Anthropology in the Teaching and Learning of Music* (MENC: Reston, VA, 1985), 46.

5. Parts of the musician interviews in my study have previously been published and discussed in my book *How Popular Musicians Learn*. I would like to thank the publishers for permitting me to reproduce portions of the interviews here. I would also like to thank the musicians for their involvement in the project and for permitting me to use their words.

6. See, for example, Lucy Green, "From the Western Classics to the World: Secondary Music Teachers' Changing Perceptions of Musical Styles, 1982 and 1998," *British Journal of Music Education* 19, no. 1 (2002): 5–30.

7. For some recent relevant research on popular music in education, underpinned by similar sentiments, see for example, Charles Byrne and Mark Sheridan, "The Long and Winding Road: The Story of Rock Music in Scottish Schools," *International Journal of Music Education*, no. 36 (2000): 46–58; Peter Cope and H. Smith, "Cultural Context in Musical Instrumental Learning," *British Journal of Music Education* 14, no. 3 (1997): 283–89; Peter Dunbar-Hall and Kathryn Wemyss, "The Effects of the Study of Popular Music on Music Education," *International Journal of Music Education*, no. 36 (2000): 23–35; Eve Harwood, "Learning in Context: A Playground Tale," *Research Studies in Music Education*, no. 11 (1998): 52–61; Eve Harwood, "'Go on Girl!' Improvisation in African American Girls' Singing Games," in *In the Course of Performance: Studies in the World of Musical Improvisation*, ed. Bruno Nettl and Melinda Russell (Chicago: University of Chicago Press, 1998), 113–26; Kathryn Marsh, "Children's Singing Games:

Composition in the Playground?" *Research Studies in Music Education*, no. 4 (1995): 2–11; Kathryn Marsh, "Mediated Orality: The Role of Popular Music in the Changing Traditions of Children's Musical Play," *Research Studies in Music Education*, no. 13 (1999): 2–12 "From T. I. to Tasmania: Australian Indigenous Popular Music in the Curriculum," *Research Studies in Music Education*, no. 13 (1999): 28–40; and Trevor Wiggins, "The World of Music in Education," *British Journal of Music Education* 13, no. 1 (1996): 21–30.

Lucy Green is reader of music education at the Institute of Education, London University, UK. She is the author of *Music on Deaf Ears: Musical Meaning, Ideology, and Education* (1988), *Music, Gender, Education* (1997), and *How Popular Musicians Learn: A Way Ahead for Music Education* (2001). She has given lectures in many countries in Europe, the Americas, and Asia and contributed articles on music education and the sociology of music to several journals and books. She sits on the editorial boards of various journals, including *Music Education Research* and *Popular Music*.

Afterword

Afterword
When We Question Popular Music in Education, What Is the Question?

Robert A. Cutietta

As I have participated in discussions regarding popular music in public schools, it has become clear to me that we are perhaps asking the easy questions and avoiding the difficult ones. The primary question we seem to be asking is whether popular music has a place in public school music education. Further, this question seems to be asked in the context of the performance environment of secondary education. Given this context, the question of whether to include popular music in our curricula should be very easy to answer. Quite simply, it should not. Popular music is not the "great" music of the system we have built and endorsed. It seems above question that the bulk of secondary music education, as we know it, should focus on the great music written from approximately 1700 to 1950. There is simply very little "quality music," as we have chosen to define it, written before 1700 or after 1950. If the question of whether popular music has a place in schools is easy to answer, there must be a more pertinent (but perhaps less obvious) question that we are choosing to ignore.

In this chapter, I want to present the framework I used for reaching the conclusions above. I present a framework for determining the relative quality of musical styles and of the compositions within those styles. Next, I examine the implications of this framework for music education. Last, I ask the question that I believe is at the core of the debate regarding popular music's place in music education.

What Is Great Music?

There are several premises from which I build my argument. Many readers may readily agree with these premises, but I want to state them (and provide a short description) at the outset.

Premise 1: All music is not created equal. Some pieces of music are of a higher quality than others. If we examine Mozart's output, for example, we will find varying degrees of quality in his work. So, too, with the Beatles. This belief is so fundamental to this discussion that if we cannot agree on it we cannot go further.

Premise 2: Almost all music written since 1700 has been written with specific instruments in mind. When Bach wrote for the organ, he did not intend for that composition to be performed on the violin. When Beethoven wrote a symphony, he usually intended the work to be performed by an orchestra, not a choir. When Liszt wrote a piano sonata, he did not intend it to be performed on the organ or harpsichord. When Lennon and McCartney wrote "Blackbird," they did not intend for it to be performed on a piano. Thus, any discussion of quality music has to include the relationship between the actual music and the instruments on which it is performed.

Premise 3: Every style of music peaks, and then a new style is born. Once a style peaks, there are no more famous composers or new innovations in that style. Bach is an example of this phenomenon. We study Bach as the height of the baroque style. He took the style to its logical heights even though the musical landscape around him had already changed. Most of his contemporaries had already started writing in the new classical style. Because there were to be no more innovations in the baroque style, there are no famous baroque composers after Bach. Likewise, we study Beethoven as the beginning of the romantic era and the end of the classical era; thus, there are no famous classical composers after Beethoven. We study Duke Ellington as the culmination of the big band era even as the rock and roll era was in its infancy. After Ellington, there were no new innovations to that ensemble.

Premise 4: A style peaks when the instruments of the time are explored and utilized to their maximum. Since musical styles are tied to specific instruments or ensembles, they tend to ebb and flow together. Thus, the great

piano music is primarily from the nineteenth century. The great organ music is from the late eighteenth century. The great symphonic literature is from the nineteenth century (when the symphony orchestra was "perfected"), and the great electric guitar music is from the late twentieth century. This progression seems to take about fifty to seventy-five years. Thus, the classical era lasted from 1750 to 1825, the romantic from 1825 to 1900, the swing era from 1900 to 1950, and the rock era from 1950 to 2000. The hip-hop era will probably end around 2050 or so. It seems to take that long for composers to fully figure out the musical potential of a new instrument.

Premise 5: After instruments peak, new instruments are created. I am not sure which comes first, the chicken or the egg in this progression, but it seems that composers take instruments to their logical limits and then switch to new instruments to explore. When the orchestra and piano had been taken to their limits, composers began exploring electronic, world, and percussive instruments in more detail. Recently, when the electric guitar was taken to its logical limits, composers switched to digital production. Whether composers demand new sounds or new sounds demand new compositions is unclear, but the progression seems to be intact.

Premise 6: When a style peaks, composers don't always know it. The result is that all new innovations within a style after the peak are simply bigger, faster, or louder variations. Composers will always push an instrument to its artistic borders while exploring every possibility along the way. Eventually, the options for innovation are greatly reduced until the only option is to write music that takes the instrument beyond its artistic limits. Usually this means playing faster, louder, or more unconventionally. Rarely do these efforts lead to the depth of subtlety necessary for great art. Instead, composers switch to new styles.

Premise 7: Most acoustic instruments peaked before 1950. The entire twentieth century passed with very few new acoustic instruments being added to the composer's palette. The only new instruments were the drum set and the saxophone, both of which were added in the first part of the century. One can argue that the instrument makers "got it right," and therefore, few new developments were needed. Indeed, we still admire violins from the eighteenth century and wind instruments from the nineteenth.

Premise 8: Since no new acoustic instruments were being created, composers moved to the new electronic-based instruments or explored instruments from non-Western cultures.

Thus, it becomes clear that any discussion of the relative value or greatness of music has to be held within the context of both the style and the instrument for which it was created. We still value the piano music of Liszt. He took the piano to its musical and physical limits. If you are a pianist, you aspire to play the music of Liszt. It is truly the great piano music. Likewise, Beethoven was able to take the symphonic orchestra, with its newly refined wind instruments, and create the ideal musical and technical balance. If you are an orchestral musician, playing the Beethoven symphonies greatly inspires you. If you are a jazz saxophone player, Coltrane wrote your great music. If you are a harpsi-chordist, your great music was written by Couperin.

Looking at music this way completely avoids the debate of "great music" from an absolute point of view. Instead, it is all relative to the era and instrument. Suddenly bluegrass and classical can coexist in an aesthetic structure that does not necessitate an "either/or." Instead, we can seek the great music of every style or instrument. If I play banjo, performing the music of Chopin probably does not hold much aesthetic weight for me.

The logical implication of this is that a musical style is only relevant if the instrument is still viable. Because of technical advances and changing social climates, instruments evolve or move out of style. For example, there is great lute music, but only lutenists know it intimately. Likewise, there is great piano music, but primarily pianists know it. Since more people play piano than lute, the piano music of Beethoven and Liszt are said to have "passed the test of time," while most lute music has not—not because of the *music*, but because the *instrument* has not survived. The same can be said of music written for the harpsi-chord, viola di gamba, and Moog synthesizer. The "test of time" may have nothing to do with the actual music, but instead be related to whether the instrument it was written for was "replaced" by a new and improved instrument.

Thus, the great music for acoustic instruments was from the early 1700s to the mid-1950s. After that time, many composers were incorporating electronic instruments of some sort into the blend. If we are looking for the great music for orchestra or band, we know in what era to find the vast repertoire of that genre.

What Does This Have to Do with Music Education?

Ultimately this discussion has to come back to the issue at hand. Should popular music be taught in the public schools? Again, to examine this point we need one more premise that is unique to music teaching.

Music teaching premise 1: All things being equal, a music teacher would rather teach a high-quality piece of music than a low-quality piece of music. I can't see that there would be much debate about this premise. It has been an assumption in festivals, contests, and educational series books for years. If we accept this and the logic for identifying quality music outlined above, the conversation immediately switches to a discussion of instruments.

When following this logic for examining music education, we need to look at more than the individual instruments. We need to view the entire ensemble as if it were an "instrument." By and large, the instrumental ensembles of public school music are the band and, to a lesser extent, orchestra.[1] These ensembles were the result of technological advancements of their day. Once the orchestral instruments evolved to their technological perfection, the resulting balanced ensemble was created. The symphony orchestra reached its "perfect" point in the mid-nineteenth century. Modifications made after that point simply enlarged, altered, or modified the "norm." One hundred years later, in the middle of the twentieth century, the band, or wind ensemble, was normalized to a point that it became

the ultimate instrument of its time. The jazz band locked into place during the 1960s.

What is interesting is that once these ensembles are created, they are basically closed systems. They evolve to provide the ideal balance of instruments. Adding new instruments would disturb this musical balance, so it is rarely done. Further, this standardization also creates a closed system between composer and ensemble. The composer knows what instrumentation to compose for, so the ensemble dictates to the composer and the composer dictates to the ensemble.

For an "instrument" to remain viable, it must have a steady stream of new compositions being written for it. This is where we run into problems. Composers want to explore new timbres and colors that they have at their disposal. These include ethnic, world, and electronic instruments. None of these are easily added to the closed-loop systems in use in schools today. Thus, we have to rely on the dwindling number of composers willing to write for these ensembles or the many arrangers who transcribe works composed specifically for a different type of ensemble and adapt them to ensembles for which the musical works were never intended. The result of this move is rarely successful musically.

In music education, we have added another closed-loop system. Since these closed ensembles are the ensembles of choice for most teachers, it follows that the only instruments they feel need to be taught are those that feed the ensemble. Thus, the mold is set in most schools in the fifth grade when students are presented with a very limited number of instruments, none of which are being used in the majority of music written in the last half century.

Once we realize this, the debate ceases to be about the relative merits of different styles of music, but instead centers on the merits of different types of ensembles or instruments. Quite simply, once the ensemble or instrument is selected, a definition of "great music" follows fairly easily. If the ensemble is an orchestra, the great music is in the symphonic literature of the eighteenth and nineteenth centuries. If the ensemble is a rock band, the great literature is from the guitar masters of the late twentieth century. For a wind ensemble, the great literature is perhaps from the mid-twentieth century. For a techno group, the great music is being written today.

The challenge for music education is to either accept or challenge the implications of the decisions that have been made. The debate about whether to incorporate pop music into the school performance curriculum is moot if the proper discussion about the appropriate ensembles is complete. Quite simply, we should not encourage wind ensembles or orchestras to perform the music of today any more than we should encourage synthesizer or rock ensembles to perform the music of yesterday. There is a complete lack of musical integrity in doing so.

As long as the primary musical ensembles in the schools are wind ensembles and orchestras, then pop music has a very limited place in our curriculum. If we want to include more contemporary music, then we must first introduce new ensembles that mandate teaching of new instruments, whether they are mandolins, guitars, synthesizers, or computers. Until that happens, there truly is no issue regarding the appropriateness of pop music.

So, the question we really need to be asking is, What are the most appropriate ensembles or instruments for teaching music in the public schools? If we decide that the ones we have as the current norm are the most appropriate, then we want to teach the best music for that ensemble. If we decide that there is a place for different types of ensembles or instruments, then we will want to teach the best music written for them.

What is clear is that the educational decisions start with the instruments and not the music. Viewing the issue from this perspective changes everything.

Note

1. For clarity, I have confined this argument to instrumental ensembles, but the same logic applies to choral music where the traditional SATB choir is not well-suited for the vast majority of music written in the past half century.

Robert Cutietta is dean of the Thornton School of Music at the University of Southern California in Los Angeles. An active electric bass player, he is also the composer and performer of the music for the weekly television series *Lost Legends of the West*. Cutietta has written multiple books and articles, including his most recent book, *Raising Musical Kids: A Parent's Guide*, published by Oxford University Press.